The Tyndale Old Testament Commentaries

General Editor:
PROFESSOR D. J. WISEMAN, O.B.E., M.A., D.Lit., F.B.A.,
F.S.A.

HOSEA

D1329152

ALISTAIR M STEWART
020796

For

RUTH

HOSEA

AN INTRODUCTION AND COMMENTARY

by

DAVID ALLAN HUBBARD,

B.A., B.D., Th.M., Ph.D., D.D., L.H.D., Lit.D.

*President, Fuller Theological Seminary,
Pasadena, California*

INTER-VARSITY PRESS

Inter-Varsity Press
38 De Montfort Street, Leicester LE1 7GP, England

First published 1989
Reprinted 1990, 1992

Text set in Linotron Baskerville
Photoset by Parker Typesetting Service, Leicester
Printed and bound in Great Britain by
Biddles Ltd, Guildford and King's Lynn

British Library Cataloguing in Publication Data

Hubbard, David Allan
   Hosea
   1. Bible. O.T. Hosea – Critical studies
   I. Title   II. Bible O.T. Hosea. *English.*
   1989   III. Series
   224'.606

   ISBN 0–85111–641–8 (hardback)
   ISBN 0–85111–843–7 (paperback)

Inter-Varsity Press, England, is the book-publishing division of the Universities and Colleges Christian Fellowship (formerly the Inter-Varsity Fellowship), a student movement linking Christian Unions in universities and colleges throughout the United Kingdom and the Republic of Ireland, and a member movement of the International Fellowship of Evangelical Students. For information about local and national activities write to UCCF, 38 De Montfort Street, Leicester, LE1 7GP.

GENERAL PREFACE

T HE aim of this series of *Tyndale Old Testament Commentaries*, as it was in the companion volumes on the New Testament, is to provide the student of the Bible with a handy, up-to-date commentary on each book, with the primary emphasis on exegesis. Major critical questions are discussed in the introductions and additional notes, while undue technicalities have been avoided.

In this series individual authors are, of course, free to make their own distinct contributions and express their own point of view on all debated issues. Within the necessary limits of space they frequently draw attention to interpretations which they themselves do not hold but which represent the stated conclusions of sincere fellow Christians.

Hosea, the prophet of love in the Old Testament, was also an outspoken critic of the religious apostasy and failure of his times which rejected God's love. The book is strongly coloured by the prophet's own experience which is interpreted with sensitivity by Dr David Hubbard, a teacher and pastor, in this detailed study. This will help readers to understand the varied and rich teaching of Hosea who offers also the hope for renewal through judgment and repentance, a message relevant in our day.

In the Old Testament in particular no single English translation is adequate to reflect the original text. The version on which this commentary is based is the Revised Standard Version, but other translations are frequently referred to as well, and on occasion the author supplies his own. Where necessary, words are transliterated in order to help the reader who is unfamiliar with Hebrew to identify the precise word under discussion. It is assumed throughout that the reader will have ready access to one, or more, reliable rendering of the Bible in English.

Interest in the meaning and message of the Old Testament continues undiminished and it is hoped that this series will thus further the systematic study of the revelation of God and his will and ways as seen in these records. It is the prayer of the editor and publisher, as of the authors, that these books will help many to understand, and to respond to, the Word of God today.

D. J. WISEMAN

CONTENTS

AUTHOR'S PREFACE

L IVING with Hosea has been an awesome privilege. For years his message has been a regular part of what I have pondered, read and taught. His remarkable role in human history and divine revelation has combined with an astounding literary skill to make an irreplaceable contribution to my life. I cannot imagine myself as a human being, let alone as a believing person, without the deposit of Hosea's political, moral and spiritual insights.

Not that I fully understand his book. Anyone who spends much time with Hosea and his fellow prophets will be frustrated as well as enriched. They lived in a culture whose contours are not easy to reconstruct. They spoke a language that will always remain foreign to us. Moreover, they dealt with a vision of God's grandeur in creation, sovereignty in history and compassion for his people, that is both massive and mysterious. But what we can grasp is infinitely worth the effort: so all-encompassing is their vision and so pertinent to human life and destiny are their words.

The work of other scholars both added to and eased my labours. The literature on Hosea produced during the past forty years (a period to which, in the main, I arbitrarily restricted myself) is voluminous. I could only scratch the surface. But it includes some of the finest biblical commentaries ever written. Writing with the works of Hans Walter Wolff, Francis Andersen and David Noel Freedman, James Mays, Edmond Jacob and Jörg Jeremias by my side has prompted not only scholarly admiration but a deeper understanding of what is meant by 'the communion of saints'.

The present commentary has sought to balance a number of emphases in fulfilling the intent of the Series. The structural and thematic unity of Hosea has been stressed, together with the variety of literary forms and stylistic techniques. The context and purpose of each passage have been examined as preparation for insights into the individual verses. The conviction that each part can be understood only in relationship to its larger setting in the flow of the prophet's work has dominated the approach. Theological implications have been sketched, and contributions to the rest of Scripture have been suggested.

The Revised Standard Version has served as a basic text. Its readings are usually italicized. The other major English versions have been particularly helpful in Hosea where the Hebrew text abounds with words, forms and structures that continue to baffle scholars. As one of the baffled, I ask the indulgence of readers who feel that they have to comb through a tangle of textual and lexical discussion to catch the gist of the prophet's meaning. Biblical exegesis is like the first rule of golf: we have to play the ball where it lies. We have to take the text as it is and make the best of it. In parts of Hosea, there is no simple way to do that.

The opportunity to share parts of this material in public lectures needs acknowledging, since discussion with friends and colleagues improved markedly the quality of my work. Particularly helpful were the conversations that accompanied the Day-Higginbotham Lectures at Southwestern Theological Seminary, the annual Theological Lectureship at the Associated Mennonite Biblical Seminaries, a seminar with the Academy of Homiletics, and the E. Y. Mullins Lectures at the Southern Baptist Theological Seminary. Add to this list the names of countless students in dozens of classes whose questions and suggestions helped me see the issues more clearly.

Thanks are due to my office team, Vera Wils, Steven Pattie, Dr John McKenna, Elsie Evans and Shirley Coe who bore patiently with my compulsion to finish the book, carried faithfully the burden of its several drafts of assembly and typing, and managed gracefully to get their other work done along the way.

The dedication to my wife, Ruth, is a token of appreciation for the fact that she has lived with Hosea's work as long as I have. More than that, her steady encouragement for me to give the commentary priority, alongside my normal administrative and teaching duties, is a chief reason for its completion. Together, we offer it with the prayers that its pages will be windows into the wonders of sovereign love and human responsibility – wonders which the prophets know from their encounter with God, and which their inspired words proclaim to their generation and the generations that have followed them for nearly three millennia.

DAVID ALLAN HUBBARD

CHIEF ABBREVIATIONS

AB   The Anchor Bible.
ANEP   *The Ancient Near East in Pictures* edited by James B.
            Pritchard (Princeton University Press, ²1969).
ANET   *Ancient Near Eastern Texts Relating to the Old Testa-*
            ment edited by James B. Pritchard (Princeton Uni-
            versity Press, ³1969).
ANVAO   Avhandlingar utgitt av Det Norske Videnskaps-
            Akademi i Oslo.
AOAT   Alter Orient und Altes Testament (Neukirchen-
            Vluyn).
BA   *Biblical Archaeologist.*
BA Rev   *Biblical Archaeology Review.*
BDB   F. Brown, S. R. Driver, C. A. Briggs, *Hebrew and*
            English Lexicon of the Old Testament (Oxford Univer-
            sity Press, 1906).
Bib   *Biblica.*
BZAW   *Beihefte zur Zeitschrift für die alttestamentliche Wissen-*
            schaft.
CAT   Commentaire de l'ancien testament.
CB.OT   Coniectanea Biblica. Old Testament Series (Lund,
            Sweden: Gleerup).
CBQ   *Catholic Biblical Quarterly.*
CHALOT   W. L. Holladay, *Concise Hebrew and Aramaic Lexicon*
            (Grand Rapids: Eerdmans, 1971).
DOTT   *Documents from Old Testament Times* edited by D.
            Winton Thomas (Nelson, 1958).
ETR   *Études Théologiques et Religieuses.*
E.T.   English translation.
EvTh   *Evangelische Theologie.*
HAT   Handbuch zum Alten Testament.
HTR   *Harvard Theological Review.*
IBD   *The Illustrated Bible Dictionary* (Leicester: IVP,
            1980).
ICC   International Critical Commentary.

IDB	*Interpreter's Dictionary of the Bible* (Nashville: Abingdon Press, 1962).
IDB Supp.	Supplementary volume to *IDB* (Nashville: Abingdon Press, 1976).
Int	*Interpretation.*
ISBE, rev.	*International Standard Bible Encyclopedia*, fully revised (Grand Rapids: Eerdmans, 1979–88).
JBL	*Journal of Biblical Literature.*
JETS	*Journal of the Evangelical Theological Society.*
JNES	*Journal of Near Eastern Studies.*
JSOT	*Journal for the Study of the Old Testament.*
KAT	Kommentar zum Alten Testament.
KB	L. Köhler and W. Baumgartner, *Lexicon in veteris testamenti libros* (Leiden: E. J. Brill, 1951–53).
mg.	margin.
NBC rev.	*New Bible Commentary*, revised (Leicester: IVP, 1970).
NICOT	New International Commentary of the Old Testament.
OTL	Old Testament Library.
OTS	*Oudtestamentische Studien.*
SBT	*Studies in Biblical Theology.*
TDNT	*Theological Dictionary of the New Testament* edited by G. Kittel and G. Friedrich (Grand Rapids: Eerdmans, 1946–76).
TDNT abr.	*Theological Dictionary of the New Testament* abridged by G. W. Bromiley (Grand Rapids: Eerdmans, 1985).
ThZ	*Theologische Zeitschrift.*
TNTC	Tyndale New Testament Commentary
TOTC	Tyndale Old Testament Commentary.
TRE	*Theologische Realenzyklopädie.*
TynB	*Tyndale Bulletin.*
VT	*Vetus Testamentum.*
VT Supp.	*Vetus Testamentum* Supplements.
WBC	Word Biblical Commentary.
WMANT	Wissenschaftliche Monographien zum Alten und Neuen Testament.
ZAW	*Zeitschrift für die alttestamentliche Wissenschaft.*
ZDPV	*Zeitschrift des deutschen Palästina-Vereins.*

CHIEF ABBREVIATIONS

Texts and versions

AV	Authorized (King James) Version, 1611.
BHS	*Biblia Hebraica Stuttgartensia*, 1967/77.
JB	Jerusalem Bible, 1966.
LXX	The Septuagint (pre-Christian Greek version of the Old Testament).
Moffatt	J. Moffatt, *A New Translation of the Bible*, 1935.
MT	Massoretic Text.
NAB	New American Bible, 1970.
NASB	New American Standard Bible, 1960.
NEB	New English Bible, 1970.
NIV	New International Version, 1978.
RSV	Revised Standard Version, 1952.
Syr.	The Peshitta (Syriac version of the Old Testament).
Targ.	The Targum (Aramaic version of the Old Testament).
Vulg.	The Vulgate (the late fourth-century Latin translation of the Bible by Jerome).

SELECT BIBLIOGRAPHY

These are the works frequently referred to and which are cited in the text by the last name of the author.

Old Testament introductions

Childs, B. S., *Introduction to the Old Testament As Scripture* (SCM, 1983. US ed. Philadelphia: Fortress Press, 1979).

Crenshaw, J. L., *Story and Faith: A Guide to the Old Testament* (New York and London: Macmillan Publishing Co., 1986).

Gottwald, N. K., *The Hebrew Bible: A Socio-Literary Introduction* (Philadelphia: Fortress Press, 1985).

Kaiser, O., *Introduction to the Old Testament: A Presentation of Its Results and Problems* (E.T., Blackwell, 1980. US ed. Minneapolis: Augsburg Publishing House, 1975).

Robert, A. and Feuillet, A., *Introduction to the Old Testament* (E.T., New York: Desclee Co., 1968).

Soggin, J. A., *Introduction to the Old Testament*, OTL (E.T., SCM, 1988. US ed. Philadelphia: Westminster Press, 1976).

Weiser, A., *The Old Testament: Its Formation and Development* (E.T., New York: Association Press, 1961). (Cited as Weiser, *Old Testament*.)

Old Testament histories

Bright, J., *A History of Israel*, 2nd rev. ed. (SCM, 1981. US ed. Philadelphia: Westminster Press, [3]1981).

Donner, H., 'The Separate States of Israel and Judah' in *Israelite and Judaean History*, ed. by J. H. Hayes and J. M. Miller, OTL (Philadelphia: Westminster Press, 1977), pp. 381–434.

Hermann, S., *A History of Israel in Old Testament Times* (E.T., Philadelphia: Fortress Press, [2]1981).

Miller, J. M. and Hayes, J. H., *A History of Ancient Israel and Judah* (SCM, 1986. US ed. Philadelphia: Westminster Press, 1986).

Works on the prophets

Blenkinsopp, J., *A History of Prophecy in Israel* (SPCK, 1984. US ed. Philadelphia: Westminster Press, 1983).

Buber, M., *The Prophetic Faith* (New York: Harper & Brothers, 1949).

Clements, R. E., *Prophecy and Tradition* (Blackwell, 1975. US ed. Atlanta: John Knox Press, 1975).

Coggins, R., 'An Alternative Prophetic Tradition?' in *Israel's Prophetic Tradition: Essays in Honour of Peter Ackroyd*, ed. by R. Coggins, A. Phillips and M. Knibb (Cambridge University Press, 1982), pp. 77–94.

Gordis, R., *Poets, Prophets and Sages: Essays in Biblical Interpretation* (Bloomington and London: Indiana University Press, 1971).

Hanson, P. D., *The People Called: the Growth of Community in the Bible* (San Francisco: Harper & Row, 1986).

Heschel, A. J., *The Prophets* (New York and Evanston: Harper & Row, 1962).

Hunter, A. V., *Seek the Lord! A Study of the Meaning and Function of the Exhortations in Amos, Hosea, Micah and Zephaniah* (Baltimore: St Mary's Seminary & University, 1982).

King, P. J., *Amos, Hosea, Micah – An Archaeological Commentary* (Philadelphia: Westminster Press, 1988).

Koch, K., *The Prophets: vol. 1. The Assyrian Period* (E.T., SCM, 1982. US ed. Philadelphia: Fortress Press, 1983).

Kuhl, C., *The Prophets of Israel* (E.T., Edinburgh and London: Oliver and Boyd, 1960).

Murray, R., 'Prophecy and the Cult' in *Israel's Prophetic Tradition*, pp. 200–216.

Nicholson, E. W., *God and His People: Covenant and Theology in the Old Testament* (Oxford: Clarendon Press, and New York: Oxford University Press, 1986).

Phillips, A., 'Prophecy and Law' in *Israel's Prophetic Tradition*, pp. 217–232.

Sawyer, J. F. A., 'A Change of Emphasis in the Study of the Prophets' in *Israel's Prophetic Tradition*, pp. 233–249.

Van der Woude, A. S., 'Three Classical Prophets: Amos, Hosea and Micah' in *Israel's Prophetic Tradition*, pp. 32–57.

Whybray, R. N., 'Prophecy and Wisdom' in *Israel's Prophetic Tradition*, pp. 181–199.

SELECT BIBLIOGRAPHY

Hosea: commentaries

Andersen, F. I. and Freedman, D. N., *Hosea*, AB (New York: Doubleday & Co., 1980).

Deissler, A., 'Osée' in *Les Petits Prophètes*, La Sainte Bible (Paris: Letouzey & Ané, 1961).

Jacob, E., *Osée*, CAT (Neuchâtel: l'Editions Delachaux & Niestlé, 1965).

Jeremias, J., *Der Prophet Hosea*, Das Alte Testament Deutsch (Göttingen: Vandenhoeck & Ruprecht, 1983).

Mays, J. L., *Hosea*, OTL (SCM, 1978. US ed. Philadelphia: Westminster Press, 1969).

Nötscher, Friedrich, *Zwölfprophetenbuch oder Kleine Propheten* (Würzburg: Echter-Verlag, 1948).

Robinson, T. H., *Die Zwölf Kleinen Propheten*, HAT (Tübingen: J. C. B. Mohr [Paul Siebeck], ²1954.

Ward, J. M., *Hosea: A Theological Commentary* (New York: Harper & Row, 1966).

Wolff, H. W., *Hosea*, Hermeneia (E.T., SCM 1974. US ed. Philadelphia: Fortress Press, 1974).

Hosea: special studies

Brueggemann, W., *Tradition for Crisis: A Study in Hosea* (Virginia: John Knox Press, 1986) paperback.

Balz-Cochois, H., *Gomer: Der Höhenkult Israels in Selbstverständnis der Volksfrömmigkeit – Untersuchen zu Hosea 4:1 – 5:7* (Frankfurt am Main and Bern: Peter Lang, 1982).

Buss, M. J., *Prophetic Word of Hosea: A Morphological Study*, BZAW 111 (Berlin: Verlag Alfred Topelmann, 1969).

Emmerson, G. I., *Hosea: an Israelite Prophet in Judean Perspective*, JSOT Supp. 28 (Sheffield: JSOT Press, 1984).

Neef, H-D., *Die Heilstraditionen Israel's in der Verkündigung des Propheten Hosea* (Berlin, New York: Walter de Gruyter, 1987).

Nyberg, H. S., *Studien zum Hoseabuch* (Uppsala: Uppsala Universitets Årsskrift, 1935).

Stuart, Douglas, *Hosea-Jonah*, WBC, 31, pp. 127–128.

Utzschneider, H., *Hosea: Prophet vor dem Ende*, Orbis Biblicus et Orientalis 31 (Freiburg und Gottingen: Universitatsverlag and Vandenhoeck & Ruprecht, 1980).

Vollmer, J., *Geschichtliche Rückblicke und Motive in der Prophetie*

17

    des Amos, Hosea und Jesaia, BZAW 119 (Berlin: Walter de Gruyter & Co., 1971).

Vuilleumier, R., *La tradition cultuelle d'Israël dans la prophétie d'Amos et d'Osée*, Cahiers Théologiques 45 (Neuchâtel: Editions Delachaux & Niestlé, 1960).

Yee, G. A., *Composition and Tradition in the Book of Hosea*, SBL, Diss. Series (Atlanta: Scholars Press, 1987).

INTRODUCTION

IT all began with a marriage. But the marriage of Hosea and Gomer was no ordinary nuptial. Initiated by the word of God, it was permeated with the purposes of revelation. A divine call was heard by Hosea that turned his life into a sanctuary where God's holy love was to be known. The tone of the book is set by God's mandate to take a wife who would become a harlot, have children who turned from God, and then know God's passion for his covenant people.

The story of the marriage is lean and spare. Of its moods, feelings, conversations, quarrels we are not told. Its blunt, bleak message overshadows all else about it: a wife and mother turning wayward, three children bearing ominous names. It is a story of judgment – a person gone wrong, just as her nation had done; children portraying doom, such as their nation deserved. It is also a story about the Lord, whose part is played by Hosea in the domestic phase of the drama. It is God who both choreographs the movement and narrates the meaning. Because he does, the story is heavy with tragedy and buoyant with hope. The restoration of the broken marriage can take place because God commands Hosea and demonstrates his promises to Israel.

The prophet's experience accounts for the sharpness of his focus. Sins condemned by Amos – abuse of power, exploitation of the poor, presumption of covenant privileges – were prevalent. Hosea makes quick sallies into those territories. Yet he and Amos are as different from each other in emphasis as they are in experiences. The Baal-worship, over which Hosea wept, had dotted the hillsides of Israel while Amos was preaching but was little reflected in his messages. The prophets were not newspaper reporters required to write all sides of the story. Nor were they scholars preparing theses that investigated all angles of their topics. They were messengers, shaped by their calls, their experiences and their reception of Yahweh's word to speak to specific issues in specific ways.

Hosea's marriage, marked as it was by tragedy and recovery beyond the tragedy, both deepened his understanding of divine passion, and narrowed the scope of his message to the single point of Israel's relationship to the covenant Lord. It is that profound pathos, let loose towards Israel in speech after speech, irony after irony, metaphor after metaphor, question after question, which gives the book its fire. It is the fire of this passion and its message that confronts the reader with Israel's Lord.

The relationship signalled in that marriage was Hosea's dominant concern. He saw that relationship *inaugurated by Yahweh's grace* in Israel's distant past. Jacob, the patriarch, was not always a grateful recipient of it (ch. 12). Israel, the people, tasted it in the Exodus (2:15; 13:4), the wilderness (2:15; 9:10) and the settlement in the land (2:15). That grace viewed Israel as special to Yahweh, cared for by him and commissioned to serve him.

Hosea also saw the relationship *jeopardized from the beginning* by Israel's forgetfulness. Like a geography teacher Hosea took his hearers from place to place reminding them of their penchant to tax the relationship by their fickleness: 'Baal-peor – here you first dallied with Baal' (9:1); 'Gilgal – here you crowned Saul king and compromised Yahweh's sovereignty' (9:15); 'Bethel – here you desecrated Yahweh's name and Jacob's memory with the golden calf' (10:5–6); 'Gibeah – here your unbridled lust stained your history book with the gruesome tale of gang-rape' (9:9; 10:9–10).

Despite that sordid past, Hosea saw in his own times the relationship *sunk to its lowest point* in Israel's unrepentant history. The cult of the Baals, the instability of the monarchy and the naiveté of foreign policies were its three chief expressions. Hosea's accusations were laced with metaphors that exposed Israel's rebellion: stubborn calf (4:16), loaf half-baked, yet mouldy (7:8–9), silly dove (7:11), baby too stupid to be born (13:13). And his announcements of judgment were conveyed in pictures of appropriate ferocity: God would be a lion, a leopard, a she-bear (13:7–8).

So sorry was the present that the near future could mean only a relationship *severed by invasion and exile*. Military intervention, with all the brutality for which the Assyrians were famous, and removal from the land, with all the pain of dislocation and deprivation – these were the necessary means of purging the nation.

Yet in the face of all of this, Hosea has a clear picture of the covenant relationship *restored at Israel's return to Yahweh*. Five times in the flow of the book, this reconciliation is intimated (1:10 – 2:1; 2:14–23; 3:1–5; 11:8–11; 14:1–7), conveying the overall intent of the book: the persistent presence of Yahweh's love despite his people's endemic waywardness. A new marriage awaits Israel in God's time and on God's terms. Because Hosea knew this, he had the courage to rebuild the relationship that Gomer had shattered, and to demonstrate both the reality and the cost of such reconciliation.

II. PLACE IN THE CANON

It was a happy choice that placed Hosea at the head of The Book of the Twelve, the Jewish description of the collection of so-called Minor (*i.e.* shorter) Prophets. Chronologically, Hosea would follow Amos by a few years (see Date, below) but logically he deserves first place. His is the longest book. But more than that it is theologically the most complete. It embraces the great prophetic themes of covenant, judgment and hope. It describes the personal relationship between Yahweh and the prophet more amply than any of its eleven companions. Its biographical lessons prepare the way for Jonah, as its magnificent interplay of judgment and hope anticipates Joel, Micah, Zephaniah, Haggai, Zechariah and Malachi.

The transition from spoken oracles to canonical book is not easy to chart. In Hosea's case some reasonable assumptions may be made. First, since Hosea seems to have completed his ministry shortly before the fall of Samaria in 722/721 BC, that event itself would have confirmed his validity as a prophet and prompted the early recording of his words. Second, the oracles and stories were probably carried to Judah by refugees from the Northern Kingdom. Third, those who transmitted the prophetic words may well have been disciples of Hosea. That he had disciples may be inferred both from the brief mention of a prophet's disciples in Isaiah 8:16, as though the presence of Isaiah's disciples needed no explanation, and from the fact that such disciples are the obvious persons to preserve his words. Two bits of evidence must be noted: (1) the biographical (third person) form of the prophetic actions, which report his marriage to Gomer and the naming of three children (1:2–9), stands in contrast to the autobiographical form of chapter 3, which we interpret as his own report of the remarriage – persons thoroughly familiar with these actions must have framed them in the form we have them; and (2) the command, 'let Ephraim alone', voiced by the prophet, may be addressed to one of his followers (see Commentary at 4:17). Fourth, Hosea's words, confirmed by the exile of the northern populace, would have gained relevance for Judah as her history began to parallel Israel's. The corruption of the monarchy under Manasseh would have brought fresh meaning to Hosea's indictments of royalty. The reforms of Josiah may have found fuel in Hosea's condemnations of Baal worship. The threat of exile to Babylon could have gained sharpness from his announcements of judgment. Hosea's impact on Jeremiah, the dominant prophet of the Babylonian period, is well-documented (see Message, below). The fact that Hosea's words contained accusations of Judah at a few pivotal spots would have enhanced their use in the 7th and 6th centuries (*cf.* on 1:7; 5:10, 14; 8:14; 12:2). Hosea and Amos must have been recognized as canonical in their authority right from the beginning, so clearly do we see their use by the prophets who followed them.

III. DATE

Dates given by various scholars for Hosea's ministry cannot be compared without adjusting them to account for the differences in the chronological systems used. One standard chronology dates Jeroboam II from 785–745 BC and sharply compresses the reign of Pekah to four years, in place of the twenty credited him in 2 Kings 15:27.[1] Dealing with the twenty years of Pekah has proved impossible to most modern scholars. In the other standard chronology, E. R. Thiele has handled this problem by suggesting that Pekah reigned first in Gilead, east of Jordan, beginning his reign at the time Menahem began his in Samaria (752 BC), and then took control of the entire state only in 740, after Pekahiah's two years on the

---

[1]Miller and Hayes, pp. 220–229.

throne.[1] Pekah continued in power until Hoshea's revolt in 732 BC, a date on which most chronologists agree. One result of the two ways of handling Pekah's dating is different dates for Jeroboam's death – 753 BC (Thiele), 745 BC (Miller and Hayes) or 747–746 BC (Wolff, p. xxi). The impact of this difference on suggested dates for Hosea is obvious, given the fact that the beginning of his ministry is linked to the closing of Jeroboam's regime. The majority of scholars, who hold to the later dates for Jeroboam's reign, would place the beginnings of our prophet's ministry from 752 BC (Wolff, p. xxi) to 750 BC (Blenkinsopp, p. 98); those who follow the earlier chronology would pose a beginning date of 755 BC (Andersen, p. 37) or a couple of years earlier.

The reference to Jeroboam II of Israel in the title fits the second prophetic action (1:4–5), where Jezreel's name signifies banishment of Jehu's dynasty. The sign was fulfilled with Shallum's murder of Zechariah, Jeroboam's son, who managed a reign of only six months (753 BC; 2 Ki. 15:8–12) and whose death ended Jehu's dynasty. Amos' ministry was so brief that it may have been completed before Hosea began his, but it is possible that the priest denounced in Hosea 4:4ff. was Amaziah of Bethel (Andersen, p. 38), Amos' opponent (Am. 7:10–17).

The royal names (1:1) suggest that Hosea's mission continued to the commencement of Hezekiah's reign (715 BC), a span of about forty years. Evidence from the book itself cannot carry us much beyond 725 BC as the final date of its prophecies, since Samaria's fall (722/721 BC) seems yet future when the book closes. If we are right in relating the oracles of Hosea 5:7 – 7:16 to the Syro-Ephraimite war (see p. 118 for date) against Judah, and in connecting the passages of priestly conspiracy against the unnamed king with Pekah's murder of Pekahiah, then one possible cut-off for the material in Hosea would be about 732 BC, the date of Pekah's death. If, however, the oven simile in 7:3–7 speaks not of Pekahiah's death but of Pekah's at the hand of Hoshea, the closing date must be moved forward to about 730 or 728 BC. Beyond that, we may find in Hosea's last chapters an urgency about the collapse of Ephraim that points to the period when Shalmaneser V

---

[1] *A Chronology of the Hebrew Kings* (Grand Rapids: Zondervan, 1977), pp. 46–51. Thiele's system will be followed in this commentary.

23

(727–722 BC) had come to the throne of Assyria, and was aggressively seeking to reduce Samaria to the status of an Assyrian province. Hosea's ministry must, then, have carried on to about 725 BC. In contrast, Andersen's (pp. 34–35) caution about the Syro-Ephraimite setting of 5:8 – 7:16 has led him to suggest the early date of 740 BC for the cut-off of the bulk of the prophecies.

Hosea's ministry began at or just before the time of his marriage when he was probably eighteen or twenty years of age. A forty year span would be entirely possible, though we would have to assume that it closed with a number of years of service in Judah during the reigns of Ahaz (735–715 BC) and Hezekiah.

IV. THE SETTING OF THE BOOK

a. Historical background

The major factors that frame the background of Amos and Hosea are these: (1) Assyria's preoccupation with affairs close to her own borders, *e.g.* protection from the mountain peoples of Urartu and Media to her north and east, a preoccupation that precluded the systematic marches to Syro-Palestine that had been her earlier pattern throughout most of the 9th century BC; (2) Assyria's domination, at the end of the 9th century BC, of the kingdom of Aram-Damascus, which had harassed Israel, particularly Gilead, and at least once destroyed her armies (2 Ki. 13:1–7, 22); (3) Jeroboam's territorial expansion and consequent economic prosperity made possible by the temporary cessation of Assyrian incursion and the partial eclipse of Aramaean aggression (2 Ki. 14:23–29);[1] (4) the resurgence of Baal worship after Jehu's partial purge (2 Ki. ch. 10); (5) the dynastic instability that plagued Israel after Jeroboam's death and saw six kings toppled in thirty

[1] Recent archaeological investigations seem to indicate that Jeroboam II was heir to rather than instigator of the impressive building projects of Samaria. The palaces and fortresses assailed by Amos (3:15; 5:11; 6:8) and Hosea (8:14; 10:14) were more likely to have been the products of the ambitious greed and regal arrogance of Omri (885–874 BC), Ahab (874–853 BC) and their successors, including Jehu (841–814 BC) who founded the dynasty in power when the two prophets began their preaching. The crime of Jeroboam, apparently, was to continue to support such self-serving affluence even when the cost was higher than the citizenry could bear. *Cf.* J. K. de Geus, 'Die Gesellschaftkritik der Propheten und die Archäologie', *ZDPV* 98, 1982, pp. 50–57.

INTRODUCTION

Summary chart

King	Dates BC	Significance	References
Jeroboam II	793–753	Supported shrine at Bethel Contributed to exploitation of the poor by sponsoring high standard of living	2 Kings 14:23–29 Amos 1:1; 5:7–11 Hosea 1:1
Zechariah	753	Death fulfilled prophecies of Amos and Hosea	2 Kings 15:8–12 Amos 7:9; Hosea 1:4–5
Shallum	752	Murderer of Zechariah Example of chaotic political life	2 Kings 15:13–15 Hosea 7:7; 8:10; 13:11
Menahem	752–742	Murderer of Shallum Oppressor of his enemies Paid tribute to Tiglath-pileser of Assyria	2 Kings 15:14–23 Hosea 7:11; 12:1
Pekahiah	742–740	Example of Israel's chaotic political life Son of Menahem Slain by Pekah	2 Kings 15:23–26 Hosea 6:7–9 7:3–7
Pekah	740–732 (as sole ruler; may have ruled Gilead beginning in 752)	Murderer of Pekahiah Conspired with Rezin against Assyria Key figure in Syro-Ephraimite attack on Judah Became vassal to Assyria Probably most prominent king in Hosea	2 Kings 15:25–31 2 Kings 16:1–9 Hosea 5:8 – 7:16
Hoshea	732–723	Murderer of Pekah Rebelled against Assyria Deposed and imprisoned by Shalmaneser V Last king of Israel	2 Kings 15:30 2 Kings 17:1–6 Hosea 10:3–8, 13–15 13:9–16

years, three of whom ruled two years or less and four of whom were assassinated (2 Ki. ch. 15; Ho. 7:7; 8:4; 10:3; 13:9–11), while the fifth was deposed (2 Ki. 17:4–5); (6) the resurgence of Assyrian power under Tiglath-pileser III (called Pul; 745–727 BC) and Shalmaneser V, who resumed the annual westward marches of their predecessors and reduced much of Syro-Palestine to vassal status (2 Ki. 15:19–20, 29; 16:7–20; 17:1–6); and (7) an altercation between Judah and Israel who, in alliance with the Damascans under their king Rezin, sought to coerce Ahaz of Judah to conspire with them against Tiglath-pileser (734–33 BC; 2 Ki. 16:5–9; *cf.* Is. chs. 7–10; Ho. 5:8–13; for a more detailed discussion of this Syro-Ephraimite conspiracy, see 'Possible historical backgrounds', p. 118 in Commentary at 5:8 – 7:16).

The first three of these historical factors shed light on the words of Amos and the beginnings of Hosea's prophecy, especially chapter 1. The last four are apposite to the oracles of judgment and hope in Hosea 4:1 – 14:9.[1]

b. Personal background

Of Hosea's own circumstances, we are told only the name of his father, Beeri (1:1) and the slimmest details about his marriage and his children (1:2–9; 3:1–3). However we interpret the marriage, it is surely the single most important element in shaping the person and message of the prophet. It was both the centre of his proclamation (or demonstration) of the divine word and the source of his understanding of the divine experience of being rejected, having to judge and discipline, and then effecting reconciliation. What the commissioning visions did for Isaiah (ch. 6), Jeremiah (ch. 1), and Ezekiel (chs. 1–3), Hosea's marriage did for him. Hosea's obedient behaviour as he received the series of commands to prophetic action in 1:2–9 and 3:1–3 suggests that he was already a prophet at the time. None of the language of recruitment, objection and reassurance found in most prophetic calls is present. It is likely, therefore, that the commands served to confirm a call already received in circumstances of which we are not informed.

No solid inferences may be drawn from the prophet's prolific use of literary imagery (see Literary Forms, below). His knowledge of agriculture, flora and fauna and hunting,

---

[1]For discussion of what is here outlined only, *cf.* the standard histories: F. F. Bruce, *Israel and the Nations* (Grand Rapids: Eerdmans, 1963), pp. 53–67; M. Noth, *The History of Israel* (E. T., London: Adam and Charles Black, [2]1965), pp. 238–262; Donner, pp. 408–434; Bright, pp. 253–276; Herrmann, pp. 226–254; Miller and Hayes, pp. 289–339.

though put to superb use in describing Israel's sins and Yahweh's punishments, do not require a specialist's knowledge to account for them.[1] Any well-informed Israelite would have been familiar with the range of activities and experiences that underlie them. It is the poetic adroitness not the technical information that is remarkable.

c. Spiritual background

If there is any area of knowledge that marks Hosea as outstanding, it is his grasp of the nature, content and language of the cult. He gives evidence of knowing it inside and out – its practices, its purposes, its perversions. He sees its theology as wrong – giving credit to the Baals for what are gifts of Yahweh, who alone has the power to spark fertility (2:5, 8–9). He brands its sacrifices as futile, offered to the wrong gods in the wrong places for the wrong reasons (4:19; 5:7). He rejects its means of revelation as lifeless instruments that can discern neither the will nor word of God (4:12). He deplores its sexual acts, brazen blends of lust and magic (4:13–14). He denounces its leaders – priest, prophet and king (4:4–5; 5:1). He mocks its hollowness – people kissing calves (13:2), adoring the products of their own craftsmen (8:6). He decries its savagery – the vicious sacrificing of little children (5:2).[2]

For all this he holds no-one but his own people responsible. No mention is made of Canaanite corruption; no blame is placed on foreign enticement.[3] Both prophet and people had ample background in their covenant traditions to know that the cult was wrong.

Hosea was certainly knowledgeable about those traditions.

[1]Buber, p. 120, summarizes what many have proposed, perhaps with more certainty than is warranted: 'he is so expert in field and village life, that there is no doubt about his being a farmer.'

[2]For details of Baal worship and its impact on Israel and Judah, see Commentary at 2:13 and 13:1. Further evidence of syncretism between Yahweh worship and the cult of Baal may be forthcoming from Kuntillat 'Arjud in northern Sinai, where a 9th to 8th century BC shrine contained evidence that Yahweh was attached to a consort named Asherah (cf. 1 Ki. 15:13; 2 Ki. 21:7). For preliminary reports of these findings, see Z. Meshel and C. Meyers, 'The Name of God in the Wilderness of Zin', *BA* 39, 1976, pp. 6–10; Z. Meshel, 'Did Yahweh Have a Consort?', *BA Rev* 5/2, 1979, pp. 24–35.

[3]Koch (p. 85); cf. J. Crenshaw, pp. 232–233: 'one searches in vain for a single confirmation that prostitution lay at the center of Canaanite religion.' If continued investigation of Ugaritic texts bears out this conclusion, then Hosea's ire and Israel's guilt are all the more understandable.

His references to history and geography in the judgment speeches of 9:10 – 11:8 and 11:12 – 13:16 speak for themselves. So do his citations of the law (4:1–2), his stress on the 'knowledge of God', which seems to be a technical term for covenant understanding and obedience (see on 4:1, 6; 6:6), his use of the Exodus events as expressions of the beginning of Yahweh's gracious relationship with his people (2:14–15; 9:10; 11:1; 12:9; 13:4–5), the self-disclosure formulas in which Yahweh introduces himself as God, the only God, of his people (12:9; 13:4), and his emphasis on the term $b^e r\hat{\imath}t$ as the technical description of the covenant (6:7; 8:1).[1] In none of these passages does Hosea reveal the need to explain his terms or justify his right to use them. Especially is this true with the key term *covenant*.[2]

Given the intimacy of Hosea's knowledge of the tradition and the cogency with which he treats of it, it may be that he brought to the task the expertise of an official of some sort. H. W. Wolff (pp. xxii–xxiii) suggests that Hosea belonged to a *Levitic* circle in Israel, was acquainted closely with the true, yet neglected, duties of a priest (4:6; 6:6; 8:12), and had a ready audience for speeches *about* Israel but not *to* them (9:10 – 10:8; 11:1–11; 14:1–8). While Wolff has supported his theory with additional lines of evidence, *e.g.* the mention of the Levite Moses as a prophet (12:13), the ties in language and thought between Deuteronomy and Hosea (see Message, below), and the use of Gibeah with its story of the Levite's concubine as part of Israel's 'sin-history' (9:9; 10:9), the theory founders on a formidable reef: our lack of clear understanding of the priesthood in early Israel and particularly of the levitical expressions of it (see Blenkinsopp, pp. 99–100).[3]

The same lack of evidence applies to theories that would identify Hosea as a *covenant-mediator*, modelled after Moses (*cf.* 12:13), responsible to speak the law of God within a cultic setting: 'Whether such a covenant-mediator ever existed, and what precisely his functions may have been, is far from being clearly attested in the Old Testament'.[4]

---

[1] See M. J. Buss, pp. 81–115, for other examples of Hosea's cultic and covenantal language, including close corollaries to the Psalms.

[2] Nicholson, p. 188. *Cf.* also Hanson, p. 158.

[3] *Cf.* also D. A. Hubbard, 'Priests and Levites', *IDB* III, pp. 1266–1273.

[4] Clements, p. 14. For the arguments that seek to reconstruct an office of covenant-mediator, see H. J. Kraus, *Worship in Israel* (E. T., Richmond, Virginia: John Knox Press, 1966), pp. 101–112.

What can we say about Hosea's spiritual background? First, he was familiar with and committed to Israel's historic relationship to Yahweh as his people and to the binding implications of that relationship. Second, such intimacy may have been the product of his devout family or of training received in a priestly or prophetic group of whose form and shape we have no knowledge, though it is clear that he viewed himself as a *prophet*, an heir to the ministries of Moses and Samuel (*cf.* on 12:10, 13). Third, Yahweh's commands to marry, have children and call them by significant names led him into an experience in which all that he had known from his past was set in fresh light and filled with new import. Fourth, the meanings of the covenant imparted to him from Israel's traditions were retranslated by him into the language of family love: he saw Yahweh as an aggrieved but constant Husband, as an offended but faithful Father. The family with its rich lexicon of loyalties and tensions became the milieu in which he reread the covenant and transmitted it to the people.

No-one before had spoken so repeatedly of God's love (*'hb*) for his people, and no-one had cast divine grace in the vocabulary of marital intimacy. Neither the realm of international treaties nor of mercantile contracts gave adequate depth, breadth, length and height to the love of God.[1] Only the realm of the family, which Hosea knew at its worst in his marriage and sensed at its best in his understanding of God's constancy, could do that. Hosea's use of a marital metaphor seems all the more shocking when set against the backdrop of the fertility cult. To call Yahweh Husband and, therefore, procreator meant that Baal was not. Hosea's answer to the harlotry with the Baals was not a prudish rejection of the love relationship but an absolute claim to it. It was not the *love* that was wrong, nor the symbolic marriage to deity; it was the ritual prostitution in which the relationship was expressed. Worse still, the union was contracted with a no-god, not one who is true and living (1:10; 2:7). In making the love-language dominant, Yahweh played Baal on his own court and

---

[1] See Clements, pp. 14–23, for a review and rejection of the theory that Yahweh's covenant with Israel was patterned after the Suzerain-Vassal treaties of the ancient Middle East.

demonstrated who was the more faithful, the truly loving Lover. Nothing less than the combination of Hosea's background steeped in covenant truth, of the tragic marital experience which put him in touch with Yahweh's own heart, and of his recognition that Yahweh not Baal was the source of all power and love, could have produced this book which by its story and oracles transposed Israel's knowledge of God into the real intimacy of a true marriage.

V. UNITY AND COMPOSITION

a. Text

In sheer difficulty of Hebrew text, Hosea ranks as the most problematic of Old Testament writings. The RSV, for instance, notes almost three times as many difficulties, uncertainties, or proposed changes for Hosea (197 verses) as for Joel and Amos combined (219 verses). The Septuagint and Syriac have been of modest use in the attempt to recover the text, as H. S. Nyberg's study demonstrated.[1] Further research has validated his basic conclusion that the Massoretic Text, problematic as it is, should continue to be the mainstay of our interpretation of Hosea. Part of the difficulty may be explained in terms of regional or dialectical peculiarities in Hosea's language, though our inventory of extra-biblical sources from the 9th or 8th centuries BC is too thin to support firm conclusions. Some puzzles have been solved by applying to the text insights gained from other Semitic languages, especially Ugaritic. Andersen's commentary abounds in such suggestions.

The approach used in the present work is to follow the consonantal text wherever it is at all possible, while reserving the right to suggest alternate pointing (*i.e.* changes in the vowels) and to divide the words differently, given the fact that ancient manuscripts sometimes lacked word divisions. Our presumption is that any given problem is more likely to be caused by the limits of our knowledge than by the alleged 'corruption' of the text. The fact that the text has survived, bristling with what we call difficulties, is itself remarkable testimony to its quality. The scribes who preserved it must have understood it much more readily than we, or they would have been keenly tempted to alter it.

[1] See H. S. Nyberg, *Studien zum Hoseabuch*, pp. 103ff.

b. Unity

By and large, the book as we have it seems to have come from Hosea or his immediate band of followers. Now that attempts to allocate the salvation passages to later times have largely been abandoned, the focus of attention has narrowed to relatively few passages which are sometimes viewed as later additions. Usually they are attributed to scribes in Judah who copied, edited and perhaps altered Hosea's original sayings somewhat in the light of the changing conditions in their own times. A typical list of the proposed alterations would include: (1) the references to the unification of the kingdoms in 1:10 – 2:1 and 3:5, thought to be added in Josiah's day as a reflection of his expansion into the north (2 Ki. 23:15–20); (2) the elaborations of the salvation oracles introduced by 'in that day' in 2:16–20, 21–23; (3) references to Judah's salvation (1:7), righteousness (11:12), caution (4:13), or condemnation (5:5; 6:11; 8:14), which are seen to be efforts to apply Hosea's words to Judah's life in the 7th century; and (4) the title (1:1) and the proverbial epilogue (14:9).[1]

Brief comments on each of these items may be useful. First, the pictures of reunion of the two kingdoms should be interpreted as expressions not of any pro-Judah leanings but of a concern for the whole people of God, rescued from Egypt, led through the wilderness and settled in the land (2:14–15; 9:10; 12:13; 13:5). These passages (1:10 – 2:1; 3:5) are manifestations of Hosea's vision that the end will be like the beginning, only better. The very language of *return* (2:7; 3:5; 14:1–2) carries this connotation. The note of hope sounded in 1:10–2:1 establishes at the outset the rhythm of judgment and salvation which shapes the book's structure, while the mention of David (3:5) is consonant with Hosea's preference of the dynastic stability of Judah to the frequent political upheavals of the Northern Kingdom. If the people were to be one again, as they had been at the beginning, there had to be a leader – 'one head' (1:11); that 'one head' was certainly not going to be patterned after Jeroboam I or any of his successors, whose actions had supported the cult that Hosea detests. *David* was the only adequate model available (3:5).[2]

---

[1] For such typical lists of proposed additions, see Crenshaw, pp. 234–235; Blenkinsopp, pp. 100–101.

[2] See Emmerson, pp. 98–113, for arguments from language, structure and contents that 3:5 'belongs to the primary stratum of material' (p. 113).

Second, both structurally and thematically 2:16–23 seems to be of a piece with 2:14–15: (1) the orientation of both sections is future; (2) the references to the Baals and to Yahweh's new name, 'My husband' (2:16) stand in obvious continuity to 2:2–13; (3) the covenant with the creation (2:18) is the reversal of the threats in 2:12 and 4:3; and (4) the final restoration announced in 2:21–23 plays on the themes of Yahweh's, not Baal's, gifts to Israel (2:8–9), of the impact of Israel's *answer* to Yahweh's courting (2:14), and of the names of the children (1:2–9; 2:1). The chief reason given for crediting 2:16–23 to a disciple of Hosea, rather than the prophet himself, seems to be the similarity in theme and style to the biographical section in 1:2–9. The unity, however, of chapters 1–3 is so evident that it is hard to drive any wedge between Hosea and a disciple who may have collaborated in the editing of the text.[1]

Third, the issue of the references to Judah (1:1, 7, 11; 4:15; 5:5, 10, 12, 13, 14; 6:4, 11; 8:14; 10:11; 11:12; 12:2) is a complex one. Each occurrence merits discussion on its own (see Commentary). But there is no *a priori* reason to eliminate Judah from Hosea's range of vision. The prophet would have been familiar with its historic role in Yahweh's programme. His commitment to the covenant, which he saw as pertinent to the whole people of God, would have sparked Hosea to apply its judgments and blessings to Judah as well as to his own northern tribes.[2]

---

[1]Mays (p. 47): 'The skilful way in which the material is ordered ... suggests that the work was done by a contemporary disciple, if not by the prophet himself.' Emmerson, pp. 21–40, argues that the salvation speeches originated with Hosea (or a close disciple) and were not the product of editing in Judah after Hosea's time. The *arrangement* of the sayings, however, she does credit to a Judean editor who sought to highlight national repentance more than divine sovereignty. See also D. J. Clines, 'Hosea 2: Structure and Interpretation', *Studia Biblica*, 1, 1978, pp. 83–103, for the conclusion that 2:2–23 is an integrated poem, whether it was originally composed that way or not.

[2]Emmerson has concluded that the references to Judah's salvation in 1:7 (p. 95), 1:11 (p. 98), and perhaps 11:12 (pp. 115–116) are from Hosea, as are the references in the context of the Syro-Ephraimite conflict in 5:10–14 (p. 70) and the announcement of judgment in 8:14 (p. 77). She reads *Judah* in 6:4 and 12:2 as a scribal substitution for *Israel* (pp. 71, 65) and is uncertain about the judgment threat in 6:11. She credits 4:15 (p. 80) and 5:5 (p. 67) to Judean reaction on the basis of their structure, and concludes that one aim of the Judean editing was to condemn Judah for aping Israel's sins.

Fourth, the title (1:1), which notes the length of Hosea's ministry as reaching into Hezekiah's reign (see 'Date' above), is obviously an editorial addition. But the authorship of the epilogue (14:9) is inconclusive. There is plenty of evidence to show that the prophets were familiar with the sayings of the wise, and Hosea's own vocabulary and style (note his use of proverbs in Literary Forms, below) may account for this verse. On the other hand, it may well reflect the concern of his later followers that their prophet's words be heeded.

c. Composition

The connections between the oracles uttered by Hosea and the written form of the book are virtually impossible to reconstruct. The threefold division of the book may hint at three stages in the process of assembling the oracles: 1:2 – 3:5; 4:1 – 11:11; 11:12 – 14:8. Whether any of these three sections had a life of its own with separate circulation we cannot tell.[1] We can, however, make some observations about the composition of the book. First, the materials that we have, especially the collections of brief speeches in chapters 4–14 are probably key fragments, prime samplings, of Hosea's total repertoire of prophecy.[2] Detached from their original settings and the occasions of their utterance, of which we have only faint traces in 4:1–4 and 5:1–2, the oracles seem cryptic and even disjointed. Second, once assembled into their collections (4:1–11:11; 11:12 – 14:8), they underwent almost no revision or expansion: 'the style is remarkably homogeneous with relatively few indications of editorial reworking' (Blenkinsopp, p. 101). The paucity of formulae, transitional phrases, or other signs of formal packaging is noteworthy, especially in comparison with Amos. Third, the fragmentary form of the sayings together

---

[1]Andersen (p. 64) proposes a separate literary history for 1:2 – 3:5 from those of the other two divisions. He posits a different hand in the collection and assembly (particularly in the case of 2:2–23 which has a very high count of prose particles) based on statistics of particle usage. Y. Kaufmann, *The Religion of Israel* (E.T., University of Chicago Press, 1960), pp. 368–371, went so far as to label chs. 1–3 'first Hosea' and chs. 4–14 'Second Hosea'. A far more complex history of composition has been recently posited, *cf.* G. A. Yee, *Composition and Tradition in the Book of Hosea.* See pp. 305–317 for conclusion and summary.

[2]Buber, p. 111, notes that the book of Hosea 'includes only a few fragments of the original corpus, saved from the destruction of Samaria and bound up together'.

with the dialectic or stylistic peculiarities (see *Text*, above) may indicate that they were circulated and collected in written rather than oral form at a very early stage. Fourth, the order in which they were assembled is both *topical* (*e.g.* the emphases on harlotry in 4:1 – 5:7, on political upheaval in 5:8 – 7:17, on cult and kingship in 8:1 – 9:6, on past history in 9:10 – 11:9 and 11:12 – 13:6; on return and restoration in 14:1–8) and *chronological*, moving from what might have been set in the last days of Jeroboam II in 4:1 – 5:7, through the Syro-Ephraimite struggle in 5:8 – 7:16, to the tumultuous years of Assyrian vassalage as the time neared for Samaria's destruction (8:1 – 13:16). Fifth, the collections are shaped so that each features a note of *accusation* (Heb. *rîb*; a quarrel, indictment, or legal case to be pressed)[1] against the people at the beginning of the oracles and so that each concludes with words of hope and salvation (3:5; 11:8–11; 14:1–7). Sixth, the thematic and stylish links between the separate short speeches and the larger clusters evince a remarkable oneness of aim, thought, vocabulary and intention throughout the book. Catchwords and catch-phrases, echoes of previous passages and anticipations of subsequent sections will be noted in abundance in the course of the Commentary. All of these lend credence to Buss' conclusion: 'It is clear that the book of Hosea contains a much sharper structure in content than has usually been thought' (p. 32).

VI. LITERARY FORMS

Hosea employs fewer set literary forms than Amos (see my Introduction to Amos), and he never reports visions. He does not specialize in stereotyped presentations of oracles, introduced by formulae and shaped to almost identical structure as found in his predecessor's book. Apart from the carefully crafted pattern of the marriage and remarriage stories and oracles in chapters 1–3, the book gives the impression of spontaneity, freedom, even passion, in its movement. Yet the style exhibits such frequent and subtle literary artistry as to evoke our admiration, surprise and excitement on every page.

[1] M. DeRoche, 'Yahweh's *Rib* Against Israel: A Reassessment of the So-Called "Prophetic Lawsuit" in the Pre-exilic Prophets', *JBL*, 102, 1983, pp. 563–574, argues that the *rib* is too personal a conflict between Yahweh and the people to be labelled 'prophetic lawsuit' or 'covenant lawsuit.'

a. Major forms[1]

Two samples of Hosea's main categories:

The judgment speech is evidenced regularly in the rhythm of accusation of sin and announcement of judgment that characterizes the book. Even the biographical narrative of prophetic actions is in fact a form of judgment speech: the accusation is 'great harlotry' (1:2); the announcement is disclosed in the names of the children (1:4–9). Hosea's patterns of judgment speech are flexible and varied, only occasionally in Hebrew using *therefore* to mark the transition from indictment to threat (*cf.* 2:6, 9; 4:3). Curiously, the AV felt more need of 'therefore' and added a dozen or so, either just to mark the transition or to translate 'and'.

Salvation speeches occur at pivotal spots in the flow of the book (*e.g.* 1:10 – 2:1; 2:14–23; 3:5; 11:10–11; 14:4–7). The autobiographical story of the remarriage (3:1–5) is a kind of salvation speech, as the closing verse intimates. A frequent characteristic of Hosea's speeches, whether on judgment or salvation, is that they speak *about* Israel more than they speak *to* her (*e.g.* 2:2–13 is addressed to the children, with the nation, as the object of judgment, described in the third person; much of the historical review in 9:10–11:7 is carried on as though Israel were not present; the promises in 1:10–11; 2:14–15, 21–23; 11:10–11; 14:4–7 are not addressed to Israel as *you*). Large portions of the book, then, are written as Yahweh's musings in Hosea's presence or Hosea's own musings, perhaps before his disciples or children. Andersen's hypothesis (p. 45) on this process of communication is that in Hosea we are frequently made privy to 'the actual deliberations of Yahweh in the divine council' (*cf.* 1 Ki. ch. 22; Is. ch. 6; Je. ch. 23), when the oracles had not yet been formulated for public delivery.

b. Other forms

Hosea used *proverbs* to underscore or summarize his message at crucial points (4:9, 11, 15; 8:7; 10:12). The force of the

[1]See Introduction To Amos, 'Literary Forms', in D. A. Hubbard, *Joel and Amos: an introduction and commentary*, TOTC (Leicester: IVP, 1989), p. 102, for an inventory of genres used by that prophet. Detailed comment on forms in Hosea will be restricted to literary types not found in Amos.

conventional wisdom was not only to sum up memorably an issue at stake but also to remind Israel, somewhat sarcastically, that the truth which they were violating or ignoring should have been so obvious that by overlooking it they had exposed their own stupidity.

Battle warnings, framed in imperatives and filled with trumpet blasts (5:8; 8:1), served to dramatize the terror, certainty and suddenness of the judgment. Wicked lives are subject to siege at any moment in history.

Exhortations to repentance (6:1–3; 10:12; 12:6; 14:1–3) reinforce the constant emphasis on *return* (*cf.* 2:7; 3:5) that punctuates the book. By quoting the actual words with which priests or prophets should have urged penitent reform, Hosea dramatizes both the hollowness of inadequate contrition (6:1–3) and the sincerity and scope of true repentance (10:12; 12:6; 14:1–3; *cf.* Am. 5:4–6, 14–15).

Prohibitions, negative imperatives (4:15; 9:1), add touches of irony to Israel's life by dashing their cultic exuberance with the cold water of reality: 'rejoice not', words that are the negation of the exhortations sometimes found in salvation speeches or 'enter not', the opposite of the normal priestly invitation (*cf.* Ps. 100).

A love song (14:5–7) seals Yahweh's pledge of healing with which the book closes. The similarities to the Song of Solomon are several and noteworthy (see Commentary).

In common with Amos, Hosea uses *woes* (7:13; 9:12b) to threaten Israel with death, and *rhetorical questions* (4:16; 9:5; 10:3, 9; 11:8; 13:10, 14; 14:8) to predetermine the answer and to fix the interest of his audience.

As much as any other form, the *divine complaint* expresses the burden of Hosea's message (2:8; 4:16; 6:4; 6:11b – 7:2; 7:13c–15; 8:5; 9:10; 10:11; 11:1–4, 8; 13:4–6; 14:8). The essence of the complaint is the inherent contradiction, whether expressed by Yahweh (the usual case) or for Yahweh (4:16), between God's merciful provision for his people and their mindless rebellion against him. The complaints usually serve as accusations in the judgment speeches but are made more poignant and condemning by their very personal character. They are a prime clue to the relational, familial thrust of Hosea's understanding of God and seem to relate to what he learned of the divine pathos from his own family tragedy.

c. Literary devices

While the two stories of Hosea's marriage and remarriage (1:2–9; 3:1–5) are clearly *prose*, though containing both narrative and speech, the sections identified as *poetry* (2:2–23; 4:1–14; ch. 9) seem to blend poetic and prosaic elements characteristic of the 8th-century prophets. Andersen (p. 65), with a detailed analysis of the ratio of words to particles, concludes that 'for the most part Hosea goes off on its own bent, a kind of free verse, or unregulated rhythmic pattern.'

At the same time, its poetic characteristics are clear. They are just not as uniformly patterned as what we may find in Psalms or Proverbs. Chief features of poetry are all present: emotional tenor; repetition in many different forms from assonance and alliteration to repetition of words, phrases and themes; parallelism frequently found in four-line or three-line entities, as well as the more standard couplets; irregular word order; compactness of expression; and imagery (see below).

Signs of open argument may be spotted in the text. See on 4:4; 5:2–3; 9:7–8. These are set in the public proclamation implied in 4:1 and 5:1 with the use of the *call to attention* that assumes the presence of an audience. These passages of open protest are the best clues we have that the prophetic word was by and large rejected, especially by those who most needed to receive it.

Like Amos, Hosea frequently inserted *quotations* of the words of those to whom, or of whom, he spoke. See on 2:5, 7; 4:15; 8:2; 10:3, 8; 12:8; 13:10. Usually the force of these citations is to add weight to the accusation by quoting the people's words as testimony against them.

Similes and metaphors are a trademark of Hosea. Harlotry and adultery are metaphors for idolatry and pervade the book (1:2; 2:4–5; 3:3; 4:10–15, 18; 5:3–4; 6:10; 7:4; 9:1), framing the picture of Israel's spiritual perfidy as symbolized in Gomer's unfaithfulness. Strikingly powerful and shocking are the figures used to describe God's pervasive and irresistible judgment: pus and infection (5:12, see Commentary); lion, panther, bear (5:14; 11:10; 13:7–8); trapper (7:12); vulture (or eagle, 8:1); farmer (by inference, 10:11). More comforting are the pictures of Yahweh as husband (2:14–23), parent (11:8–9), lover (14:3–7), and verdant tree (14:8) that convey messages of hope. Hosea's descriptions of Israel are equally vivid, pin-pointing the almost infinite variety of Israel's sins: stubborn heifer (4:16); snare and net (5:1); heated oven (7:3–7); bread half-baked and mouldy (7:8–9); silly dove (7:11); treacherous bow (7:16); useless vessel (8:8); grapes and fig-tree (9:10); luxuriant vine (10:1); trained heifer (10:11); crooked merchant (12:7); stupid baby (13:13). Israel's lack of stability is pictured as mist, dew, chaff, smoke (13:3), the futility of her foreign policy as riding herd on the wind (12:1), and the fate of her calf-idol as bobbing like a chip on the water (10:7). To a people used to thinking in visual terms, nothing must have been more needling than to have these word-pictures from everyday life thrust before them as mirrors of their wickedness and folly.

Puns were part of Hosea's arsenal of irony. They were used not as artistic embellishment but for pungent emphasis: *Jezreel* with its double meaning, 'God will scatter' like seed in judgment (1:4) and 'God will sow' (or inseminate) in restoration (2:22–23); the play on 'put an end' (Heb. *šbt*) and *sabbaths* (Heb. *šbt*, 2:11); the repeated interchange between *Ephraim* and *wild ass* or ideas of *fruitfulness* (Heb. *'pr*, *pr'*, and *pry*; 8:9; 13:15; 14:8); use of verbs (Heb. *'qb* and *swr*) related to their ancestor's double name, Jacob and Israel (12:3–4); the mocking of Bethel by the use of Beth-aven (10:5) and Beth-arbel (10:14); the jeering at *Gilgal's* future as 'stone-heaps' (*gallîm*, 12:11 [Heb. v. 12]); the labelling of *princes* as *rebels* (Heb. *śārîm*, *sor'rîm*, 9:15) – these are just a few of the significant word-plays that punctuate the book. Their biting force will not have escaped Hosea's hearers.[1]

---

[1] On the role of irony, sarcasm, dramatic tension and other literary ingredients of tragedy or comedy, see M. J. Buss, 'Tragedy and Comedy in Hosea', *Semeia*, 32, 1985, pp. 71–82. D. Robertson, 'Tragedy, Comedy, and the Bible—A Response', *Semeia*, 32, 1985, p. 106, rightly concluded that neither 'tragedy' nor comedy is an adequate literary label for what we find in the great prophets.

VII. MESSAGE

a. Major themes

We are not left to guess about the person of God in Hosea. Yahweh introduces himself in words that feature his uniqueness and sovereignty (12:9; 13:4). It was Israel's failure to make proper response to these introductions that prompted the divine judgment and Hosea's preaching of it.

God's unique sovereignty had two massive ramifications for Israel's common life. First, idolatry was absolutely prohibited, since Yahweh's uniqueness as the Holy One (11:9) meant that all replicas were lifeless caricatures, utterly incapable either of revealing the divine person or of channelling the divine power (8:6; 10:5–6; 13:2). Since adoration of God's name alone was the only appropriate reply to the self-introduction of the Exodus (Ex. 20:2–3), any other worship drew divine wrath and prophetic fire like no other sin. For the prophets, worship was the 'center, the heart of the people's life'.[1] The implications of compromise and corruption at this centre were grasped and amplified by Hosea: (1) almost at the outset of his message he relayed the divine announcement that the religious structures themselves had to be put to an end (2:11; 3:4); (2) enthusiasm without true understanding had led Israel from Yahweh into spiritual harlotry with the Baals (4:6–12); (3) so perverted was their worship that the shrines themselves were to be boycotted (4:15); (4) sacrifices were a sham when Yahweh's uniqueness was forgotten (5:6–7); (5) they had so failed to come to grips with that uniqueness that they actually kissed calves as an act of adulation (13:2); and (6) in consequence of all this, the acts, centres and objects of worship were a prime target of judgment (4:19; 5:7; 8:6; 9:1–6; 10:2, 5–8).

Second, Yahweh's unique sovereignty meant that all of life was within his control, whether creation, history, politics, international affairs, social relationships, or religious activities. All that the people did was under the authority of the one true God; all that they needed was in his power to supply. The contrast between this unity of life and the world-view of Israel's polytheistic neighbours who lived in 'a world of many

---

[1]C. Westermann, *Elements of Old Testament Theology* (E.T., Atlanta: John Knox Press, 1982), p. 132.

gods with as many minds' was startling. For Israel, 'this divine authority is concentrated in a single personal will, which takes complete hold of the man addressed by it, and tolerates no other claim'.[1] This unified understanding of authority and obligation accounts for the range of topics touched by Hosea as well as for the ways in which the topics are inter-related. The one God who had introduced himself to his people in the Exodus had kept on introducing himself through the prophet as Lord of history, fertility, domestic politics, international affairs and national life.

To Hosea, God's *lordship of history* was not so much a display of power as of loving yet frustrated relationship. No mention do we find of the destruction of the tall, sturdy Amorites (Am. 2:9), smitten by the divine hand. The pictures, rather, are of a farmer's nurture (9:10), a parent's instruction (11:1–4), a guardian's protection (13:4–5), or a lover's wooing (2:14–15). The Exodus is seen as a time when Israel defected from her relationship with God. Her present sin is understood to have its beginnings in that time,[2] and is linked to the future in the descriptions of judgment which, in part at least, reverse the course of history: judgment is a 'return to Egypt' (9:3, 6; 11:11) or a reversion to the wilderness (2:5; 12:9).

The picture of God's *lordship of fertility* contributes to the book's unity. From the pun on Jezreel's name (*cf.* on 1:4, 11; 2:22–23) to the metaphor of the fruit-giving cypress (14:8), Hosea reminds Israel that Yahweh, not Baal, is the source of all that sustains their lives: He is the One who gives them crops and wealth (2:8), who initiates 'a cosmic covenant' to set at peace the animal kingdom (2:18),[3] who provides their pasture (4:16), who brings the rain (6:3), who will restore their verdure (*cf.* 10:1) in the end (14:4–7), and who, in the meanwhile, names their true source of righteousness and steadfast love (10:12). Hosea's eye is single: who is responsible for fertility and should therefore receive the worship and gratitude of the people? Fertility without myth or magic was what the prophet wanted his audience to understand. He deliberately combined the themes of lordship of history and of fertility: 'the authentic source of all fertility was also the

---

[1] W. Eichrodt, *Man in the Old Testament*, *SBT*, 4 (E.T., SCM Press, 1951), p. 15.
[2] C. Westermann, *op. cit.*, p. 135.
[3] See Murray, pp. 209–210, for discussion of this covenant and its expressions in Je. 33:20, 25; Ezk. 34:25–31; Jb. 5:22–23 (RSV 'league').

Deity whom Israel revered as champion of enslaved people.'[1]

Hosea's depiction of God's *lordship of domestic politics* is as clear and specific as his dealing with the other expressions of sovereignty. In contrast to Amos who frequently directs his words at the national leadership (Am. 4:1; 6:1; 7:9, 10–17), most of what Hosea says about the monarchy is levelled at priests who have conspired against the monarchy (6:7 – 7:7) or at the people in general, who have changed kings as though they were changing clothes (8:4, 10; 10:3; 13:10–11). Where the kings themselves were culpable in their domestic leadership, two major wrongs seem to be in view. First, as sponsors of the shrines they were guilty of complicity in adulterous religious activities (5:1–7). This involvement underlies the close link between the collapse of the monarchy – 'we have no king' – and the loss of 'Samaria's king', *i.e.* the calf-god in 10:3–7; (*cf.* also 8:4 where dynastic instability and destructive idolatry are condemned in parallel lines). Second, the kings were held accountable for lack of justice and covenant compassion in the land (10:4). They should have set the example for sowing righteousness. Instead, as sponsors of military enterprises, they 'ploughed iniquity' and must 'be utterly cut off' when the judgment comes (10:12–13, 15). But Hosea's quarrel does not seem to have been with the monarchy *per se*, as though Israel should have had some other form of governance,[2] but with its support of the corrupt worship inaugurated by Jeroboam I (I Ki. ch. 12), its refusal to exercise righteous leadership, and its perpetuating of a pattern of dynastic changes which could be remedied only by the collapse of the entire political structure (3:4) and the reestablishment of a Davidic dynasty (1:11; 3:5; *cf.* Am. 9:11).[3]

Hosea's way of dealing with God's *lordship of international*

[1]Crenshaw, p. 240. *Cf.* P. D. Hanson, p. 167: 'Hosea could remain true to the triadic confession of his heritage [worship, righteousness, compassion], even as he combined it with the freshness of a natural order revivified by the one true God, who was the Sovereign One not only of history but of nature as well.' *Cf.* Ho. 10:12.

[2]The reference to Gilgal's evil (9:15) may well refer to Saul's coronation as first king (1 Sa. 11:15). Hosea certainly contends that the monarchy as developed has not turned out well in serving God's purposes. Yet the fact that he looks to a new kingship beyond the present (1:11; 3:5) indicates that he did not advocate an abandoning of the whole system.

[3]See Emmerson, pp. 105–113, for a discussion of 'Hosea's attitude to monarchy'.

affairs again differs sharply from Amos'. No speeches against the other nations, no allusions to their exoduses and no invitations for them to come to Samaria as witnesses of her crimes, are found on Hosea's pages. The nations are either instruments of *judgment* by invasion (1:5; 7:16; 8:14; 10:8–10, 14–15; 11:6–7; 13:15–16) and exile (2:6–7; 3:4; 8:13; 9:3, 6, 15, 17; 10:6; 11:5, 10–11) or *of temptation* by enticing Israel to foolish treaties (5:13; 7:11; 8:9; 12:1) and wicked military build-ups (8:14; 10:13–14). So prevalent and persistent were these temptations and so glibly did Israel succumb to them that renouncing them was a key condition of Israel's return: 'Assyria shall not save us, we will not ride upon horses' (14:3).[1] Yet Yahweh did not hesitate to use the foreign powers for his purposes. Indeed, they are the direct means of judgment in Hosea who, unlike Amos, does not employ cosmic disasters like earthquakes or other natural catastrophes. Hosea kept the punishment suited to the crimes: either hob-nobbing with pagans too closely or fearing them unduly would be dealt with when God marched with the pagans. Hosea spends no effort justifying this or predicting the judgment that in turn will fall on the judging nations (*cf.* Is. ch. 10; Hab. ch. 2).

At the root of all that Hosea says is his declaration of God's *lordship of national life* in Israel. It is a lordship that Hosea defines in personal terms: Yahweh is husband and parent to the people; they are wayward spouse and stubborn child to him. It is a lordship built on a relationship described as: *covenant love* (Heb. *ḥesed*, 2:19; 4:1; 6:4, 6; 10:12; 12:6), the commitment to live in terms of the bond that unites parties with as much goodwill and care as possible; *faithfulness* (Heb. *ʾᵉmûnâ*; *ᵉmet*, 2:20 [Heb. v. 22]; 4:1), utter reliability in word and deed; *mercy* (Heb. *rḥm*, 1:6–7; 2:1 [Heb. v. 3], 4 [Heb. v. 6], 19 [Heb. v. 21], 23 [Heb. v. 25]; 14:3 [Heb. v. 4]), tender compassion like a mother's for her child; *knowledge of God* (Heb. *daʿat*, 4:1–6; 6:6; Heb. *ydʿ*, 2:8 [Heb. v. 10], 20 [Heb. v. 22]; 5:4; 6:3; 8:2; 11:3; 13:4), the intimate, loyal, consistent fidelity to all that the covenant embraces (*i.e.* living in terms of an historic and personal relationship to God and of all the

---

[1]Y. Kaufmann, *The Religion of Israel*, p. 375, flags Hosea's concern about armament as innovative: 'The first biblical author, indeed, the first man in history, to condemn militarism as a religious-moral sin was Hosea.'

instructions about life's conduct that go with it).[1] Righteousness and justice are his ways of summarizing the covenant
response (Am. 5:7, 24; 6:12; *cf.* Ho. 2:19; 10:4, 12; 12:6).
Personal language should be, in this relationship, understood
to refer primarily to the nation and not merely to individuals
within it. The wife and the child stand for all the people, not
just those who appropriate the significance of the terms. In
fact, we have no evidence in the book apart from the prophet
himself of any pious remnant standing free of the condemnations that dominate the speeches.

Writing a commentary on Hosea towards the close of the
20th century carries with it the opportunity and responsibility
to say something about the feminist implications of Hosea's
use of female imagery to describe Israel's spiritual promiscuity. That there are patriarchal features to the story should
readily be acknowledged: (1) the marriage of Hosea and
Gomer would not have been described as a partnership in our
understanding of the term: (2) Gomer, in her corrupted
sexuality, does become the figure of fallenness, a feminine,
not a masculine figure; and (3) it may be possible to see her
treated like an object as her sexuality becomes the vehicle to
display the sins of the nation.[2] Some other observations from
the text may broaden our perspective a little: (1) Gomer does
not stand for the *women* of Israel but for the nation, both
genders of which, and especially the men, were indicted for
their perverseness (4:14); (2) Gomer seems not to be a typical
Israelite woman, as though Hosea were bracketing all of her
sex with her, but an exception – a person whose harlotry was
blatant and public; (3) if *wife* is one dominant image for Israel,
son is the other (11:1–4), so that masculinity comes in for
censure along with femininity;[3] (4) the story of Gomer's

[1] On the relationship between 'instruction' (Heb. *tôrâ*) and 'knowledge of
God', see Koch, p. 91: 'For *torah* feeds the knowledge of God; and ... this is the
concept which provides the guide for conduct. Here knowledge ... is an
understanding, with emotional and sympathetic connotations and practical
consequences, which is possible only as a result of close personal community
with what is known.'
[2] For a reading of the story of Gomer that makes points like these, see T.
Drorah Setel, 'Prophets and Pornography: Female Sexual Imagery in Hosea'
in *Feminist Interpretation of the Bible*, ed. by Letty M. Russell (Philadelphia:
Westminster Press, 1985), pp. 86–95.
[3] J. J. Schmitt, 'The Gender of Ancient Israel', *JSOT*, 26, 1983, pp. 115–125,
points out that the Hebrew text, including that of Hosea, encourages us to use

relationship with Hosea does not intend to teach us about marriage but about God's dealings with Israel, and to do so in these intimate terms it has to work within the cultural framework of the time; (5) yet it transcends that framework with its emphasis on *Go, love* (3:1) which implies forgiveness and reconciliation in a legal setting, where capital punishment might have been the normal outcome; (6) the personal relationship, as mutual as Hebrew can make it, between God and Israel is signalled by the substitution of 'My husband' for the pagan-sounding and more hierarchial 'My Baal' (lit. 'my master', 2:16); and (7) both the training and nurture of Ephraim (11:1–4) and the language of compassion and mercy involved in Not-pitied's name (Heb. root *rḥm* related to *womb*) may be maternal more than paternal figures. In these last three points we may pick up clues that, rather than being a deposit of patriarchal prejudice that objectifies female sexuality, Hosea's story was a stage on the way to an enriched understanding of womanhood that came into full blossom in the Christian gospel.[2] For Yahweh to have used sexual terms to picture his relationship to the people surely was to elevate our understanding and appreciation of human sexuality.

Two final observations may be in order about the familial covenant-language in which Yahweh's lordship of Israel's life is couched. First, looking at the texts from a form-critical standpoint indicates that in the judgment speeches reasons are given, in the form of accusations, to account for the announced judgment. In the passages of hope, however, no explanation is forthcoming of the divine love that proffers forgiveness and waits for Israel's return. Succinctly put, 'God's judgment needs a reason; his compassion does not.'[2]

Second, the intimacy depicted in the book is seen as an expression, not a compromise, of Yahweh's holiness. As this survey of his lordship suggests, his transcendence is affirmed at every point – over history, over creation, over his people,

---

they or *he* for Israel, rather than *she*, even when female imagery may be involved.

[1]See S. Terrien, *Till the Heart Sings: A Biblical Theology of Manhood and Womanhood* (Philadelphia: Fortress Press, 1985), pp. 53–58.

[2]C. Westermann, *op. cit.*, p. 144. A somewhat different tack is taken by Emmerson, p. 164, in her conclusion that Judean redactors overlaid 'a theology of repentance in which the initiative lies solely with the forgiving love of Yahweh with the call for man's prior response.' Her evidence for this Judean emphasis on repentance is less than convincing.

over the nations. He is holy Lord, unique in every way possible. And he shows his holiness by entering into the midst of his people and healing them with his love, after he has judged them in the wrath that is also a manifestation of his loving holiness (11:8–9).

The depth of what God feels, as Hosea understands those feelings, can never be separated from the height of who he is. The sharpness of the pain that registers in the divine complaints (see Literary Forms, above) is directly related to the majesty of the Person who is suffering. And that language of suffering takes on its pathos from the familial relationship which controls Hosea's prophecy. No shepherd could feel that pain over his sheep, no judge over his defendant, no king over his subjects. Spouses and parents know special kinds of pain. Into these, the magnificent Holy One of Israel entered without balm or panacea. Not until Jesus weeps over Jerusalem, endures the betrayal of a disciple, and complains against the withdrawal of the Father, do we see a clearer picture of wounded majesty.[1]

b. Use in the Old Testament

Martin Buber (p. 110) has called *Jeremiah* Hosea's 'posthumous disciple'. In language (see Commentary, *passim*), imagery and theological concepts, Jeremiah seems to have seen himself as heir to Hosea's mission, especially as an interpreter of the covenant. And both of their lives became parables of suffering for the sake of love: God's onerous command to Hosea to marry was matched by his command to Jeremiah not to marry (16:1–2).

Hosea's *dominant metaphors*, Israel as bride and son to Yahweh, are given significant play in Jeremiah (3:1–5, 20; 3:19–22). The *wilderness* motif, with its overtones of honeymoon, is found in both prophets (Je. 2:1–3). Key *theological terms* are picked up by Jeremiah and used in ways almost

---

[1]Treatments of divine suffering, in contrast with the classical category of the *impassivity of God*, may be found in E. S. Gerstenberger and W. Schrage, *Suffering* (E.T., Nashville: Abingdon, 1981), pp. 98–102; T. E. Fretheim, *The Suffering of God: An Old Testament Perspective* (Philadelphia: Fortress Press, 1985); J. Moltmann, *The Trinity and the Kingdom of God: The Doctrine of God* (E. T., SCM, 1981. US ed. San Francisco: Harper & Row, 1981), pp. 21–60. Moltmann cites A. J. Heschel's concept of *divine pathos* as one influence in his thinking about God's love (pp. 25–30).

identical to Hosea's: covenant love (Heb. *ḥesed*, Je. 2:2); harlot or harlotry for idolatry (Heb. *znh*, Je. 3:2–3); knowledge of God (Je. 2:8; 4:22; 31:34); return (Heb. *šwb*, Je. 2:19; 3:1, 19, 22; 4:1, *etc.*). Similarities in *literary forms* may also be noted: (1) lists of commandments (Ho. 4:2; Je. 7:9); (2) law-suits or legal quarrels (Heb. *rîb*, Ho. 2:2 [Heb. v. 4]; 4:1; 12:2; Je. 11:20; 20:12); (3) divine complaints (Ho. 6:4; 11:8; 14:8 [Heb. v. 9]; Je. 8:4–7; 8:22 – 9:3; 12:7–13); (4) exhortations to repent and return (Ho. 6:1–3; 14:1–2; Je. 3:22–23); (5) confessions of sin (Ho. 14:2–3; Je. 14:7–10, 19–22); and (6) admonition to sow righteousness (Ho. 10:12; Je. 4:3).[1]

In the case of *Ezekiel*, the question is whether the influence of Hosea was passed through Jeremiah or came independently. The chief parallel is the theme of harlotry/idolatry in chapters 16 and 23. As Zimmerli has noted, the list of gifts which Yahweh gave to the bride (Ezk. ch. 16) is not recorded in Jeremiah and may indicate that Ezekiel had direct contact with the text of Hosea chapter 2.[2] But the figure of Israel as 'the vine' is so widely used that we should not argue strongly for a direct connection between Ezekiel chapter 15 and Hosea 10:1 (*cf.* Is. 5:1–7; 27:2–6; Ps. 80).

The relationship of Hosea to *Deuteronomy* is one of the thorniest in Old Testament studies. Wolff's approach (p. xxxi) would be typical of the majority opinion which holds that Hosea's circle of followers 'were forerunners of the Deuteronomic movement.' Through them, Hosea's ministry had deep impact on the forms and message of the book of Deuteronomy which was the 'Book of the law' discovered in the Temple in Josiah's day (2 Ki. 22:8–10). Among the themes which Wolff traces to Hosea's influence are these: God's providence in the Exodus, wilderness journeys and conquest of the land; Israel's satiety with God's blessings and consequent presumption upon his grace, which led to their forgetting of him; the condemnation of political alliances; and the use of the terms *tôrâ*, 'instruction', Yahweh's 'love', 'redemption', and 'brotherhood'.

[1] These similarities are described more fully by J. A. Thompson, *The Book of Jeremiah*, NICOT (Grand Rapids, Eerdmans, 1980), pp. 81–85. For *šwb* 'return', see pp. 76–81; for 'covenant', see pp. 59–67. M. J. Buss, p. 81, thinks that Hosea's influence on Jeremiah was more subtle than direct: they were 'part of the same tradition'.

[2] W. Zimmerli, *Ezekiel*, Hermeneia, I (E.T., Philadelphia: Fortress Press, 1979), p. 44.

But these connections between Hosea and Deuteronomy are not readily explained. This is not the place to debate the date of the completion of Deuteronomy,[1] but there is a growing consensus that believes the core of Deuteronomic teaching was preserved in the Northern Kingdom so that Hosea's work drew from these materials.[2] Such a view would account for the fact, already noticed by E. W. Nicholson (p. 188) in connection with Hosea's use of *covenant* (Heb. *berît*), that the major themes of Hosea, especially his appeals to law, history and standards of right living, are teachings familiar to his audience and thus demand no explanation. The issue is so complex and the tangible evidence so thin that dogmatic conclusions are unwise and continued research is welcome.

c. Use in the New Testament

Hosea's specific contribution may be found in the number of his *phrases* echoed in the New Testament, inserted in the text, whether consciously or unconsciously by the authors, yet serving as clues to continuity in the movement of divine revelation: the apocalyptic prediction of people calling for the rocks to cover them from judgment (Lk. 23:30; Ho. 10:8); harvest of righteousness (2 Cor. 9:10; Ho. 10:12); fruit of lips (Heb. 13:15; Ho. 14:2); 'I am rich, I have prospered' (Rev. 3:17; Ho. 12:8).

Most of the *direct quotations* have been discussed in the Commentary. We list them here: the changing of the children's names from negative (1:6, 9) to positive (1:11 – 2:1; 2:23) becomes a prophecy of the inclusion of Gentiles into the church (Rom. 9:25; 1 Pet. 2:10); God's account of his care for Israel in the Exodus (11:1) is said to be fulfilled in Christ's descent into Egypt (Mt. 2:15); God's ironic summons to Sheol and death to work their judgment (13:14) becomes for Paul a cry of resurrection victory (1 Cor. 15:55).

Some motifs from Hosea have been used to shape *basic themes* in New Testament theology. First, the priority of relationship and compassion to ritual became a dominant theme

---

[1] See J. A. Thompson, *Deuteronomy*, TOTC (Leicester: IVP, 1974. US ed. Downers Grove, Illinois: 1974), pp. 47–68.

[2] M. Buss, p. 81: 'It seems to be possible, on the basis of vocabulary and thought, to show that there is a stream of tradition which includes Hosea,

in Matthew's account of Jesus' mission. 'Mercy not sacrifice', carried over *verbatim* from Hosea 6:6 in the LXX, expressed the indictment against the legalism of the Pharisees, who may have been viewed as playing a role akin to that of the priests in Hosea. Second, the idea of the 'knowledge of God' with its strong connotations of obedience, loyalty and intimacy seems to have been seized in the Johannine literature especially and used to describe a major aspect of Christian discipleship (Jn. 17:3, 7–8; 1 Jn. 2:4, 13–14; 3:1). Third, the marriage metaphor is applied to the relationship of Christ to the church and (1) plays a dominant role in the notes of joy and newness that the gospel brings (Mt. 9:15), (2) helps to provide a context of love and sacrifice for the mutual subjection required of partners in Christian marriage (Eph. 5:21–33), and (3) captures the radiance of the church's triumphant and eternal union with the Saviour (Rev. 19:7–9; 21:1–4).

Deuteronomy, the Asaph psalms, the Deuteronomistic historians, Jeremiah and Ezekiel,' *cf.* van der Woude, p. 47.

ANALYSIS

I. HOSEA'S EXPERIENCES (1:1 – 3:5)
  a. Title (1:1)
  b. A significant family (1:2 – 2:1)
     i. Action I: a harlot for a wife (1:2–3a)
     ii. Action II: a son that speaks of judgment (1:3b–5)
     iii. Action III: a daughter shown no pity (1:6–7)
     iv. Action IV: a son that signals divorce (1:8–9)
     v. Salvation speech I: an initial glimmer of hope (1:10 – 2:1 [Heb. 2:1–3])
  c. A tragic separation: judgment speech I (2:2–13 [Heb. 2:4–15])
  d. A gracious restoration (2:14 – 3:5 [Heb. 2:16 – 3:5])
     i. Salvation speech II: renewal with cosmic consequences (2:14–23 [Heb. 2:16–25])
     ii. Action V: reconciliation with disciplinary constraint (3:1–5)

II. HOSEA'S MESSAGES: PART ONE (4:1 – 11:11)
  a. Introduction: general indictment of the nation (4:1–3)
  b. The covenant shattered (4:4 – 5:7)
     i. The rejected law (4:4–10)
     ii. The corrupt religion (4:11–19)
     iii. The culpable leadership (5:1–7)
  c. The politics run amok (5:8 – 7:16)
     i. Folly and greed in foreign affairs (5:8–15)
     ii. Song of feeble penitence (6:1–3)
     iii. Divine complaint of fickleness (6:4–6)
     iv. Illustration of covenant infidelity (6:7–11a)
     v. Divine complaint of deceitfulness (6:11b – 7:2)
     vi. Judgment simile of the heated oven (7:3–7)
     vii. Judgment metaphor of the inedible bread (7:8–10)
     viii. Judgment simile of the senseless dove (7:11–12)
     ix. Double divine complaint of rebellion (7:13–16)

COMMENTARY

The book of Hosea is about judgment and hope. Each of the three major sections of the book begins with the threat of divine judgment of Israel and ends with the promise of divine restoration:

(1) the story of Hosea's marriage illustrates the sins of Israel and the consequent judgment, 1:2 – 2:13, while the account of the reconciliation of Hosea and his wife in response to Yahweh's promise to restore Israel, his own bride, exemplifies the hope that Yahweh, as loving husband, offers beyond the judgment, 2:14 – 3:5;

(2) the oracles of judgment – sparked by corrupt worship, savage politics and foolish foreign alliances – spell Israel's doom, 4:1–10:15, while the divine complaint raised by Yahweh, as the offended parent of a delinquent child, culminates in an offer of forgiveness and a call to return, 11:1–11;

(3) the closing speeches of judgment continue to sound the alarm for Israel's fate, as they depict God's wrath in virtually unparalleled terms of ferocity, 12:1–13:16, while the prophecy reaches its climax in a love-song in which God's husbandly love triumphs over all of Israel's unfaithfulness, 14:1–9.

I. HOSEA'S EXPERIENCES (1:1 – 3:5)

To grasp the overall message of this first section, we must catch the significance of its *literary structure*. These three chapters are a two-part story (1:2–9; 3:1–5) wrapped around a three-part oracle (1:10 – 2:1; 2:2–13; 2:14–23). This structure produces a literary unit that can be described by the scheme A B' B B' A', where A (1:2–9) is the story, whose point is judgment and A' (3:1–5) is the story whose point is hope, while B (2:2–13) is the oracle whose announcement is judgment, and the B¹ (1:10 – 2:1; 2:14–23) are the oracles whose proclamation is hope.

The envelope or *inclusio* formed by the two-part story with which the section opens and closes is not only a graceful literary device but an important theological pointer. This structure – in which Gomer's waywardness is described before Israel's sin is denounced, and Yahweh's restoration of Israel to full covenant privileges is promised before Hosea is commanded to demonstrate that restoration – packages the gist of the section: Gomer's betrayal of Hosea may foreshadow Israel's defection from Yahweh, but no human act of forgiveness can take priority over divine forbearance. When it comes to the exercise of grace God is mentor to us all. Four *interpretative guidelines* underlie our reading of these three chapters.

Guideline one: *The account of Hosea's experiences is literal not allegorical.* We seem not to be dealing with a made-up illustration like a parable, but with actual episodes in the life of the prophet. Granted that the three children are given symbolic names and that Gomer and Hosea represent Israel and Yahweh respectively, however, there are present other details in the story which signal no allegorical meaning, *e.g.* Gomer's and Diblaim's names (1:3) and the price of redemption paid by Hosea in 3:2. Furthermore, the moral problem encased in God's command that a prophet should marry a harlot (or a woman who would become one) is not eased by an allegorical reading. A divine command that is reprehensible in actual experience is no less so in an illustrative story. Moreover, something of the poignancy, power and pathos is drained from the book, if we are not dealing with an actual story where a suffering prophet learns and teaches volumes about the pain of a God whose people have played false with him.[1]

Not allegory, then, but *enacted prophecy* is the proper genre in which to classify these accounts. Not only does Hosea's account issue from divine directives (1:2; 3:1), but the basic prophetic reason for the command is contained in explanations explicit to the commands (1:2b; 3:1b). Hosea is to act in God's place as well as to speak for him. Like Isaiah (*e.g.* ch. 20),

---

[1]See Heschel, p. 53, for a summary of the basic arguments for a literal interpretation.

Jeremiah (*e.g.* chs. 27–28), and Ezekiel (*e.g.* chs. 4–5; 12:1–16; 24:15–27), Hosea himself is a sign to the people (*cf.* Is. 8:18; Ezk. 24:27), a prophetic symbol of God's wrath in judgment and of his love in restoration. This means the story is not an illustration gleaned from human experience and then applied as a spiritual message, but an actual personal history plotted by Yahweh, in which Hosea executes at exquisite personal cost God's holy purposes.[1] Thus an emphasis on the symbolic role of the story should be complemented by calling attention to the impact of these episodes on Hosea's appreciation of Yahweh's dealings with Israel: 'Only by living through in his own life what the divine Consort of Israel experienced was the prophet able to attain sympathy for the divine situation.'[2]

Guideline two: *The autobiographical account in chapter 3 is the sequel to the biographical account in chapter 1.* The reason for the switch from third person ('so he went and took Gomer', 1:3) to first person ('so I bought her', 3:2) is lost in the dust of antiquity but is probably related to an editorial process that preserved some accounts of a prophet's life in his own words (autobiography) and others in the words of his followers (biography). (For other examples of these two patterns, compare Is. 6:1–8 with 7:3–8; Je. 1:4–19 with 20:1–6; Am. 7:1–9 with 7:10–17.) In any case, the change in person between chapter 1 and chapter 3 is not strong enough evidence on which to build a case, either that chapter 3 describes an event *prior* to chapter 1, or that chapter 3 is an alternate record of the events in chapter 1 and is, therefore, simultaneous to it.

The details of chapter 3 seem to argue for a sequential interpretation: (1) the word 'again' (Heb. *'od* 3:1) suggests an advance on the previous narrative, whether we attach it to 'And the Lord said to me' (Andersen; Mays) or to 'Go, love' (LXX; AV; RSV); (2) the absence of the woman's name implies that the reader ought to be familiar with that detail; (3) the

---

[1]For a recent survey of the meaning of symbolic acts for the Hebrew prophets, see William Leng, 'Prophetic Actions in the Book of Jeremiah', *The Tyndale Paper*, 30 (July, 1985). Using insights from contemporary anthropologists to elucidate the text, Leng concludes that prophetic acts were not influenced by 'imitative magical actions' but were—whether applied to Israel's future, past or present—'descriptive and illustrative, a dramatic means of confronting Israel with the will of Yahweh' (pp. 9–10).
[2]Heschel, p. 56.

lack of reference to the children points towards a movement in the stories, when the judgment conveyed in their names has run its course and the focus has been placed on the restored relationship of Gomer-Hosea/Israel-Yahweh; (4) Hosea's purchase of the woman almost certainly builds on the threats of Hosea's banishment of Gomer (2:3) and her abandonment of him (2:5); and (5) the picture of covenant loyalty in 3:3 (but with implied discipline; see comments below) makes most sense when seen as the prophet's demonstration of the renewed covenant depicted in the salvation oracle of 2:14–23.

Basic to the sequential interpretation is, of course, the assumption that the unnamed woman of chapter 3 is the well-known Gomer of chapter 1. Any other reading would break the analogy which carries the basic message of this section: the Lord of Israel will judge his idolatrous people and afterwards renew his relationship with them. To introduce a second woman would derail the entire train of thought and make wreck of the hope which the prophet would convey to Israel.

Guideline three: *When Gomer married Hosea she was an ordinary Israelite woman who later became an adulteress and a prostitute.* This guideline assumes that the description of Gomer as 'a wife of harlotry' (1:2) anticipates what she will later become, just as the reference to the 'children of harlotry' describes the three offspring to be born to Gomer after the marriage (1:3–4).

Gomer was probably not a cult prostitute in an official or professional sense (*cf.* Mays, pp. 25–26 for arguments to the contrary). The technical vocabulary available to describe persons set apart for such religious duties within the fertility cults is not employed to describe Gomer, though it does describe the cultic consorts of Israel's men in 4:14 (Heb. *qᵉdēšâ*; *cf.* Gn. 38:21–22; Dt. 23:18). Moreover, the picture of family life sketched in the accounts of the conception, birth, naming and weaning of the children does not accord well with the lot of one set apart for cultic sexual services. Yet the cult could well have been one setting where Gomer practised her promiscuity, given the general involvement of Israelites of both sexes in such pagan rituals (*cf.* 4:13–14).

An alternate interpretation, argued by Wolff (p. 14), holds that the harlotry ascribed to Gomer and the children refers to a rite of bridal initiation supposedly practised in Israel, as it was later in the Graeco-Roman world. By this custom, in gross defiance of biblical laws of chastity (Dt. 22:21) all Israelite brides would have been defiled in some sexual rite prior to their marriage to their partners. Gomer would have been an ordinary Israelite woman who had undergone the customary initiation, and thus experienced the sexual and religious defilement which symbolized the nation's apostasy. Biblical evidence for such an initiation is thin. Beyond that, the graphic descriptions of Gomer's adulterous escapades in chapter 2 seem out of place if her behaviour was standard practice for all Israelite women. Part of the prophetic symbolism hinges on her situation being unusual not typical (see Andersen, pp. 157–169, on these various theories, including a critique of Wolff's approach to Gomer's promiscuity).

Guideline four: *The oracles of chapter 2 are an essential comment on and expansion of the two calls to prophetic action described in 1:2 and 3:1.* As such they are an integral part of the structure of the first section of the book, drawing light from the prose stories and casting light on them. In a sense the two calls set the theme for the entire book: (1) *the call to marry,* fortified by the description of the land's harlotry, shapes the tone of pending judgment – judgment which the prophet seeks to avert (2:2–3, 6–7); and (2) the *call to remarry* in love, strengthened by the assurance of Yahweh's love for Israel, keynotes the theme of hope by giving concrete, visible form to the wonder of divine forgiveness – a wonder which the prophet celebrates.

Another way that the oracles comment on the story is in the negative and positive use of the children's names. The *negative* force of each name, so clearly a harbinger of judgment in 1:3–9, is alluded to in the threatening speech of 2:4–5; the children, representative of the individual Israelites, partake of the iniquity and therefore of the fate of their mother, who symbolizes the nation as a whole. The *positive* use of the names is anticipated in the brief promise of 1:10 – 2:1, where Jezreel is reinterpreted to mean not 'God will scatter in judgment', as in 1:4–5, but 'God will sow in resettlement', and, where the 'nots' are removed from the other two names to declare the return of God's mercy on Israel and his renewal of the covenant with his people. What is anticipated in 1:10 – 2:1 is made the climax of the salvation speech in 2:21–23, when the covenant renewal is described in cosmic terms that stretch from heaven to earth and issue in the specific promises to Jezreel that Israel will be resown in the land; Not-pitied will be pitied and Not-my-people will again be God's people.

These interpretative guidelines are far from comprehensive and do not resolve all the questions present in the crucial sections with which the book commences. The prose narratives are lean and spare, and what they do not say is as tantalizing as what they do. The cultural, social and religious backgrounds are almost beyond our reach. Any help, therefore, we should welcome. The pointers summarized above do not say everything, and what they do say may not be entirely accurate. But they represent a solid consensus of much recent study of Hosea and will not lead us far astray in our efforts to develop a consistent interpretation of the prophet's experiences and messages.[1]

a. Title (1:1)

The precise form of the title is unique to Hosea. With Amos, Hosea lists monarchs from both Israel and Judah, while Isaiah and Micah mention only Southern kings, reflecting the fact that their messages were directed more consistently towards the Southern Kingdom, while the writings of Amos and Hosea deal mainly with the North. Hosea's title includes no mention of visionary experience but puts its entire emphasis on *The word of the Lord*, which is the true label of the book (*cf.* Joel 1:1; Mi. 1:1; Zp. 1:1; Zc. 1:1).

As with Isaiah, Joel and Zechariah, we are given the name of Hosea's father. *Beeri*, 'My well' or 'My spring' (*cf.* Gn. 26:34) seems to play no role in the text, save to distinguish our Hosea from others of identical or similar name (*cf.* Joshua, Nu. 13:8, 16; Dt. 32:44 or the last king of Israel, Hoshea, 2 Ki. 15:30; also *cf.* the longer form of the name in Ne. 12:32; Je. 42:1; 43:2). The emphasis on salvation or deliverance (Heb. *yš‘*) implicit in Hosea's name (a variant of Joshua, meaning 'Yahweh saves') was as appropriate to his life and message as it was

---

[1]In addition to the major commentaries cited, further interpretative background on this section may be gained from G. W. Anderson, 'Hosea and Yahweh: God's Love Story', *Review and Expositor*, LXXII, 1975, pp. 425–436, from H. H. Rowley, 'The Marriage of Hosea', *Men of God*, 1963, pp. 66-97, and from Gordis, pp. 230-254.

unsuited to Israel's weak and unsuccessful king, whose ill-fated policies contributed to his kingdom's collapse in 722–21 BC (*cf.* 2 Ki. 17:1–6).

The chronological references to the kings of Judah and Israel serve to anchor Hosea's mission in the heart of his people's history. The Judean list shows two things: (1) Hosea's ministry was carried on over a lengthy span of years, embracing parts of the reigns of *Uzziah* (Azariah) — 790–740 BC (2 Ki. 15:1–7), *Jotham* — 751–732 BC (2 Ki. 15:32–28), *Ahaz* — 732–715 BC (2 Ki. 16:1–20), *Hezekiah* — 715–686 BC (2 Ki. chs. 18–20), all kings of Judah; and (2) the impact of Hosea's prophecies continued to be felt in Judah long after the tumultuous collapse of Samaria; indeed the very fulfilment of his sad oracles encouraged those who had preserved them to continue to hear in them the living word of God.

The catalogue of Judean kings contrasts with the lone mention of *Jeroboam, son of Joash* (so described to distinguish him from his earlier namesake, the son of Nebat; 1 Ki. chs. 12–14) as a ruler of Israel. The last significant leader of the Northern Kingdom, Jeroboam II was noted both as an instrument of divine rescue in an era of political helplessness and the perpetrator of the sins of Jeroboam I (2 Ki. 14:23–29). It is clear from Hosea's later references (7:7; 8:4; 13:11, *cf.* 2 Ki. ch. 15) to the rough parade of kings that followed Jeroboam's death that the prophet's ministry continued for at least two more decades and possibly three.

Why, then, is there no mention of Jeroboam's successors in the title? Three reasons can be suggested: (1) Hosea's mission may have been concentrated during the early years of the span of time marked out in the title; the experiences with Gomer and the children, and many of the oracles that interpret them, undoubtedly date them in Jeroboam's last years; (2) with the death of Jeroboam, chaos set in; kings rose and fell, and none was dominant enough to warrant mention in the title; and (3) there was a direct connection between Jeroboam's family and the judgment symbolized by Jezreel's name (1:4–5), since Jehu's crimes had to be punished and God's way of doing that was to bring Jehu's dynasty to a close with the assassination of Jeroboam's son, Zechariah, whose royal tenure lasted just six months (2 Ki. 15:8–12).

b. A significant family (1:2 – 2:1)

This section encapsulates the message of the entire book:
verses 2–9 sound notes of accusation ('great harlotry by
forsaking the Lord', v. 2) and of threat (the names of the three
children ring with announcements of judgment, vv. 4–9); the
promises of hope and salvation that mark the major divisions of
the book (2:14 – 3:5; 11:1–11; ch. 14) are anticipated. The
sharp reversal of tone between verse 9 and verse 10 is a
reminder that we are dealing, not with the events and messages
of Hosea in the order of their historical occurrence, but with a
beautifully edited composition in which the thematic order of
the theology – the relation of hope to judgment and judgment
to hope – takes priority over the sequence of events in history.

The literary form of verses 2–9 is a biographical *memorabile*
(to use Wolff's word) or *memoir*, a third person account of a
series of four episodes in the life of the prophet. Here it consists
of commands to prophetic actions (see discussion of enacted
prophecy or prophetic symbolism above, p. 55). Though the
names of Gomer and her three children are featured in the
drama, centre stage belongs to Yahweh and his quartet of
imperatives, which call for Hosea to take a harlot for a wife
(action I: 1:2–3a) and to father and name a son that speaks of
judgment (action II: 1:3b–5), a daughter to be shown no pity
(action III: 1:6–7) and finally a son that signals divorce (action
IV: 1:8–9).

The shift in tone and form between 1:2–9 and 1:10 – 2:1
[Heb. 2:1–3] is abrupt. The divinely commanded prophetic
actions are completed, and the text draws our eyes to the
distant future with a *prophecy of restoration* that turns on a
reversal of the meanings of the children's names from negative
to positive. The language of the promises of hope is not first
person singular as were the threats of judgment. 'I will' gives
way to 'they shall', as though the prophet were relaying the
divine message in his own words. The sharp contrast between
this section and what precedes it may serve as an indicator that
Hosea's book is about both judgment and hope – judgment in
the near future, and hope after judgment has revealed God's
justice and reminded Israel of their waywardness. The brief
but bright word of hope here helps to prepare for and interpret
the more detailed pictures of hope that punctuate the book and
mark its three major divisions (2:14 – 3:5; 11:1–11; 14:1–9).

i. Action I: a harlot for a wife (1:2–3a). The first clause may be the title of the sequence of prophetic commands, 'the beginning of Yahweh's speaking through Hosea' (LXX; Vulg.; AV; NEB; Jeremias; Mays; Wolff), or more likely a temporal clause, 'when Yahweh began to speak through Hosea'. *When* Hosea was called to be a prophet, we are not told. Our book contains no record parallel to the accounts that mark the commissionings of Isaiah (ch. 6), Jeremiah (ch. 1), or Ezekiel (chs. 1–3). We can assume that Hosea may still have been an adolescent, based on what we know about patriarchal tribal societies and the relationship of some of Judah's kings and the ages of their first sons; Amon and Josiah, for instance, both seem to have married at fourteen (2 Ki. 21:19; 22:1; 23:31).[1] Hosea's apparent youth makes his experience akin to Jeremiah's and marks his quiet obedience to the divine command as even more notable.

God's word was to come *through* or *by* (Heb. *b* with *dbr* 'speak' indicates that Hosea is the agent of the message) Hosea. The whole sequence of commands was not a private word to the prophet but a word through the prophet to the house of Jehu (action II), the Northern and Southern Kingdoms (action III), the entire land and people (actions I, IV). 'Go, take for yourself' is a standard expression for marriage (*cf.* Gn. 4:19; Ex. 34:16), and the repetition of the verbs in verse 3 shows how promptly, staunchly and totally Hosea followed the divine word. Absent here is any mention of courtship (*cf.* 2:14–15) or betrothal (2:19–21) which play prominent roles in the oracle that promises remarriage. Nothing is said of Hosea's feelings nor of the process by which he implemented the command. The effectual word of Yahweh was at work. Disobedience was unthinkable (Am. 3:8; 7:14–15).

The marriage and the subsequent procreation of children were viewed as one event in action I. *Go, take* are the only verbs in the clause. No additional word of bearing or begetting is included in the Hebrew. The wife and the offspring, though their appearance was staged in the sequence of conception and birth outlined in 1:4–9, were all part of one revelatory event: the public exposure of Israel's unfaithfulness to

[1]See R. De Vaux, *Ancient Israel* (E.T., London: Darton, Longman & Todd, 1961), pp. 24–38, for a summary of Hebrew marriage customs, including probable ages of marriage for both boys and girls.

Yahweh, her covenant Husband. 'Wife of harlotries' or 'whoredoms' (Heb. plural shows how repeated, how characteristic, such infidelity was) is best interpreted in the light of 'children of harlotries'. In both cases the reference is not to past but future conduct. The children born of such a mother were affected by her corruption and the corruption of the vast bulk of Israel's citizenry. The wife, thus, may well have been chaste when Hosea married her but succumbed to her lust afterwards. This initial command has, therefore, been phrased after the fact.

The divine interpretation introduced in verse 2 by *for* indicates that the wife and the children are illustrations of the whole *land* – a term that may well embrace both the Northern and Southern kingdoms, as action III (1:6–7) suggests. The choice of *land* as the subject of the outrageous adultery/ idolatry is suggestive. *Land* recalls the promises to Abraham (Gn. chs. 12; 15; 17) as well as the Exodus, conquest and settlement under Moses, Joshua and the Judges. It pricks the consciences of Israel with the reminder that their land was a gift from God, to be used in celebration of his covenant, and to be retained only by total loyalty to him. Now that *land*, together with its people, was wantonly (the Heb. use of infinitive absolute and finite verb connotes excessive and extreme conduct: *great* harlotry) engrossed in spiritual fornication.

Verse 2 introduces us to the double meaning carried by the word harlotry, a meaning that sets the theme for chapters 1–3 and, indeed, for the entire book: (1) *harlotry* may describe *literal* acts of illicit lust, often with financial or material gain involved (*cf.* 2:5 for the mention of lovers who provided compensation to the wanton one); (2) *harlotry* may also describe *religious* acts of infidelity, the abandoning of worship of the one true God for the idols and myths of paganism, notably in Hosea's day the worship of the Baals; it is this religious meaning that is obviously intended (*cf.* 4:12, 18; 5:3–4).

The relationship between these two meanings, literal and religious, should not be missed. Much of the message of Hosea turns on it: (1) the wife's literal harlotry is a persistent illustration of Israel's religious fornication; indeed in the flow of the judgment oracle in 2:2–13, what begins literally with a call for the wife's repentance (2:2) ends figuratively with descriptions of Israel's religious lewdness (2:10–13); (2) in those festivals literal fornication was moreover a part of the religious liturgy, aimed to move the Baals to engender the fertility of the land upon which Israel was dependent (2:12; see Commentary at 4:12–15).

Hosea's unquestioning obedience to the first command (v. 3) starkly echoes the divine imperative, *Go, take* (v. 2; for *take*, Heb. *lqḥ* as a description of choosing a bride, *cf.* Gn. 4:19; 6:2; 11:29; 12:19). The various attempts to explain the meaning of Gomer's name by its alleged derivation from a root *gmr* 'to complete', 'to achieve' have neither gained a scholarly consensus nor contributed to our understanding of the story. The same is true of *Diblaim*, which is more likely the name of Gomer's father than of her home town. The contrast between these names and those of the three children is striking: the whole point of the babies' names is to symbolize judgment, as the explanatory clauses in each of the last three actions reveal. Absence of any such explanation in the names of Gomer and her father suggests one thing alone: the story is real – Hosea took to wife an Israelite girl, who, whatever her beginnings, was to etch her name in the infamy of the nation.

ii. Action II: a son that speaks of judgment (1:3b–5). The narrative hurries to describe the fulfilment of the second object in God's command (v. 2), the pregnancy of Gomer and the birth of the first son (v. 3b). All other details are stripped away, even the traditional Hebrew expressions 'he knew her' (Gn. 4:1, 17) or 'he entered her' (Gn. 16:4).

The focus in actions II–IV is on the *name*, which in each case is the direct object of Yahweh's command to Hosea: 'Call (the imperative form is masc. singular) his/her name...'. The text explains the name first chosen, *Jezreel*: (1) it was the place where Jehu was swept to power over all Israel on a mighty tide of bloodshed (2 Ki. 9:21–28, 30–37; 10:1–10), here called graphically *the blood of Jezreel* (the Heb. word is plural and should be translated 'bloodshed'; *cf.* Gn. 4:10–11; Hab. 2:8, 17); (2) it was the locale chosen – by the principle of *lex talionis*, where the punishment is portioned out appropriately to crime for the execution of judgment (Heb. for *punish* is *pqd*, literally 'visit' which may have the positive meaning of 'look after', 'care for' as in Ps. 8:4 or the negative meaning 'punish' or 'avenge' as here; *cf.* 2:13; 4:9, 14; 8:13; 9:9; 12:2). The location of Jezreel in a valley-plain between the mountains of Samaria and Galilee, and its close proximity to the valley of

Megiddo, mark it as one of the prominent battle sites in Palestine, one of the few places where chariotry, cavalry and marching armies could be manoeuvred (*cf.* Gideon's defeat of the Midianites there, Jdg. 6:33); it was the appropriate place for the *bow of Israel, i.e.* Israel's foolish dependence on military might (*cf.* 14:4), to be broken. *Bow* was the most accurate and wide-ranging weapon of antiquity.

Though Jehu's accession to the throne had been blessed by Elisha, even to the sanctioning of bloodshed to accomplish it (2 Ki. 9:1–10), it is obvious that Jehu (c. 841–814 BC) and his descendants had overplayed their hand; (1) their zeal for bloodshed exceeded all bounds; (2) the ambition of Jehu outstripped any sense of divine commission; (3) his rule, though retarding the Baal worship, which had been sponsored by Ahab and Jezebel, did little to bring a return to the worship of God which Omri's dynasty had compromised (885–874 BC); and (4) in short, as the prophet-historian who recounted his story in Kings put it: 'Jehu did not turn aside from the sins of Jeroboam the son of Nebat, which he made Israel to sin, the golden calves that were in Bethel, and in Dan... But Jehu was not careful to walk in the law of the Lord the God of Israel with all his heart' (2 Ki. 10:29, 31). The political, spiritual and social chaos recounted in Amos and Hosea is ample testimony to the justice of this verdict.

The fulfilment of the Jezreel judgment came in due season (note the *yet a little while,* v. 4; *cf.* Ps. 37:10 for the identical phrase and its implied counsel to patience) and marked the beginning of the swift slide (six kings in thirty years) to the collapse of the Northern Kingdom, prophesied so forcefully by Amos (7:9). After the four decades of Jeroboam's reign (c. 793–753 BC), his son Zechariah barely had time to warm the throne when he was cut down by the conspirator, Shallum (2 Ki. 15:8–12). The site of the assassination was significant: Ibleam, (adopting the LXX reading with many of the versions), a town about thirteen kilometres south and west of the city of Jezreel, at the southern tip of the valley where Jehu had murdered Ahaziah (2 Ki. 9:27).

Jezreel warrants two other comments. First, its ambiguity makes it an effective symbol both of judgment and restoration: it can mean 'God will scatter' as one may scatter chaff or other undesirable litter and so 'destroy', the implied meaning here; it can also mean 'God will scatter' as one may scatter seed in ploughed furrows for planting and so 'restore', the clear meaning in 2:22–23 [Heb. 2:24–25]. Second, it forms a word-play with Israel (Heb. *yiśrā'ēl* sounds much like *yizr'ēl*), the implication being that Jezreel is more than a place name; like Not-pitied (v. 6) and Not-my-people (v. 8), it is a figure descriptive of the whole nation, ripe for judgment, yet to be restored to a covenant-relationship when the judgment has done its necessary work.

iii. Action III: a daughter shown no pity (1:6–7). The absence of the word 'him' (Heb. *lô*) in contrast to 'bore him' (v. 3) has raised questions about the daughter's legitimacy. Was Hosea the father? Does the slight change in wording, which is also found in verse 8, signal that Gomer's harlotry had begun? We cannot be sure, but it is more likely that the omission of the 'him' is part of the scheme of increasing compactness in the use of formulas to describe the four actions.

Not pitied (Heb. *Lô ruḥāmâ*) is even more terrifying than Jezreel, because the name is not at all ambiguous and needs much less explanation. It marks a sharp change in Yahweh's attitude towards his people (*house of Israel* means Northern Kingdom), whose very national identity was built on God's compassion, his tender commitment as the stronger to the weaker (Heb. *rḥm* is related to the words for 'womb' and 'lower abdomen' and connotes deep physical as well as emotional feeling), which was demonstrated in his constant parental care for them (Ps. 103:13). The keystone of such care was, of course, forgiveness (Dt. 13:17), and the judgment conveyed by Not pitied's name is made all the more harsh by the terrible promise that all forgiveness will be withdrawn.[1]

The mention of the house of Judah in verse 7 has been

[1] The Hebrew is ambiguous at two points: (1) the meaning of the word *kî* that introduces the final clause of v. 6; (2) the object to be supplied for the strong verbal clause that translates literally, 'I shall truly take away (unstated object) for (or 'from') them'. Since 'sin' is often used as the object of 'take away' (Heb. *ns'*; *cf*. Ho. 14:3; Mi. 7:18; Is. 2:9; Ps. 99:8) it seems most reasonable to supply it as the unstated object and to read the clause as an explanation of what Yahweh means by his promise 'no longer to deal mercifully with the house of Israel'. In this case *kî* must mean 'rather' or 'instead', so that the final clause contrasts with, instead of explaining, the previous clause. The LXX and Vulg. support Wolff's reading of *kî* as signalling contrast but give us little help beyond that.

considered an addition to the text from the hand of a Judean scribe who made some editorial notations after Samaria had fallen (721 BC) and before Judah collapsed (586 BC).[1] Wolff (p. 9, note h; p. 21) calls attention to the absence of references to Judah in actions II and IV and reads verse 7 as 'a parenthetic note' that encourages the reader 'to view the threatening verses of this chapter in terms of the entire saving history', not just in terms of the collapse of the Northern Kingdom. Thus interpreted, the passage helps to explain why Israel, which trusted in bow and horse, was swept away, while Judah was preserved from Assyrian captivity by 'Yahweh their God'.

It is possible, however, to credit Hosea himself with this contrast between Israel's forfeiture of any right to mercy and Judah's deliverance by the mercy of God, 'as the preserver of the continuity of the people of God' (Emmerson, p. 94). There is ample evidence in Hosea's speeches to document his distress over Israel's peculiar problems of dynastic instability, Baal-dominated shrines, and foolish trust in military defences and weaponry (2:18; 10:14; 14:3). The cluster of expressions for war and its instruments with which verse 7 closes has a superlative force: nothing that the human mind can frame, tame or employ can bring victory when God's plan is defeat (Pr. 21:31).

The interpretation that may best serve to explain the place and meaning of verse 7 in the text is that of Andersen, who argues cogently that the negative particle 'not' (Heb. *lō'*) carries over from verse 6c to the first two verbs of verse 7 and makes them negative as well, so that the basic relationship of verses 6–7 is parallel not contrasting: Israel and Judah will have a common fate, though not necessarily at the same time.[2] Treating these references to 'house of Israel' (v. 6, Northern Kingdom) and 'house of Judah' (v. 7, Southern Kingdom) as parallel prepares for the coupling of both, 'sons of Judah' and 'sons of Israel', in the oracle of salvation (1:10 – 2:1 [Heb. 2:1–3]) that follows these four actions of judgment in 1:2–9. If the thrust of verse 7 is negative, then the preposition *by* (Heb.

---

[1] See Emmerson, pp. 88–95, for a survey of interpretative options.

[2] Andersen, pp. 188–9, cites Je. 3:2 and Nu. 23:19 as structural parallels that demonstrate the way in which an initial *lō'* can cast its negative on the following clause or clauses.

b) may be translated 'from', with the result that the weaponry listed is the enemy's, *from* which God promises no rescue (Andersen, p. 155).

iv. Action IV: a son that signals divorce (1:8–9).

Weaning is mentioned, presumably to suggest the elapsed time, two to three years (*cf.* 1 Sa. 1:21–28; 2 Macc. 7:27), between the births. The time frame may serve both to show the continuity of Hosea's family life and to hint at the forbearance of God, who, though announcing judgment through the first two births, was demonstrating his long-suffering love. Accordingly, Wolff (p. 21) connects the author's insertion of 'and she weaned' with the space needed to implement the possibilities of 'return' held out in 2:7 and 3:5.

With the naming of the third child the signs of judgment have reached their climax. 'Not my people' signals a total change in God's relationship to Israel: the waywardness of the nation has effectively annulled the covenant; the son's name not only described how Israel had behaved – as if they did not belong to Yahweh – but also declared God's response of separating himself from them.

The explanation introduced by *for* (v. 9) makes this clear. Its language echoes the events of the Exodus at two key points: (1) it negates God's great pledge to Moses not only to rescue Israel from Egyptian bondage, but to take them for his people and to be their God (Ex. 6:6–7); and (2) it withdraws from them all the providential care carried in the name by which God first revealed himself to Moses (Ex. 3:14), since a literal translation of the last clause of verse 9 reads 'and I (am) not I am (or I will be) to you' – the Hebrew *'ehyeh* is the same in both Exodus and Hosea.[1] The sting of this passage is sharpened by the recognition that one meaning of the divine name assures the continuity of covenant; Moses' *Ehyeh* is none other than the God both of the patriarchs and of Israel's national future, both Northern and Southern Kingdoms. What greater threat than for that name to be unknown? The threat is intensified by its directness. For the first time in the sequence of signs, the Lord speaks to the people. From 1:2 through

[1] For a survey of the background and meaning of the divine name see B. S. Childs, *The Book of Exodus*, OTL (Philadelphia: Westminster, 1974), pp. 47–89. It may well be that the use of the verb 'to be' in 11:4 and 14:6 are implicated with the divine name.

1:9a, he has spoken to Hosea *about* Israel; now he speaks *to* Israel in the second person plural, announcing the plight they have brought on themselves and the verdict they have forced him to declare.

v. Salvation speech I: an initial glimmer of hope (1:10 – 2:1 [Heb. 2:1–3]). The tone changes: (1) Yahweh, whose commands dominated the signs in 1:2–9, is no longer the speaker; Hosea's prophetic voice becomes prominent; and (2) the theme turns positive, with salvation not judgment as the intended message. In the book's basic structure announcements of judgment and promises of hope alternate. Here the rhythm is set for the rest of the book, even though the impersonal language, devoid of the 'I wills' of 2:14–23; 11:9; 14:4–5, distinguishes this speech from other words of salvation in Hosea.[1]

The promises of restoration are framed in terms reminiscent of the covenants of Israel's past. First, the divine pledge to Abraham and his family shapes the wording of verse 10a: despite whatever destruction or decimation reduces their numbers in judgment (*cf.* Am. 5:3; 6:9–10), God will keep his word to the patriarchs and restore Israel's populace to a size beyond counting – *like the sand of the sea* (*cf.* Gn. 32:12 [Heb. v. 13]; 15:5; 22:17). Wolff (p. 26) notes that the hearers would have understood the fulfilment of this promise as a miracle, given the paucity of their populace in comparison, *e.g.,* to Assyria's. The first hearers would also have recognized it as a promise of a return to a Solomonic scale of national grandeur, given the similarity of wording between verse 10a and 1 Kings 3:8.

The promise that follows (verse 10b) is an expansion and an explanation of this miracle: the vast increase in size is the result of a new relationship with God which Hosea describes in a phrase he may well have coined: *sons of the living God* (*cf.* Mt. 16:16 for a similar description of Jesus and Rom. 9:26 for the application of the phrase to gentile Christians). The phrase, which catches us off guard when we expected to hear 'my people,' carries two points: (1) the living God is the one who will effect the miracle; and (2) it anticipates the defeat of

---

[1]Mays (p. 31) hears in the 'impersonal idiom' an effort 'to concentrate on the events themselves as the truly significant revelation'.

the Baals announced in 2:11–12, 16–17, by attributing a self-sustaining, life-giving character to Israel's God that exposes the impotence of the fertility cult to which Israel was so fatally attracted. *In the place where* (v. 10b), whether interpreted logically, 'instead of' (Wolff, p. 27), or geographically, *i.e.* in a public place where naming ceremonies were held (Andersen, p. 203), illustrates Hosea's conviction of intimate connection between past and future: God's redemption tomorrow takes place by the restoration and surpassing of his redemption yesterday (*cf.* 2:14–15).

The second reminder of Israel's covenants comes in verse 11, where the reuniting of the kingdoms and the appointment of *one head, i.e.* leader, harks back to Yahweh's pact with David, announced by Nathan in 2 Samuel 7 (*cf.* the specific mention of David in Ho. 3:5). As sin had marred the kingdoms and led Yahweh to withdraw his pity (see comments on 1:6–7), so divine grace and consistency will triumph and redeem them, though the judgment on the house of Jehu (v. 4) will not be rescinded. This reunion of the kingdoms takes on a miraculous cast in the light of the sharp conflict between them which Hosea personally observed: the Syro-Ephraimite struggle of 734 BC, which seems to underlie 5:8 – 7:16. The *one head*, a more general term used here perhaps to avoid the negative connotations of kingship in Hosea (*e.g.* 7:3, 5, 7, 16; 8:4; 9:15; 10:3, 7; 13:10, 11), must be from David's dynasty (3:5; for 'head' = 'King', see Ps. 18:43 [Heb. v. 44]).

Harder to discern is the precise meaning of *and they shall go up from the land*. (v. 11). First, we can read *land* to mean Assyria, the place of captivity and understand the passage to picture a return from exile there. The word *land* (Heb. *'āreṣ*) in the singular without a modifying noun, however, is not used in the Old Testament for a foreign nation. *Land*, in our context, almost inevitably means the 'promised land', given by God as Israel's home, so long as her covenant loyalty remained strong.[1]

Second, we can read the clause *they shall go up* (Heb. *'lh*) *from* as an idiom for military conquest, meaning 'they shall take

[1]For discussions of the role of the land in God's redemptive programme, see W. Brueggemann, *The Land* (Philadelphia: Fortress Press, 1977) and E. A. Martens, *God's Design: A Focus on Old Testament Theology* (Grand Rapids: Baker, 1981), pp. 97–115, 175–189; UK edition: *Plot and Purpose in the Old Testament* (Leicester: IVP, 1981).

possession of', as some scholars have done on the basis of Exodus 1:10.[1] But that reading of Exodus 1:10 has not gained strong support.[2]

Third, we can understand 'the land' as the Underworld, the realm of the dead (*cf.* Gn. 2:6; Jb. 10:21, 22; Ps. 139:15; Is. 44:23) and interpret the passage as a reference to Israel's resurrection from the death of captivity and judgment (*cf.* Ezk. 37:1–14, where the description of the revival of Israel's bones is followed immediately by a prophetic sign that promises the reunion of the two kingdoms under David the king, vv. 15–28). Andersen (p. 209) blends this interpretation (which he finds compatible with Ho. 5:8 – 6:6) with a picture of return from exile and finds such a reading in line with 'Hosea's capacity for using language with more than one level of meaning'.

Fourth, 'go up' has been translated 'spring up' (*cf.* Dt. 29:23 [Heb. v. 22], for this sense of the Heb. *'lh*), like an abundant crop bursting forth from the land. On this reading the clause in verse 11 reaches back to the mention of Israel's immeasurable size (v. 10) and looks forward to God's bountiful sowing – a time hinted in the mention of Jezreel and made explicit in the 'I will sow him for myself in the land' of 2:23.[3]

As different as each of these interpretations is from the others, all of them convey the same general sense: the glory of the united people, kindled in their splendid past, will blaze even brighter when the judgment is over and the full work of God's restoration is underway. The climactic character of that restoration is celebrated in the exclamation with which verse 11 closes, 'How great is the day, O Jezreel.' This translation, following Andersen's reading (p. 209) of Hebrew *kî* (usually 'for') as 'how' and of 'Jezreel' as a vocative, not a noun dependent on 'day', has the advantage both of heightening the climax and preparing for the direct addresses to the brothers and sisters which close this salvation speech.

Jezreel (v. 11) begins, then, the sequence in which the name of each child is transformed from a sign of judgment to a sign

---

[1]G. Beer, *Exodus*, *HAT* 1, 3 (Tübingen, 1938) p. 14. Mays (p. 33) has argued for this interpretation partly on the basis of an alleged reference to 'holy War' in the phrase 'day of Jezreel'.

[2]See B. S. Childs, *The Book of Exodus*, p. 5.

[3]This interpretation, suggested by Th. C. Vriezen, *Hosea, profeet en cultuur* (Gronigen: 1941), pp. 13, 22, has been adopted by Wolff (p. 28).

of grace. The names were coined with this reversal in mind: (1) Jezreel is deliberately ambiguous – God will both scatter in judgment and sow in restoration (see on v. 4); and (2) beginning the other two names with 'not' meant that their negative force could be removed with the stroke of a pen – which is precisely what happens in 2:1.

Though there may here be a slight allusion to the geographical sense of Jezreel (some have compared day of Jezreel to day of Midian, Is. 9:4 [Heb. v. 3]), it is its etymology, bright with the joy of sowing a bumper crop, and its pun-like similarity to the word Israel that radiate from the text. The judgment on Jehu's house (v. 4) and Israel's foolish trust in weaponry (v. 5) are not reversed; indeed they could not be without nullifying the specific purpose of the judgment. What is reversed is the way God deals with his people. What once he had to scatter he will again be ready to plant.

If *Jezreel* is being addressed (v. 11), then the real break in the text should be after *land* in verse 11, and the final clause should be connected to 2:1 as the word which set the stage for Jezreel's declaration to the other two children. These addresses intrude on the impersonal tone of the speech (see above) and confront the hearer again with the realities of Hosea's family, whose plight as omens of judgment has temporarily been ignored.

The plural imperative *say* and the plural nouns in Hebrew 'brothers' and 'sisters' (made singular in RSV, following LXX) are directed to clusters of persons within the reunited nation not to Hosea's children personally, a transition begun with the plural *you* of 1:9. Groups within Israel (here called Jezreel) are commanded to declare Yahweh's pardon to the men and women of the nation in name-changing language based on actions III and IV of 1:6–9. The fact that change of name reflects change of status, character and destiny (*e.g.* Abram to Abraham, Gn. 17:5; Sarai to Sarah, 17:15; Jacob to Israel, 32:28) makes the proclamation all the more powerful.

Additional Note: Fulfilment of Hosea's prophecies

The major words of judgment signalled in the names of the children and detailed in the indictments and threats that dominate the book (2:2–13; 4:1 – 10:15; 12:2 – 13:16) were fulfilled in the Assyrian invasions that marked Israel's last dozen years (733–721 BC) and especially in the final collapse of Samaria and her incorporation within the Assyrian Empire. How and when the words of hope (1:10 – 2:1; 2:14–23; 11:1–11; 14:1–8) were accomplished are more complicated questions, answerable only in several stages.

A reminder of Hosea's own time-frames may be useful: (1) the *present* for him is the time of harlotry in all its forms – total rejection of God's will and ways; the present is the time in view in virtually all his accusations; (2) the *near future* is the time of judgment to be inflicted by God through the agency of the Assyrian armies; and (3) the *more distant future* is the time of hope when the meaning of Israel's names will be changed from negative to positive and they will be transformed in the glory predicted in 1:10 – 2:1.

The first stage in that hopeful future is the *return from exile* (*cf.* 11:10–11) begun in the days of Cyrus (c. 539 BC) and continued for nearly a century, through the times of Ezra and Nehemiah. The return was viewed as a reunion and restoration of the two kingdoms. The term 'Israel' dots the pages of Ezra-Nehemiah and describes the post-exilic nation in Malachi 2:11 (*cf.* Zc. 8:13 for 'house of Judah and house of Israel', a reminder that the Old Testament knows nothing of the 'ten lost tribes'). Yet the post-exilic era lacks both the royal leader promised in Hosea 1:11 or 3:5 and the expansive splendour announced in 1:10. Both Haggai and Malachi call attention to the austerity, even poverty, of life in the Persian period. Indeed, the Old Testament closes by reaching beyond itself and longing for the day when the promises of righteousness, glory and prosperity found in almost all the prophets will be fully realized (*cf.* Hg. 2:6–9; Zc. ch. 14; Mal. ch. 4).[1]

Small wonder, then, as a second stage, that devout women and men found in *the birth of Jesus as the Messiah* the fulfilment of the promises to Abraham (Lk. 1:55), to David (Lk. 1:32–33) and to the people through the prophets (Mt. 1:23; 2:6). The only specific citation from Hosea in the infancy-narratives suggests that Matthew (2:15) saw in Jesus a new Israel rescued from a new Pharaoh (Herod) by a new exodus (see on Ho. 11:1), and thus he used for his argument a passage which in Hosea is not a prediction but a divine reflection on Israel's past. Still it is likely that the promises of national unity under

---

[1]*Cf.* D. A. Hubbard, 'Hope in the old Testament', *TynB*, 34, 1983, pp. 33–59.

David's headship (Ho. 1:11; 3:5) were part of what helped to shape Jewish expectation of a Messianic King, even though Hosea's promises were not verbally cited in the New Testament.

The *formation of the church* is the third stage. Here the New Testament snatches the word-plays on the names of the last two children and applies them to the incorporation of Gentiles into the covenant, as the new people of God (Rom. 9:25–26; 1 Pet. 2:10). The removal of the 'nots' is seen by Peter and Paul, not as the restoration of Jews to a renewed covenant relationship, but as descriptive of Gentiles who had previously received no mercy nor had been included in the people of God. In this way prophecies that in their first setting had been directed to Israel are rechannelled to describe the life of the Christian church and especially its gentile expression. In the movement of biblical prophecy the Old Testament not only stretches forward to the New Testament, but the New Testament also reaches back and claims from the Old Testament those passages which suit its theological understanding of what God was accomplishing. Biblical prophecy comprises thematic unity and verbal affinity, as well as clear prediction.

The fourth and culminating stage is the *return of Jesus Christ*, the full display of God's sovereign love and perfect judgment. What this will mean spiritually to national, ethnic and religious Israel is hard to say. The same section of Romans (chs. 9–11) that applies Hosea's prophecy to the gentile Christians holds out long-term hope for the people of Israel, 'the natural branches' to 'be grafted back into their own olive tree' 'and so all Israel will be saved' (Rom. 11:24, 26). Paul seems to say that, though the bright promises of Israel's future can be broadened to embrace Gentiles within the church, the formation of the church does not exhaust these promises. Something will be left over as an experience of redemption for the original covenant people. Whether this will have political and geographical dimensions has been the subject of heated debate. The pro or the con depends on whether or not the debaters believe that one act in the drama of Christ's return will be a millennium, a period in which Christ reigns on earth to demonstrate his divine glory, vindicate his lordly claims, and give literal fulfilment to the prophetic promises, including Hosea's.

c. A tragic separation: judgment speech I (2:2–13 [Heb. 2:4–15])

This section fulfils the prediction implied in action I where Yahweh commanded Hosea: 'take to yourself a wife of harlotry and (have) children of harlotry' (1:2). There repeated acts of harlotry were a prospect; here they have become a reality. Harlotry and adultery have the wife in their iron grip (2:2, 5). The children, too, have been contaminated by her corrupt ways (2:4). The odds of reconciliation seem long.

A link to the previous context is forged in the continued use of imperatives: *say* (v. 1); *plead* (or 'argue') (v. 2). And the allusions to Hosea's family that dominate 1:2–9 and are echoed in salvation speech I (1:10 – 2:1) appear again; *plead* must be addressed by Hosea to his children, as the mention of *your mother* (2:2) makes clear. The subject matter, however, displays drastic change. The *time-setting* which had leapt to the far future in the 'great day' of restoration is dragged back to the dreadful realities of Israel's present, and the *subject matter* which had glowed with expectations of spiritual and political prosperity now turns dark under the storm clouds of judgment. What was succinctly mentioned in 1:2, the harlotries, now becomes blatantly exposed, a foretaste of the judgment speeches that will govern the book, beginning at 4:1.

2–3. The repetition of the command 'plead' or 'make your case against' signals the finality of the opportunity. Gomer's flagrant sin must be dealt with now or never. The parallel negative lines, *for she is not my wife, and I am not her husband*, seem to be more than a statement of fact. They have an official ring to them, not unlike a divorce formula, which in the ancient Middle East was usually uttered by the husband alone, with the wife forced to accept the verdict. The facts that verse 2 holds open the possibility of change (and also v. 7) and that verse 3 begins with *lest* which introduced a potential threat, not a settled act of judgment, would indicate that the divorce is contemplated but not yet decided, hence the urgency with which the children are to put their arguments to their mother.[1]

---

[1] For a recent discussion on Jewish divorce and marriage formulae, see M. A. Friedman, *JBL* 99, 1980, pp. 199–204. One form of the wedding ceremony cited by Friedman is from an Aramaic Jewish wedding document preserved at

The nouns describing her infidelity are plural in Hebrew and may allude to the intensity of her behaviour (*cf.* on 1:2). But more likely they refer to objects or ornaments which brand her as lewd and which, therefore, she should remove from her face and breasts to signify her needed change of heart. Some biblical clues as to the specific form of ornamentation or markings may be found in Jeremiah 4:30, which apparently pictures a prostitute's lurid use of dress, jewelry and facial cosmetics, in the Song of Solomon 1:13, where the woman compares her lover's embrace to a 'bag of myrrh, that lies between my breasts,' and in Genesis 38:15, where Judah judged Tamar to be a harlot, 'for she had covered her face.'[1] The key to the objects *that she put away* (lit. 'let her remove', Ho. 2:2) may be found in the *ring* (nose-ring?) and *jewelry* of 2:13 (see comments), which were accoutrements of her lascivious behaviour.

Lest (v. 3) introduces what is probably best understood as a series of threats of discipline in which Gomer, unless she makes a clean break with her adultery and its trappings, will be stripped naked and removed from the blessings of her present life to a wilderness setting that will threaten her very existence. Public exposure, accompanied by corporal punishment, was one Assyrian way of dealing with harlots who broke the law.[2] Here the nakedness seems part of a rite of embarrassment (*cf.* Jb. 17:6, for the use of Heb. *ysg*, the second verb in v. 3, in a context of ridicule), akin to what Yahweh promised Jerusalem in Ezekiel 16:37: 'I will gather them against you from every side, and will uncover your nakedness to them, that they may see all your nakedness,' (*cf.* Ezk. 23:10).

Make her as in the day she was born may reach both backward and forward. It obviously restates and underscores *I strip her naked* with which it is in parallel. It may connect with *wilderness* and *parched land* (*cf.* Je. 2:6), in which we hear intimations of Israel's desert experiences of thirst (*e.g.* Ex. 17:1–7; Nu. 20:2–13).[3] The point is this: *day she was born* has a double

Elephantine in Egypt: 'She is my wife and I am her husband from this day and forever.'

[1] The Heb. *ki* can also mean 'even though' and hence suggest a parallel to the Assyrian custom which forbade prostitutes to be veiled. See Andersen (pp. 224–225) for discussion.

[2] J. B. Pritchard, *ANET²*, p. 183.

[3] For a summary of both the positive and negative meanings of 'wilderness' in Hosea, see R. Adamiak, *Justice and History in the Old Testament* (Cleveland: John T. Zubal, 1982), pp. 34–35.

meaning, (1) Gomer's natal day on which she arrived stark naked; and (2) Israel's natal day, *i.e.* the Exodus and the wilderness wandering, when Yahweh formed her as his people. The context, in which *wilderness* obviously refers to Exodus (Ho. 2:14–15), argues for this interpretation against the other possible readings, *viz.* that the wilderness language is a punishment of drought on the land (Mays, p. 38) or infertility of the people, a common Middle Eastern idiom. *The day she was born* marks, then, the beginning of the transition from a focus on Gomer-Hosea to one on Israel-Yahweh (Andersen, pp. 225–27). The preposition *like* must then mean 'as in' the *wilderness* and the *parched* land (*cf.* Andersen, pp. 225–226).

4–5. As God made clear in the beginning (1:2), the children are wrapped in a bundle with their mother's sin and judgment. What Israel as a nation (the mother) has done leaves its mark on every individual or group (the children). At least three senses have been suggested for 'children of harlotries': (1) The children are illegitimate; Hosea/Yahweh is not their father; (2) the children themselves engage in fornication; note the conduct of the priests and their daughters in 4:13–14; or (3) the children are contaminated by their mother's fornication. Though a case may be made for each of these suggestions, the third is the most likely because there is less specific evidence for the other two. Ideas of corporate as well as individual guilt were part of Israel's view of life, as the punishment of Achan's family illustrates (Jos. 7:22–26). Both the entire context of the children's lives and also the dominant person in their lives were steeped in harlotry; the shame and guilt of that rubbed off on them to such an extent that their father felt constrained to withdraw his compassion, an obvious reference to the judgment proclaimed in the daughter's name, Not pitied (1:6).

In this accusation nothing is said about the actual misbehaviour of the children: the sole explanation of their involvement in harlotry is the conduct of their mother (v. 5), whose own words are cited as part of the evidence against her. The lovers whom she blatantly chases are the Baals, from whom she believes she receives the sustenance of her life: *bread* of barley or wheat; *water* for drink and irrigation; *wool* and *flax* for warmth and clothing; olive *oil* for cooking, fuel for lamps, medication, cosmetics and cultic ceremonies; alcoholic *drink* like beer or wine.

With Israel's quotation the horror of her harlotry becomes clear. She has pursued the Baals (see on 2:13), the local or regional expressions of the Canaanite fertility gods (who are not named until v. 8). She has engaged with their priestly representatives in acts of fornication whose purpose is to assure the fertility of the land. She has, in an error of cosmic dimensions, credited the Baals with what can only be gifts of Yahweh.[1] The participial style with which she chants the lists of gifts virtually makes her words a hymn to the Baals (a close parallel in a hymn to Yahweh is Ps. 136:25: 'he who gives [is giving] bread to all flesh'). Graspingly, she has claimed all this beneficence as her own, with the Hebrew suffix *my* attached to every noun. A two-fold error this: credit to the wrong giver; possessiveness by a selfish recipient. Part of the threatened judgment will be God's correction of the double error, when he takes back what is ever and rightly his (vv. 8–9).

6–7. The judgment (introduced by *therefore*; *cf.* vv. 9, 14; 13:3) appropriate to Israel's lustful chase is to cut her off from her lovers – a case of judgment by frustration (*cf.* 5:6). Its purposes are positive and gracious, no matter how vexing it may have seemed to Israel: (1) it sought to protect her from her wanton urges which could only produce further harm for her and her children (v. 6); and (2) it was aimed so to thwart her heated pursuits of the Baals that she would change her mind and return to Yahweh (v. 7). The enforced chastity, described in the thorn bushes and stone walls (*cf.* the firm hand that God has to keep on 'the stubborn heifer' of 5:16) that block the paths to the shrines and cut her off from the Baals, anticipates the period of discipline and sexual continence in the second part of action V (3:3–4). Yahweh's assertiveness in confining Israel and personally seeing to her discipline is seen in the 'Behold I' with which the first clause begins and in the fact that he is the subject of the wall-building as well.[2]

Not that Israel's ardour is cooled by all of this (v. 7). Her desire to *pursue* (literally 'hunt down') and to seek satisfaction in the pagan worship is as strong as ever, but the divinely placed impediments frustrate the chase. Deprived, she is

---

[1]See Andersen (p. 233) on the Sumerian legal requirement that a man must support with gifts of grain, oil, and garments a prostitute who has born him children; for the text of Lipit-Ishtar, see *ANET²*, pp. 159–61.

[2]RSV, NIV omit the 'behold' for stylistic reasons: NASB retains it.

again quoted directly (*cf.* v. 5), not this time in words that prove her guilt but in terms that evidence repentance: 'I will return' (*cf.* 3:5; 6:1; 14:1). Both quotations begin – the style is surely deliberate – with *I will go* (the Heb. form is a bit more emphatic: 'Let me go'; 'I want to go'), but the sentences end worlds apart: verse 5, in the orgies of the Baal shrines, verse 7, in the *better* of the living God, the first and only true Husband.

8–13. Much has to happen before that repentance is a reality. The closing verses in this first judgment speech unpack the meaning of verses 4–5: the replacement of pity with judgment, and the perils of Baal worship which has summoned that judgment. Accusations (vv. 8, 12b, 13b) intertwine with announcements in a fabric of crime and punishment boldly woven by divine artistry.

For the first time (v. 8), Hosea uses the word 'know' (Heb. *yd'*, *cf.* 2:20; 4:1, 6; 5: 3, 4; 6: 3, 6; 13: 4, 5), which as much as any single term captures the essence of his understanding of what God wants and what Israel is lacking. Intimacy, loyalty and obedience – the three-fold cord of the covenant – are braided together in this word. To 'know' is to act as the covenant requires; not to 'know' is to fly in the teeth of covenantal allegiance, both in letter and spirit. Ignorance may more readily be excused; forgetfulness of the covenant and its Sovereign can not. *She* (emphasized by the pronoun in Heb.) *did not know* of verse 8 is recapitulated by the *and me* (emphasized by the Heb. word-order) *she forgot* of verse 13.

Verse 8 reaches back to verse 5 for its substance and expands upon it. The list of staple crops – *grain* (Heb. *dāḡān* can denote a range of grains, especially wheat, millet, barley and spelt),[1] new *wine* (may be grape-juice, or an old poetic word for 'wine'; Heb. *tîrôš*) and olive *oil* (Heb. *yiṣhār*) – shows both how fundamental God's provision was and how basic was Israel's error in not acknowledging her full dependence on him. Wolff's point on the use of these three words is well-taken (p. 37): they, in contrast with their counterparts in verse 5 (bread, wine, oil [Heb. *šemen*]), describe food come 'directly from Yahweh' not yet processed by human hands.

Not only commodities but luxuries were God's gifts, given in magnificent abundance (literally 'multiplied' in Heb.; *cf.* Dt. 8:13; 17:17): *silver* and *gold*. Such bounty was put to shameful

---

[1] R. K. Harrison in *ISBE*, rev., II, p. 553.

use by the smiths that fabricated idols. In Hosea's day, silver may have outpriced gold, as its priority in the sentence suggests.[1] Both were highly valued in Palestine because they had to be imported: silver from Asia Minor, the Aegean islands, Armenia or Persia; gold from Ophir and Egypt.[2] Yahweh, to whom belonged the 'earth and what fills it' (Ps. 24:1), was responsible for the creation of these rare metals, for the economic prosperity that enabled their purchase, and for the technological skill that allowed their refinement. To debase their use was to despise God.

Therefore (v. 9) introduces the inevitable consequence of such rejection. *I will take back* is literally 'I will return and take'. The 'return' (Heb. *šwb*) plays off the quotation placed in Israel's mouth in verse 7: she has not yet mustered the will to return to God in repentance; he will take the firm decision to return to her in judgment (see full discussion on *šwb* in Andersen, pp. 244–5) and to *take back* what he had previously given.

Grain and *wine* are the very words listed in verse 8, while *wool* and *flax* recall the prized list of goods in verse 5. *Time* and *season* refer to the periods of harvest: May–June for the grain; July–September for the grapes. The threat of judgment could be fulfilled by drought (*cf.* Am. 4:7–8) or invasion, when it was the custom of the Assyrians, for example, to time their annual westward marches between the end of the spring rains and the beginning of the grain harvest. This tactic assured an army more than 1000 kilometres from home adequate provision (including young lambs born in the spring) for their troops and compounded the devastation inflicted on their enemies or vassals.

The picture is almost vicious. *Take away* (Heb. *nṣl*) means to 'snatch away', 'tear off' as one would snatch prey from the mouth of an animal (Am. 3:12). The absence of wool for colder weather and flax (linen) for warmer makes for physical deprivation. But more than that, it is the shame and disgrace in being unclothed that the passage points to, as is indicated by *nakedness* (Heb. *'erwâ*, which can mean genitals; *cf.* Noah's scene of drunken shame in Gn. 9: 22–23) and by the elaboration in verse 10, introduced by 'and now' (*cf.* 5:3; 10:3; 13:2). The exposé of Gomer/Israel's nakedness threatened in 2:3 is

---

[1]See P. L. Garber in *IDB*, IV, p. 355.
[2]See A. Stuart and J. Ruffle in *IBD*, II, pp. 1002–1003.

made more explicit in verse 10. The force of the passage is in the combination of (1) *lewdness* (Heb. *nablutâ*, whose root *nbl* intimates that brazen folly may result in such gross nudity); (2) *uncover* (Heb. *glh* to 'reveal', 'lay bear', 'totally disclose', a word used of divine revelation in a positive sense) as the antonym to *cover* in verse 9; (3) *in the sight of her lovers*, *i.e.* before their very eyes – maximum exposure of her shame before the Baals (and their priests?) with whom she had behaved so shamelessly and (4) inability of anyone to *rescue* or snatch her (again Heb. *nṣl*; *cf.* v. 9; 5:15) from God's *hand*, symbol of his power (Gn. 49:24; Is. 50:2).

Any doubt about the central role of the corrupt cult is dissipated in verse 11. The forceful language is continued by the uncompromising *I will put an end* (Heb. *šbt* in a form that means literally 'cause to cease'), an expression already used of the annihilation of Jehu's dynasty (1:4). There may be a direct connection between the disgrace witnessed by Israel's lovers (v. 10) and the destruction of the feasts (v. 11). The feasts in all their forms were so degraded by Israel's Baal worship that they no longer belonged to God; they were *her mirth*, her occasions of unbounded joy (Heb. *māśôś* is used of a bridegroom in Is. 62:5), but they were utterly dependent on Yahweh's bounty. Once the land, at his command, withheld its crops, no offerings and, hence, no feasts were possible; Israel stood bare before the Baals whose favour she courted.

Mirth describes the divinely ordered purpose of the festivities: they were to be celebrations of thanksgiving for the gifts of God in crops and the mighty works of God in redemption. *Appointed feasts* speak of the divinely fixed schedule which governed the timing of the feasts, a schedule built into the order of creation in the sun and moon (Gn. 1:14; the Heb. word for 'seasons' is the same word Hosea uses for *appointed feasts*) and by divine example and fiat in the sabbath (Gn. 2:2–3). The three words sandwiched between describe specific regular festivals: *feasts* are the annual events calling for pilgrimage to a central shrine for their celebration (Dt. 16:16–17; *cf.* Ex. 34: 22–23); *new moons* are monthly gatherings first noted in 1 Samuel 20:5ff., mentioned by Amos (8:5) as a time when no business was transacted, and described more fully in Ezekiel 46; *sabbaths* were the weekly days of rest prescribed in the Old Testament law codes (*e.g.* Ex. 23:12; 34:21) and connected with Yahweh as a 'sabbath to the Lord

your God' (Ex. 20:10), a point that made its use in Baal
worship all the more tragic.[1] *Sabbath* forms a sarcastic pun
with the opening verb of the verse, *I will put an end*; both use
the same Hebrew letters (*šbt*).

All these God-given occasions were co-opted by Israel for
her (note the repetition of the pronouns) pagan purposes. The
agricultural character of the pilgrimage feasts made them
readily adaptable to the fertility cult whose purpose was to
assure regularity of harvest and abundance of produce. The
new moon and *sabbath*, which had counterparts in other Middle
Eastern religions, may well have become corrupted by the
astrological practices of Israel's neighbours as well as by the
sexual rites against which Hosea inveighs.

God's appalling devastation (*I will lay waste*) moves (v. 12)
from the perverted feasts to Israel's familiar symbols of
prosperity and security, the grape *vines* and *fig trees* (1 Ki. 5:5;
Mi. 4:4; Zc. 3:10), which were often grown together in the
same plot and were picked at the same time in the late sum-
mer harvest. The celebrating of that harvest capped the agricultural year (though it coincided with the beginning of the
Hebrew calendar year) and closed the cycle of fertility for
which the Baals got the misplaced credit.[2] Again (*cf.* 2:5),
Israel's words are cited in testimony against her. The quotation reinforces the picture of possessiveness implied in the
pronouns *her vines* and *her fig trees:* she claimed to be entitled to
them, to own them as her rightful pay (the Heb. form *'eṭnâ* is
used only here and may be a word-play with *tᵉ'ēnâ*, *fig tree*
[Wolff, p. 38]; the other form of 'hire' or prostitute's 'pay' is
'eṭnān [Dt. 23:19; Ezk. 16:31, 34, 41; Ho. 9:1]), her reward for
giving herself to the Baals, again called *my lovers* (*cf.* 2: 5, 7).
The devastation will be accomplished by God's causing the
vineyard/orchard to go to seed and be invaded by all manner
of unproductive shrubs and trees. The mention of the animals
(*cf.* the lion and bear in Am. 5:19) helps pave the way for the
picture of restoration in 2:14–23, which includes a covenant
with the *beasts of the field* (v. 18) and the subduing of their
destructive urges. The judgment speech closes with an attack
(for *punish*, Heb. *pqd*, see 1:4) on the feasts and all they stood

[1]For descriptions of the feasts of the Hebrew calendar, see H. J. Kraus,
Worship in Israel (Richmond: John Knox Press, 1966), pp. 45–88.

[2]J. Mauchline in *DOTT*, p. 201. We have a good idea of the rhythm of sowing
and harvesting in Palestine's agricultural year from the Gezar Calendar.

for (v. 13). Their character is exposed: in verse 11 God had disowned the feasts and credited them to Israel – *her* feasts; in verse 13 the overt connection with the Baals is made and, simultaneously, the identity of the *lovers*, hinted in verse 8, is announced.[1] (See Additional Note on 'The Baals' on p. 81).

Burned incense is the likely translation of the verb (Heb. *qṭr* 'send sacrifices up in smoke'). No specific object is stated and some versions have supplied other objects for the verb – 'offerings' (JB), 'sacrifices' (NASB; NIV). Since the Hebrew root is the base of several words for incense and altars of incense, it is probably better to assume that the object is incense when no other object is stated (*cf.* Ex. 30:7; 40:27; 2 Ch. 2:5; 26:18, 19; Je. 7:9, where Baal is named as the recipient).

The use of ornamenting (*cf.* the bride in Is. 61: 10) jewelry seems to connect verse 13 with verse 5. Here Israel is pictured preening herself with *her ring*, probably of gold (Gn. 24:22; Jdg. 8:24–26) and worn in either the nose (Gn. 24:47; Is. 3:21) or ears (Gn. 35:4; Ex. 32:2–3, where the form is plural), and *her jewelry* (a similar Heb. word is used with erotic connotations in Song 7:2), which may have resembled the bands worn by the goddesses Ishtar and Anat which draped their torsos so as to emphasize the breasts and the pubic area (see Andersen, pp. 260–262 for a detailed description).

And went after her lovers brackets this verse with verse 5. This parallel, centring in Israel's passion for idolatry/harlotry, argues against Wolff's suggestion (p. 40) that verse 13 pictures a formal procession at the shrine where the worshippers paraded behind leaders who carried standards emblematic of the pagan gods.

Forgot me for Hosea is the counterpart to *know* the Lord in 2:20 (*cf.* especially 6:6, where the rejecting of the knowledge of God and the forgetting of the law of God are parallel ideas) and combines the characteristic attitudes with which Yahweh faces his need to judge – firmness and sadness (*cf.* 11:1–9). To

---

[1]This interpretation of the structure and meaning of 2:12 follows the consensus of most modern commentators (Jacob, pp. 26–29; Jeremias, p. 45; Mays, pp. 42–43; Wolff, p. 14). Andersen (pp. 215, 252–54) ends the first sentence after fig trees and identifies the children (*cf.* 2:4) as the prostitute's hire on whom Yahweh's ire will fall in the form of wild thicket and roaming beasts, an application of the punishment threatened in Lv. 26:21–22: 'Then if you walk contrary to me . . . I will let loose the wild beasts among you which shall rob you of your children.'

forget God is to act as though he had never made himself known, never redeemed his people in the Exodus, never provided for them in the land, or laid his gracious and constraining claims upon them. The oracle formula *says the Lord* (Heb. *n^{e}'um Yahweh*; cf. 2:16, 21; 11:11) makes crystal clear what we began to suspect as early as verse 3 of this judgment speech: while Hosea may have begun the passage addressing his children, Yahweh's voice soon replaced the prophet's and Israel, not Gomer, became the target of the judgment.

Additional Note: The Baals

Hosea's use of the plural *Baals* (cf. 2:17; 11:2), is best interpreted (1) in terms of the multiplicity of shrines where Baal worship corrupted the worship of God; and (2) in the light of the tendency for the name Baal to be attached to various cities or regions in the land – Baal-berith at Shechem (Jdg. 8:33; 9:4); Baal-gad (Jos. 11:17) in the valley of Lebanon west of Mount Hermon; Baal-hamon (cf. 8:11), location unknown; Baal-hermon (Jdg. 3:3; 1 Ch. 5:23), near that northern mountain; Baal-peor (Nu. 25:1–9; Ho. 9:10) in Moab. The singular form, apparently referring to an idol, was used by Hosea, (cf. 2:8) in keeping with the typical Canaanite understanding of Baal as the lord of the storm, who is pictured wearing a bull-like helmet, wielding a thunder-bolt with a spear-sharp point in one hand and a battle mace in the other.[1]

A series of stories about Baal is preserved in Ugaritic literature, and the more than fifty years of research since the discovery of those texts at Ras Shamra (ancient Ugarit) in northwest Syria have aided our understanding of the nature of Baal worship, as Hosea viewed it.[2] Salient to our study are the accounts of Baal's victory over Yamm, the sea-god, who represents chaos and its constant threat to destroy order, and of Baal's on-going struggle, in which he needs the help of his sister-wife, the goddess Anat, to keep Mot the god of summer-drought and death at bay, lest fertility fail and Baal's sovereignty be overthrown. Central to that fertility is Baal's

---

[1] *ANEP*, p. 40; *ISBE*, rev., I, p. 377.
[2] A handy guide to the impact of the Ugaritic discoveries on the Old Testament is found in P. C. Craigie, *Ugarit and the Old Testment* (Grand Rapids: Eerdmans, 1983).

sexual encounter with Anat, who gives birth to a calf.[1] Cultic prostitution seems to have developed in imitation of that cosmic act of intercourse between Baal and Anat, although extra-biblical evidence of ritual sexual activity in Syro-Palestine is scarce. Hosea is the best single source we have. The connection between myth and ritual, nevertheless, is well attested in the ancient Middle East. The myth told the basic story and the ritual was designed to keep it happening.

The history of the amalgamation of Yahweh worship with the veneration of Baal is not easy to trace. There may have been pockets throughout the countryside where Canaanite religion was never stamped out. Furthermore, some confusion between Baal and Yahweh was encouraged by the Hebrew language itself, which, at least until Hosea's time (*cf.* 2:16–17), allowed Baal (literally 'owner', 'master', husband') to be used as a title for Yahweh (*cf.* the theophoric names of sons of Saul – Eshbaal, 1 Ch. 8: 33; of Jonathan – Merib-baal, 1 Ch. 8:34; of David – Beeliada, 1 Ch. 14:7). Furthermore Baal in various forms was a standard title of deity from the coasts of Philistia to the Mesopotamian Valley (*cf.* Bel). It was Ahab, however, cheered on by his wicked spouse Jezebel of Tyre in Phoenicia, who attempted to combine the cult of Baal with the worship of God so that the former would supplant the latter: (1) temples to Baal were built in Jerusalem (2 Ki. 11:18) and Samaria (1 Ki. 16:21); (2) Baal altars of incense were set up in Jerusalem (Je. 11:13), possibly on roof-tops (Je. 32:29); (3) Ahab's retinue counted 450 Baal priests (1 Ki. ch. 18) and sundry prophets; (4) Elijah detested Baal worship sufficiently to stake his ministry on God's power to expose the impotence of Baal and his priests (1 Ki. ch. 18); (5) by Jehu's time (see on 1:4) Baal worship had regained the initiative it lost to Elijah (2 Ki. chs. 9–10); and (6) Judah, too, was contaminated with it by Athaliah, Jezebel's daughter (2 Ch. 17:3; 21:6; 22:2), by Ahaz's molten images (2 Ch. 28:2), by Manasseh's altars (2 Ki. 21:3), by vessels of Baal which had to be purged from the temple and by priests who had to be deposed in Josiah's reform (2 Ki. 23:4–5).

---

[1]For information on Baal, see K. G. Jung in *ISBE*, rev., I, pp. 377–379; Craigie, *Ugarit and the Old Testament* (Grand Rapids: Eerdmans, 1983), pp. 61–66; for the texts, see G. R. Driver, *Canaanite Myths and Legends* (Edinburgh: T. & T. Clark, 1956).

d. A gracious restoration (2:14 – 3:5 [Heb. 2:16 – 3:5])

At 2:14 the cloud of judgment over Israel, evident in Hosea's doomed marriage (1:2–9) and God's accusations and announcements (2:2–13), is lifted. As the judgment was described in actions and then speech, so now the hope is affirmed in speech (2:14–23) and then action (3:1–5).

Hosea's responses to divine commands (1:2–9) set the stage for Yahweh's speech (2:2–13) of condemnation; Yahweh's oracles of promise (2:14–23) pave the way for Hosea's response in reconciliation (3:1–5). When judgment is the theme, illustration precedes actuality; when hope is in view, actuality takes priority over illustration (see beginning of comments on 1:1 – 3:5).

i. Salvation speech II: renewal with cosmic consequences (2:14–23 [Heb. 2:16–25]).

The movement of the text finds us unprepared for the surprise at 2:14. The accusation *and forgot me* (v. 13) leaves us ready for a corresponding announcement, 'I will forget her and her children'. This is precisely what happens in the indictment of the priests who forget God's law (4:6). *Therefore* (*cf.* vv. 6, 9) steels us for the fateful announcement. But it does not come. Instead, we are startled by a bouquet of promises whose components include: (1) a second Exodus and conquest (vv. 14–15); (2) an eradication of all mention of the Baals (vv. 16–17); (3) an assurance of security from attacks of man and beast (v. 18); (4) a new betrothal and marriage (vv. 19–20); and (5) cosmic prosperity as the sign of the renewed covenant (vv. 21–23). Each promise in this bright array is highlighted by the words of future assurance, *I will.*

14–15. The common strain between the words of judgment and the notes of hope is the divine initiative, now heard as the language of love. *Allure her* can be so strong as to suggest enticement (Jdg. 14:15; 16:5) or even seduction (Ex. 22:16); *speak tenderly* (lit. 'upon her heart') can be used in romantic contexts (Gn. 34:3; Ru. 2:13); Israel's *answer* to such courting must be 'yes', as it was on her honeymoon in the Exodus (*cf.* Je. 2:2).

Intertwined with the love language are the reminiscences of the Exodus: the *wilderness* is the site of Yahweh's wooing, as far removed from the tree-shaded shrines of the Baals (*cf.* 4:13) as it was from the brickworks of Egypt. Promises in the desert, of wedding gifts, will be repeated and transform the scenes of Joshua's conquest of Canaan: new vineyards, blessed by Yahweh not Baal, will teem with grapes. And the *Valley of Achor* ('trouble'), plagued for half a millennium by the memory of Achan's disobedience to the command to put everything in Ai to the ban (Jos. 7:26), will be gifted to Israel with a new name, a new beginning: 'a portal (spacious door-opening) of hope' (*cf.* Je. 31:17; La. 3:29).[1] For Hosea, God's memories of the wilderness are poignant (9:10; 13:5). The Exodus (literally 'her coming up'; *cf.* 'they shall go up' in 1:11) is mentioned last because it embraces the other two historical references, the wilderness wandering and the possession of Canaan, and epitomizes the divine love for Israel that was celebrated in those events.

From the land of Egypt prepares the way for the stellar role that Egypt plays in Hosea's messages. As in verse 15, *Egypt* may be a reminder of God's loving rescue of an enslaved people (11:1; 12:9, 13; 13:4). In contrast, *Egypt* for Hosea's hearers carried the threat of return to that house of bondage, an eradicating of the Exodus (*cf.* 7:16; 8:13; 9:3,6; 11:5,11). In all these passages except the first, Egypt is paired with Assyria as the land of potential captivity. The reason for such pairing may be found in a third sense that *Egypt* carries for our prophet: it speaks, along with Assyria, of the ambivalent foreign policy that dogged Israel's last decades before the Assyrians conquered the land under Hoshea (2 Ki. 17:1–6). Some of Hosea's choicest language is reserved to mock this ambivalence (7:11; 12:1). To court either country at the price of disloyalty to Yahweh was to invite disaster. Poised between her past deliverance *from* Egypt and her threatened return *to* Egypt, Israel had to find a wiser course than political equivocation.

16–17. Bountiful vineyards and hope-filled valleys will be possible only when all vestiges of Baal worship are cleared from the land (see on 2:13, for the influence of the Baals). *In that day* (*cf.* 1:5; 2:18, 21) links this facet of salvation to the preceding one: a renewed Exodus stripped of references to Baal are all part of that great future, whose surety is

[1]See D. A. Hubbard, 'Hope in the Old Testament', *TynB*, 34, 1983, pp. 33–59. The Heb. root *qwh* suggests 'waiting with expectancy' and possesses none of the uncertainty so often associated with our English word 'hope'.

underscored by the oracle formula, *says the Lord*, (see on 1:13). Another link between verses 14–15 and verses 16–17 is the language of marriage. What God predicts, even commands, is more than a turning from the use of the name *Baal* ('lord' or 'master') for Yahweh; it is also the gift of a warmer, more intimate name: *my husband*, (my [special] man *cf*. 2:9; Gn. 2:23–4). As with the new Exodus and conquest, the latter period will outshine the former. The bright tomorrow of *in that day* will see Israel more lovingly related to God than ever before.

The new name, *my husband*, drives out the old. The removal of the names means the eradication of any existence, any influence the Baals may have had. It reduces them to the ciphers they really were.[1] The ending of verse 17 recalls the words of verse 13 with which the first judgment speech concluded. The 'and me she forgot', as Israel spent herself in lustful pursuit of her lovers/Baals, has been replaced by 'their names (the Baals) shall not be remembered again'. A literal fulfilment of this prophecy is found in the zeal that goaded Israel's scribes sometimes to replace 'Baal' in Israelite names with *bōšet*, 'shame' (*cf*. Meribbaal, 1 Ch.8:34; Mephibosheth, 2 Sa. 21:8; Ho. 9:10, seems to harbour such substitution, RSV mg.).

18. Two specific threats of judgment are reversed here, with all the certainty of a divine *covenant*. The result is complete security: (1) no danger to person or crop is to be feared from wild animals, foraging birds, or poisonous reptiles (*cf*. 2:12, which promised such devastation to vine-yards; *cf*. also Am. 5:19); and (2) no military invasion will be tolerated, since the instruments of war – *bow, sword* and other weapons (so *war*, Heb. *milhâmâ*, must mean here; *cf*. 1:7; Ps. 76:3; Is. 3:25; 21:15, and see F. Zorell's *Lexicon Hebraicum*)[2] – will be broken and removed from Israel's land.

On that day firmly ties this promise both to the preceding one and to the climax of the oracle in verse 21. The combined peril of animal and military devastation is noted elsewhere in the Old Testament (*e.g.* Jb. 5:19–23; Je. 15:2–3). War meant

[1] For the force of *name* in the Old Testament, see H. Michaud in *A Companion to the Bible*, ed. J. J. von Allmen (New York: Oxford University Press, 1958), pp. 278–279; G. W. Bromiley, *TDNT*, abr., 1985, pp. 695–696.
[2] Franz Zorell, *Lexicon Hebraicum Veteris Testamenti* (Rome: Pontificium Institutum Biblicum, 1966), p. 441a.

both the neglect of the fields and the destruction of the walls and watchtowers, providing opportunity for the ravaging by the animal kingdom. That all the inhabitants of the land (the 'for them' [NEB, NASB, NIV], which RSV, in a misguided desire to harmonize the pronouns with what follows in v. 19, reads 'for you') would be affected by this two-fold assault is obvious. The third plural pronouns (*cf.* also 'I will make *them* lie down in safety') point to Israel as a group of individuals and families, vulnerable to disaster, while the second (vv. 19–20) and third (v. 17) feminine singular pronouns describe Israel as Yahweh's bride.

The picture of shattered weapons reflects the second judgment action in 1:4–5 as well as the promise not to deliver Israel or Judah by military intervention in 1:7. The judgment symbolized in Jezreel's name necessarily entailed military aggression: it took Assyrian bows to break Israelite bows. Now in 2:18 the promise holds that Assyrian and all other brands of weaponry will be swept from the land. We can imagine what hope that pledge held for Israelites who almost annually from 743 BC to the capture of Samaria in 721 BC had felt the sting of Assyrian arrows.

Hosea couched the promise in *covenant* language both to assure its solemnity and to link it with past covenants. References to covenant sacrifices which ratified the agreement and bound the partners to it on pain of death (*cf.* Gn. 15:7–20; Je. 34:18) are retained in the basic verb of covenant-making: 'to cut' (Heb. *krt; cf.* 2:18; 10:4; 12:1 [Heb. v. 2]). The closest biblical parallels to verse 18 are Genesis 9:9–10 and Ezekiel 34:25. God strikes an agreement with his creation to provide permanent benefit to his people. The picture of total harmony in creation recalls Genesis 1:30 and its Edenic setting before the symphony turned discordant at the initial act of human disobedience (Gn. 3:15; 17–19; *cf.* Is. 11:6–9; 35:9).

This reference to *covenant* (Heb. *bᵉrît*, probably from a root that has to do with 'binding' or 'tieing together') differs from Hosea's other two uses of the term: (1) it is applied to treaties or compacts made foolishly or treacherously with foreign nations (10:4; 12:1 [Heb. v.2]); and (2) it remembers the covenant and its stipulations laid upon them by Yahweh at their founding as a people (6:7; 8:1; both passages use the verb 'transgressed' [Heb. *ʿbr*] to depict the cavalier way in which the people had overridden their obligations). The future needed a new kind of covenant initiated by Yahweh and guaranteed by his sovereignty. Such we find beginning to be described in verse 18, though it was left to Jeremiah (31: 31–34), who owed Hosea a measurable debt for his ideas and emphases (see Introduction), to spell out its specific components and its larger significance.

19–20. The switch from *them* to *you* (2nd feminine singular) in the pronouns and the move from the language of security to that of betrothal mark this passage off from verses 14–18 and 21–23, though it is intimately connected with both: (1) it picks up in detail the renewed relationship of verses 14–15 and describes what will make it different from the bond that Israel so badly ruptured by her sin; (2) it shows the intimacy and integrity of the union symbolized in the new name, *my husband*, of verse 16; (3) it reflects the context of peace and security warranted by the new covenant of verse 18; and (4) it sets the stage for the re-entry of the children whose changed names are the centre-piece of verses 21–23.

The focus in verses 19–20 is on the legal and contractual nature of the new relationship. *Betroth* is a much more formal term than 'go, take' (1:2) or 'go, love' (3:1) or 'I will speak tenderly' ... and 'she shall answer' (2:14–15). In Israelite marriages *betroth* would involve negotiations with parents or their representatives (2 Sa. 3:12–15), including settlement of proper bride-price which the suitor would pay to the bride's family (2 Sa. 3:14). An interval of time would pass between the betrothal and the consummation of the relationship (Dt. 20:7; 28:30), but in that interval she is considered to belong officially to her intended (Dt. 22:23–27) and to belong to him for life (as the *for ever* of Ho. 2:19 should be interpreted; *cf.* Ex. 21:6). The intensity of Yahweh's betrothal to Israel is conveyed by Hosea's three-fold use of the term.

Grammatically, the five nouns which describe the nature of the relationship may be considered the price paid by Yahweh for his bride (the Heb. preposition *b* has this meaning in 2 Sa. 3:14). But the contractual aspects of this should not be pressed: to whom would Yahweh pay such a fee? He is Israel's only parent (11:1). What these words do depict is everything that Yahweh brings to the relationship, all the attributes which make for a covenant stamped by loyalty and integrity and love. Without reserve, in the fullness of who he has shown himself to be, he renews his permanent commitment to his bride.

Righteousness and *justice* are the first pair of attributes (*cf.* Am. 5:7, 24; 6:12). *Righteousness* describes Yahweh's commitment to be all that his covenant role as Sovereign and Saviour demands and to relate to her in strength, loyalty and uprightness in all his dealings with her. The Hebrew word *ṣedeq* points to the straightness of God's own character (Jb. 36:3), his administration of justice (Je. 11:20), and his vindication in, or rescue from, enemy attack (Ps. 35:24, 28). *Justice* centres in Yahweh's fairness in all his relationships to his people, as he honours their obedience and corrects their waywardness, without whimsy or arbitrariness. The Hebrew *mišpāṭ* implies rectitude in decision-making (Gn. 18:25), concern for compassionate redress of grievance (Is. 30:18), desire to seek the best for his creatures wherever possible (Ps. 36:6).

Steadfast love and *mercy* form the second pair. *Steadfast love* rings with the tones of covenant loyalty, describing both the attitude and the behaviour of the Lord who made a pledge to his people in full freedom. The Hebrew *ḥesed* may connote God's guidance and protection (Ex. 15:13), and the motive for his rescue (Ps. 6:4), or forgiveness (Ps. 25:7) or covenant-keeping (Dt. 7:9, 12; Mi. 7:20). *Mercy* glows with tenderness and compassion, especially as it shows itself to the weak, the needy, the oppressed. The Hebrew *raḥ°mîm*, recalling the daughter's name built from the same root (1:6–7; 2:1; *cf.* 2:23), is an affective term, akin to the word for womb (Gn. 49:25; Ho. 9:14) and conveying deep, motherlike, feelings; the Old Testament attributes such compassion more frequently to Yahweh (*e.g.* 2 Sa. 24:14; Is. 63:7, 15; Je. 16:5) than to human beings (Pr. 12:10; Am. 1:11).

Faithfulness, the final price of the betrothal, conveys Yahweh's utter dependability, the reliability of all his words and deeds, especially his covenant promises. The Hebrew *°mûnâ* shows itself in restoration after judgment (La. 3:21ff), in the integrity of his works (Ps. 33:4), in the unmatched height (Ps. 36:5) and length (Ps. 100:5) of his credibility. Hosea's clustering of this quintet of divine qualities resembles passages from Israel's hymnody where all the words except *mercy* appear together (*e.g.* Pss. 33:3–4; 36:5–6; 89:14).

The climax of this section is reached in the one-line promise, *and you shall know the Lord* (v. 20). Though *know* is appropriate to the intimacy of marriage (Gn. 4:1), its meaning here is that the bride will make the appropriate response to the Bridegroom by committing herself as fervently and faithfully to the terms of the covenant as he has. Such lack in Israel's present devotion was simply stated by Hosea in 2:8, 13 and will be greatly expanded in 4:1, 6; 5:4; 6:6. Covenant loyalty and obedience are the core of knowing Yahweh. And they manifest themselves in precisely those qualities that Yahweh pledges to bring to the marriage. What he offers is what he asks of Israel in permanent commitment: *righteousness* – the fulfilment of all covenant requirements to him and each other (10:12); *justice* – the safeguarding of the rights of every member of the community (12:6); *steadfast love* – the extending of covenant grace to others with the same good will Yahweh had shown to them (4:1; 6:6; 10:12; 12:7); *mercy* – warm concern for others, especially those in distress (only here in Hosea); and *faithfulness* – reliability in the keeping of promises, in the fulfilment of obligations, and in the constancy of upright conduct (only here in Hosea; but compare the cognate word *ᵉmet* in 4:1). Hosea's restoration of Gomer to their marriage (3:1–2) would demonstrate how profoundly Israel needed God's bride-price and knowledge of him.

21–23. Two great promises bring the salvation speech (2:14–23) to a glorious conclusion: the restoration of fertility to the land and the changing of the children's names to declarations of salvation. The mention of *Jezreel* is the hinge between these promises (v. 22b), announcing fertility by its very etymology (*cf.* on 1:4–5) and beginning the sequence of renaming. The eschatological formula *in that day* and the oracle formula *says the Lord* (v. 21) bind this segment to the previous ones (*cf.* 1:16, 18) and infuse it with the divine authority appropriate to its cosmic message and its pledge of covenant renewal.

The promise of fertility recalls the judgments of deprivation in 2:9, 12. Its form is a dramatic sequence of communication from Hosea to the *heavens*, the source of rain, from the heavens to the *earth*, the source of crops, from the earth to the crops themselves (for *grain, wine* and *oil*, see on 2:8), from the crops to *Jezreel*, a pun now for Israel and a slap at the Baals in the world where it is God who is the source of all well-being. The key to the drama is *answer*, whose importance to the work of salvation was suggested in verse 15. When Israel gave her *answer* to Yahweh's intimations of love (v. 14), the way was prepared for him to *answer* the yearnings of his creation to produce the fertility which he had purposed for it. The wilderness period was past and his promise of vineyards (v. 15) needed fulfilment. *Answer* can best be understood as a shout or gesture in response to a crying need. We can picture the cries rising upward – Jezreel (Israel) to the crops, the crops to the soil, the soil to the heavens, the heavens to Yahweh – and the response being signalled downward.

The word-play on Jezreel's name is continued in the promise 'I will sow her for myself in the land' (v. 23). The pronoun 'her' refers to Israel, carried over from vv. 19–20, and implied in the pun Jezreel = Israel (v. 22).[1] The clause reverses the judgment of 1:4–5 and echoes the positive use of Jezreel's name in 1:10. Beyond that, it implies Yahweh's gift of fertility in the land (*cf.* Nu. 5:28 where the Heb. *zr'* describes pregnancy). Not pitied's name (*cf.* 1:6–7) is reversed without any response; but Not my people's (*cf.* 1:8–9) name-change calls for the answer of the people, since a covenant-ceremony of some kind seems to be in view (*cf.* Je. 30:22; 31:1; Ezk. 36:28; 37:23; Zc. 2:11; 8:8). Israel's response closes this salvation speech, as Israel's answer in the wilderness began it (v. 15). This reversal of the judgment, accompanied by this change of the children's names, thus expands the prophetic hope of 1:10 – 2:1 (see note on Fulfilment of prophecy following comments on 1:10 – 2:1) and shapes the intimate unity of 1:10 – 2:23 with 1:2–9. (For the New Testament use of these changed names in 1 Pet. 2:10 and Rom. 9:25, see on 1:10 – 2:1).

ii. Action V: reconciliation with disciplinary constraint (3:1–5).

Some differences between action V and the first four (1:2–9) need noting: (1) there is no statement of sequence, except for the word *again* which probably should be read with the formula of divine speech, 'said to me *again*' (*cf.* Andersen, Mays) rather than with the divine command, 'go again' (Jacob; Jeremias; Wolff; LXX; Vulg.; most English versions); this interpretation best suits the word order and puts the spotlight on the fact of Yahweh's speaking, rather than on the command itself; (2) Hosea's response, coming in two parts (vv.

[1] RSV emends the pronoun to *him* because of Jezreel's masculine gender in 1:4–5; NIV, NASB read 'her' with MT.

90

2–3), is much more central here than the terse 'so he went and took Gomer' (*cf.* 1:2); (3) Hosea speaks directly to Gomer (v. 3) for the only time in the book (in 2:2–3 he speaks to her through the children); (4) the memoir in 3:1–5 is in the first person singular, with Hosea as narrator, while actions I–IV are in the third person; (5) Gomer is not named in action V (*cf.* 1:2; reasons for identifying the 'woman' of 3:1 with Gomer are given in Guideline two in the introduction to 1:2 – 3:5 above); and (6) the command is reworded: 'go, take' (1:2) has become 'go, love' (3:1); this changes the whole message from the corruption of Israel's idolatry to the constancy of Yahweh's love.

1–2. These verses jerk the hearer back to the sinful realities of the present, after the tantalizing look at the future in salvation speech II (2:14–23; *cf.* the same sequence of 2:2–13 to 1:10 – 2:1). The situation in Gomer's life seems precisely what it was when the children were commanded to plead with her in 2:2; the picture of Israel's life – 'turning to other gods' – looks frozen where it was at 2:5; no words like 'I will go and return to my first husband' (2:7) have been forthcoming; Gomer is branded an *adulteress* (*cf.* 2:2), and as having a *paramour* (cf. 2:5, 7, 12, 13). Apparently her promiscuity has focused at this point on one person, called in verse 1 by the Hebrew word usually translated 'friend' (*rēa'*; *cf.* Song 5:16, 'lover'; Je. 3:1, 'paramours'; Je. 3:20, 'husband'). Israel is still captivated by the sensual cult, as her love for *raisin cakes* suggests (*cf.* 2 Sa. 6:19); she undoubtedly treasured them as gifts from the Baals (*cf.* 2:5, 12), part of her harlot's hire, and perhaps a sexual stimulant (Song 2:5).

Into this bleak situation came the stark command, *go, love*, explained by the strong affirmation, *even as Yahweh loves*. Few places in Scripture tell us more about divine love: (1) it is constant in all circumstances, present even while the people (probably both Israel and Judah are included; *cf.* on 1:6–7, 11) are enmeshed in their idolatry/harlotry (*cf.* 4:12, 19; 5:3–4 for expressions of the degree to which Israel's perversion held her captive); (2) it contrasts utterly with the triviality of human affections, especially when these affections are diverted to unworthy objects – while Yahweh is loving the Israelites, what are they loving? Raisin cakes! (3) it can be illustrated through human love when that human love has grasped something of the power and pathos of the divine – the command to Hosea assumes a correspondence between the divine and the human; what Hosea has learned about the forgiving, restoring love of Yahweh from the salvation speech (2:14–23) he is to teach others by his love for an adulteress; (4) it is commitment and action (v. 2), commanded with a divine imperative; and (5) it is strong as well as tender and has the courage and integrity to exercise discipline when that is necessary (vv. 3–4).

The word 'love' (Heb. *'hb*) has for Hosea something of the range of meaning it occupies in modern English: (1) it can mean 'to gain pleasure from' – as did Gomer's paramour from her company (3:1), Israel from her raisin-cakes (3:1); (2) it can describe a misguided relationship like Israel's with the Baals (2:7, 12, 15; 9:10) or with Assyria to whom she paid tribute as a lover's hire (8:9); (3) it can connote loyal and costly love like that of Hosea's, which God commanded for Gomer, despite her infidelity (3:1); and (4) it can illuminate the many facets of Yahweh's commitment to Israel from the Exodus call to his people (11:1), through the guidance, training and care he offered in their youth (11:4), and the forbearance he showed in the midst of her infidelity (3:1), to the forgiveness that turns aside divine anger and heals their inconstancy (14:4). The divine imperative that commands true love is a lesson never lost on those who truly know their God (1 Jn. 4:8).[1]

Hosea's response (v. 2) shows both how costly love can be and how degraded Gomer's condition had become. Note that the response to 'go, love' (v. 1) is not 'so he went and loved' (*cf.* 1:2–3), but *I bought* – love in action. It is love that bears all that is necessary to accomplish the divine purpose.[2]

---

[1] For a comprehensive survey of the nuances and significance of love in the Bible, see L. Morris, *Testaments of Love: A Study of Love in the Bible* (Grand Rapids: Eerdmans, 1981).

[2] See D. J. Wiseman, 'Weights and Measures', *IBD*, III, pp. 1634–1637; O. R. Sellers, *IDB*, IV, pp. 832ff.; Wolff, p. 61. The exact nature of the transaction is hard to pinpoint: (1) the verb form is awkward and has prompted most modern translations to settle for *bought* (RSV; JB; NASB; NIV; Wolff), as much from the context as from a precise understanding of the Hebrew form; some have used more general terms that allow for the possibility that Hosea paid a fee to hire her long-term ('got her back,' NEB; 'acquired', Jeremias; Mays; 'procured', Andersen); (2) with whom the transaction took place is not stated—presumably the 'paramour' of verse 1, who claimed some right to Gomer, perhaps by virtue of his provision for her; and (3) the meaning of the price (introduced by Heb. *b*; *cf.* on 2:19–20) is not clear—the combination of silver and grain suggests that Hosea may have had difficulty obtaining it; *shekels* are measures of weight,

3-5. Hosea's response to Yahweh's command (v. 1) came in two parts: the action that gets her back (v. 2) and the speech that lays down the terms of the reconciliation (v. 3). Those terms are not easy to discern from verse 3 alone, and most interpreters have invoked the help of verses 4–5 to understand them. *Many days* must mean a period of temporary duration in verse 4, because the *afterward* of verse 5 points to a joyful, climactic event when the *many days* have passed. The terms of verse 3, then, are *temporary* guidelines for the restored relationship. They also seem to be *disciplinary* guidelines: Gomer's activities are to be sharply restricted – she is to dwell (or 'remain') with Hosea (the same verb describes the period of waiting for purification after childbirth, Lv. 12:4–5), refrain from the fornication that had become her passion and from any other sexual intimacy, including intercourse with Hosea (*cf.* Wolff, p. 56; RSV; NEB; JB; NASB; Mays, p. 58). This interpretation turns on two assumptions: (1) 'and you shall not belong to a man' means 'any man' not 'another man'; and (2) 'I also [will not be] unto you' describes Hosea's parallel celibacy. An equally commendable translation is Andersen's (p. 291), who reads the first verb of the sentence as 'wait' (not *dwelt*), the two prohibitions as describing Gomer's temporary sexual abstinence, and the last clause, as the promise of a fully restored relationship – 'then indeed I will be yours', a reading that has the advantage of anticipating the full restoration of Israel to Yahweh in verse 5.

The disciplinary period in the marriage is a prophetic action designed to symbolize a time of chastening and deprivation through which Israel is to pass. That verse 4 is an explanation of the purpose of verse 3 is signalled in the *for* (Heb. *kî*) at the beginning (*cf. for* in 1:2, 4, 6, 9). Gomer is to be deprived of intercourse; Israel of *king, prince, sacrifice, pillar, teraphim* and *ephod*.[1] The deprivation is suitable and thorough:

---

perhaps in coin form, calculated by some to be just under half an ounce; *homer* and *lethech* are volume measures for grain, probably contained in woven baskets; the *lethech* is thought to be half an *homer*; precision escapes us, since the homer's size is variously estimated from five to eleven bushels; a reasonable guess is that the combined silver and grain value was about thirty shekels of silver and thus equivalent either to the worth of a female slave (Ex. 21:32; *cf.* Lv. 27:4 for the monetary equivalent of a woman vowed to the Lord) or to the cost of acquiring a cult-prostitute (Jeremias, p. 55).

[1]For Ephod, see R. K. Harrison, *ISBE*, rev., II, pp. 117–118; for Teraphim, see J. A. Motyer and M. J. Selman, *IBD*, III, p. 1535. The pillars may originally

every political and military (*princes* may be battle leaders; see on 13:10) office, cultic entity, or substitute for direct dependence on Yahweh's revelatory word (*cf.* Ho. 4:12) will be stripped away.

Two great verbs telegraph the end of this deprivation, which can best be interpreted as an experience of exile (as Hosea often threatens, *e.g.* 8:13; 9:3, 6; 11:5): *return* and *seek*. Both have positive and negative connotations for Hosea. Negatively, *return* (Heb. *šwb*) is used of Israel's turning back to false gods (7:16) with a consequent cancellation of the Exodus resulting in exile to Egypt (8:13; 9:3; 11:5); *seek* also may imply a negative object (*lovers* = Baals, 2:7) or a negative manner (with animal sacrifices, 5:6). Positively, both mean to return to full covenant loyalty on the terms of repentance, trust and obedience: *return* is what is needed but refused by Israel (5:4; 7:10) despite God's prompting (2:7), what they profess to do without full sincerity (6:1), what they will do only when judgment has run full course (14:1–2); *seek* is what God patiently waits for (5:15) and what Israel finds itself incapable of doing despite all the evidence to the contrary (7:10), until the *afterward* described in verse 5. Where *return* and *seek* occur together, they reinforce each other – to return with the full desire for fellowship with God on his terms (*cf.* 7:10). In the present context, where the returning and seeking follow a time of intense political and spiritual deprivation, *return* may carry with it not only the idea of repentance but of return home from exile.

Mention of *David their king* conveys a number of thoughts in the context of Hosea: (1) the reunion of the two kingdoms under one head (*cf.* 1:11); (2) the reversal of Israel's pattern of dynastic instability (7:3–7; 8:4; 10:3); (3) the rejection of the foreign alliances which served as a buffer against their own political weakness (7:8–9, 11, 16); and (4) the covenantal continuity promised to David by Yahweh and violated by Jero-

have been memorials to mark the hallowed sites of Israel's history like Bethel (Gn. 28:18, 22; 35:14) and Shechem (Gn. 33:20; Jos. 24:26) but proved akin to the Canaanite columns that symbolized male deities and were forbidden (Dt. 16:21–22); the *ephod* may be connected with the high priestly garment which contained the urim and thummim for divination (Ex. 28:4–40; 35:27; 39:2–30), and may have been an image (*cf.* Ex. 32:4; Jdg. 8:27), a garment used to adorn idols (2 Ki. 23:7), or a figurine akin to *teraphim* (*cf.* Jdg. 17:5; 18:14), which were usually small terracotta figures of deities thought to grant protection and guidance (1 Sa. 19:13; 21:21; 2 Ki. 23:24; Ezk. ch. 16).

boam I and all his successors (*cf.* on 8:4). Like Amos (9:11) and
the great prophets who followed him (Mi. 5:2; Is. 11:1–5; Je.
23:5–6; Ezk. 37:24–28; Zc. 12:7), Hosea connected Yahweh's
future victory to the renascence of Davidic rule. For Hosea,
the return to Yahweh carried with it the reversal of all that
Jeroboam's splitting of the kingdom had wrought. The
spiritual return and the national reunion were of a piece – a
reminder that the Old Testament sees Israel as a flesh and
blood entity whose loyalty to Yahweh is lived not in an
otherworldly realm but in the real economics, politics and
geography of history. (For the ways in which such prophecies
are fulfilled, see note at end of 1:2 – 2:1.)

The passage concludes with words on the manner, the
benefits and the timing of the return. *The latter days* should be
read as counterpart to *many days* (vv. 3–4). *The latter days* are
not primarily the 'end times' in an absolute sense, but a time
after the days of discipline have done their work. *Goodness* is
not only a recovery of fellowship with Yahweh but the restoration of all his generosity in the produce of the land which
Israel's foolishness credited to the Baals (2:5; *cf.* Gn. 45:18, 20,
23; Je. 2:7 for this meaning of *ṭûb*); *goodness* may stretch
beyond material blessing to the total renewal and covenant
keeping described in salvation speech II (2:14–23; *cf.* Ne.
9:25; Is. 63:7). *Fear*, the manner of their coming, is pivotal to
the scene. Nothing less than such reverent awe is appropriate
for Israel, who has learned in deprivation both who Yahweh is
and who Baal is not, both the importance of covenant loyalty
and the terror of its absence.

We are left to surmise what happened to Hosea and Gomer.
As dramatically as they appear, they are dropped from the
concerns of the prophecy. They have grasped our attention,
sharpened our understanding of God's judgment and grace,
and left us ready for the further messages of the prophet.

II. HOSEA'S MESSAGES: PART ONE (4:1 – 11:11)

This section starts again the journey from judgment to hope,
from Israel's tragic present to her brilliant future. This time
the author calls us to linger long in the present to hear in
artful detail how bad Israel's harlotry (1:2) had become (4:1 –
11:7). Only when we have observed the crimes of Israel with

an intimacy and at an intensity almost beyond our absorbing, are we allowed to hear a fleeting soliloquy of hope (11:8–9) and catch its meaning for Israel's future (11:10–10).

If an outline of the complexity of this struggle were to be ventured, we might understand the materials in this way:

> Introduction (4:1–3)
>
> (1) The covenant shattered (4:4 – 5:7);
> (2) The politics run amok (5:8 – 7:16);
> (3) The cult ripe for destruction (8:1 – 9:9);
> (4) The calling unfulfilled (9:10 – 11:11)

The specific themes and style of each section will be noted in their place. Though it is not easy to propose an historical background for these sections, there is good reason for suggesting that many of the speeches were delivered in the latter part of Hosea's ministry (*c.* 735–730 BC) in contrast with his family experiences (1:2 – 3:5) which must have occurred in the latter days of Jeroboam II, two decades earlier.

a. Introduction: general indictment of the nation (4:1–3)

This is clearly a new section: (1) marked by a call to attention – 'Hear the word of Yahweh' (*cf.* 5:1; Am. 3:1; 4:1; 5:1); (2) addressed to Israel, who had been discussed as *they* in 3:4–5; (3) phrased in poetry not prose; and (4) directed to the present sins of the people not to future rescue. It is a comprehensive judgment speech indicting sin in sweeping terms (vv. 1–2) and announcing a judgment of cosmic scope (v. 3). The formal opening, the use of *controversy* (Heb. *rîb*; *cf.* on 2:2), and the legal tone of the indictment have been interpreted as the frame-work of a covenant lawsuit (Wolff, p. 66). Since a number of ingredients are lacking – a summons to witnesses (*cf.* Mi. 6:3–5), questions and answers about divine requirements (*cf.* Mi. 6:6–8) – it is more likely that the literary form compresses an argument or quarrel between Yahweh and the people rather than a scene of formal legal charges.[1]

The quarrel announced in verse 1 centres in the absence of

[1]M. Deroche, 'The Reversal of Creation in Hosea', *VT*, 31, 1981, p. 400. For descriptions of covenant lawsuits, see Kirsten Nielsen, *Yahweh as Prosecutor and Judge, JSOT* Supplement 9 (Sheffield: 1978).

covenant virtues and the breach of covenant stipulations (v. 2). It reaches back to the accusations of 1:2b, 'great harlotries by forsaking Yahweh', and 2:2–13, the lust for the Baals, and spells out their consequences. Her harlotry with the Baals has seduced Israel away from her basic covenant commitments: (1) *no faithfulness* describes lack of truth-telling and truth-doing which result in instability, infidelity and unreliability; (2) *no kindness* speaks to the lack of concern for needy neighbours, which the covenant insists on as the appropriate response to the steadfast love Yahweh has shown his people; and (3) no *knowledge of God* sums up the whole theme of covenant revelation of who God is, what he has done for his people in redemption and what he requires of them. It is the absence of these qualities and this knowledge *in the land* (a reminder that the gift of the land to Israel warranted better behaviour) which helped to shape the betrothal terms that will determine Israel's future with Yahweh. He, in the end, will bring these qualities to the marriage and, by so doing, evoke them from Israel (*cf.* on 2:19–20; *ʾemet* in 4:2 is closely related in derivation and meaning to *ʾemûnâ*, 'faithfulness').

If virtues are lacking, vices are present, each of which is expressed in terms plucked *verbatim* from Israel's law codes: (1) *swearing* (Heb. *'lh*) breaks the commands against unworthy uses of the divine name (Ex. 20:7; Dt. 5:11) by damning others and attaching Yahweh's name to the curse (*cf.* 10:4; Ex. 21:17,20; Jdg. 17:2); (2) *lying* (Heb. *khš*) violates the personal and legal rights of others, especially when it entails false witness in legal deliberations, financial transactions, or religious vows (7:3; 10:13; 12:1; Lv. 19:11; *cf.* Ex. 23:1–3, 6–9); (3) *killing* (Heb. *rṣḥ*) is murder, the taking of human life without due process of law (6:9; Ex. 20:13; Dt. 27:24); (4) *stealing* (Heb. *gnb*) originally implied kidnapping and was expanded to include crimes of appropriating the valuable possessions of another (Ex. 20:15, 17; Lv. 9:11; note the death penalty for it in Ex. 21:16); and (5) *committing adultery* (Heb. *n'p*; see on 1:2; 2:2; 3:1) caps the list as the expression of Israel's spiritual and physical promiscuity (*cf.* 4:13–14; 7:4; Ex. 20:14; Lv. 20:10).

The last clauses of verse 2 are troublesome: (1) *they break all bounds* may be the verb for which the previous five words (all infinitive absolutes in Hebrew, putting emphasis on the act itself without reference to subject or time of action) serve as subject; the quintet of legally proscribed acts *break all bounds*; (2) if the verb (Heb. *prṣ*; *cf.* 4:10 for its use in childbirth; 2 Ch. 24:7, for breaking into a house; Mi. 2:13, for breaking through a wall) stands by itself, then it may depict some general yet vicious mayhem that violates human rights in letter and spirit; and (3) if linked with the final clause – *murder* (lit. 'bloodshed', Heb. *dāmîm*) *follows* (lit. 'bumps against', Heb. *ngʻ*) *murder* – it may connote either lavish, wanton bloodshed or more specifically the activity of armed troops breaking into households to seize victims for the human sacrifices that fed the altars of the Baals (Andersen, pp. 338–339), a savage breach of divine law like that described in Psalm 106:37–39. Since ordinary *murder* is catalogued under *rṣḥ*, some such explanation as this would suit the context well and prepare for the indictments against the priests that dominate the next section, 4:4 – 5:7, especially 5:1–2.

These thoroughgoing violations of the terms of the royal covenant call for a commensurate judgment. *Therefore* (v. 3) steels the audience to hear it but hardly prepares them for its scope. The judgment seems to take the form of drought – a sentence appropriate to crimes committed in search of fertility through the Baals (*cf.* on 2:3–13) – as the second verb 'withers' (NIV 'wastes away'; *cf.* Is. 16:8; Joel 1:12) indicates and the first verb (Heb. *ʼbl* mourns, seems to mean 'dries up' in Je. 12:4; 23:10; Am. 1:2) may suggest. The thoroughness of the drought, wiping out *all who dwell in* (*cf.* Ps. 24:1) the land and the entire animal kingdom – *beasts, birds* and *fish*, gives clues that the devastation is not just natural: the crimes of the *land* of Israel (v. 1) will result in judgment for the whole 'earth' (*so land* may be read in v. 3), just as it is Yahweh's intention that Israel's faithfulness shall bring blessing to the rest of the world (Is. 2:1–4; Mi. 4:1–4). The annihilation of the animal kingdom is pictured in language that outstrips the flood-story, where at least representatives of each species were preserved (Gn. 6:18–22). Hosea's holocaust resembles closely Zephaniah's (1:2–3) and echoes Genesis 1:30 in such a way that the appointed judgment for Israel's sin is nothing less than the 'reversal of creation'.[1] Thus, Yahweh's restoration, promised in 2:15–23, must include a renewed covenant with the entire animal kingdom (v. 18).

[1]See M. Deroche. 'The Reversal of Creation in Hosea', *VT*, 31, 1981, pp. 400–409.

b. The covenant shattered (4:4 – 5:7)

In this section the focus narrows from the people as a whole, with whom Yahweh has sharp controversy, to the priests – especially the high priest – who regulate the cult and interpret its terms to the people (*cf.* 4:4, 6, 9; 5:1 for specific references to the priests). The crimes mentioned here are entirely fitting to this sacerdotal context: (1) failure to teach the law (4:6); (2) use of the cult to feed their own appetites (4:7–10); (3) practice of forms of divination (4:12); (4) offering of sacrifices at the high-places (4:13a); (5) participation in ritual orgies of sex (4:13b–14); (6) encouragement of drunken lewdness in connection with idol worship (4:17–19); (7) false trust in the sacrifices at the shrines (5:6); and (8) bearing of bastard children as the fruit of the pagan orgies (5:7).

i. The rejected law (4:4–10).

The passage places the blame for the sins of 4:1–3 squarely on the shoulders of the priests, in the person of their leader, although not without some sharp debate indicated in verse 4. The passage breaks into two sections: verses 4–6, and verses 7–10. Both are judgment speeches in which accusations are interleaved with announcements. In the first section, the indictment is failure to keep the law; the punishment is the rejection of their priestly status. In the second section, the crime is hedonistic greed in the celebration of the cult; the judgment, accordingly, is deprivation of any source of joy.

4–6. The puzzling text of verse 4 is usually interpreted in one of two ways: (1) Yahweh is heard as speaker, rebuking (v. 4a) some unnamed party who protested the sweeping indictment of 4:1–3, and forbidding him to argue back (Heb. *rîb*; see on 2:2; 4:1) or to 'accuse' Yahweh of unjust charges against the people; or (2) the chief priest is the speaker, whose words rebuking Yahweh are cited in verse 4a; Yahweh's rebuff begins, then, at verse 4b and points the finger of accusation at the priest himself. There is not much to choose between these options. Both assume a dialogue between Yahweh and a protester; both give Yahweh the last word in singling out the priest to be tried as a culprit.[1]

---

[1] In limiting the discussion to these two options, I have set aside the third alternative (represented in MT; LXX; Vulg.; AV; NASB; NIV) that has the people

If our account of a debate is reasonably accurate, the setting for the speech may have been one of the major shrines, perhaps Bethel (12:4), the royal shrine sponsored by the court of Samaria (*cf.* Am. 7:10–13). This setting explains the inclusion of a *prophet* in the condemnation, since cult prophets, who assisted in worship and pronounced oracles of hope or doom to needy worshippers, seem to have been among the religious personnel at such centres of worship.[1]

Stumble (v. 5) is a favourite word in Hosea to describe the disasters that beset those who do not walk in God's ways. The wayward fall on their faces so hard that it is impossible to get up without outside help (*cf.* 5:5; 14:1, 9). The timing – priest *by day* and prophet *by night* – is not designated so much to distinguish between the falls as to indicate that either may stumble at any time, whether night (when one might expect it) or day (when one would ordinarily feel safe). The expression may be a *merism* in which contrasts of time are listed so as to cover the whole range of possibilities.

The threat, '*and I will destroy your mother*' (v. 5c), clearly marks God, not Hosea, as the speaker in this section. The clause should be taken as parallel to verse 6a (against Andersen, p. 352) and interpreted accordingly: *mother* is not the mother of the chief priest (against Wolff, p. 78) but is the nation Israel, mother of all its individuals (*cf.* 2:2, 4–5), who is called *my people* in verse 6a. The structure, then, of verses 5–6 is a sequence of four two-line parallel statements:

---

contending with the priest. For a recent defence of this reading, which has the advantage of not emending the мт, see M. Deroche, 'Structure, Rhetoric, and Meaning in Hosea IV 4–10', *VT*, 33 (1983), pp. 185–198. Part of the argument rests on the questionable premise that *prophet* in verse 5 and *priest* in verse 6 refer to Israel herself in her failure to fulfil these offices to which Yahweh had called her (*cf.*; Ex. 19:6; Nu. 11:29; Joel 3:1–2); the resultant conclusion is that the entire speech attacks the people and is a direct continuation of verses 1–3. The options presented in the commentary seem to fit better the flow of the entire passage and entail the modest emendations of changing a vowel in the word 'your people' (to read 'with you') and dividing another word into two (*kimrîbêy* to *kîmā* ['indeed'] *rîbî*); see Andersen, pp. 344–351 for this suggestion and further discussion of the textual options.

[1]On cult prophets, see A. R. Johnson, *The Cultic Prophet in Ancient Israel* (Cardiff: University of Wales, 1962), *Ibid.*, *The Cultic Prophet and Israel's Psalmody*, (1979).

5a you shall stumble, O priest, by day;
5b shall stumble also the prophet with you by night.

5c And I shall destroy your mother;
6a Shall be destroyed my people from lack of the knowledge
   [of God];

6b Since you the knowledge [of God] have rejected,
6c I will reject you from [being] a priest to me.

6d As you forgot the instruction of your God,
6e I, yes I, will also forget your children.

This over-literal rendering demonstrates both the parallelism
in the structure and the progress in thought. The collapse of
the priest and prophet, key ministers of law and word, leads
inevitably to the disastrous destruction.

The knowledge, so specified with the Hebrew definite article,
can only link to *the knowledge of God* in 4:1 and refer to the
failure of the priesthood to give the covenant instruction
which was its duty. It is a fierce failure, as *rejected* and *I reject*
announce (Heb. *m's*; *cf.* 9:17, 'cast off'; also Am. 5:21). Note
that *the knowledge* is clearly paralleled by *the law* (*i.e.* tôrâ,
'instruction') *of your God*. The magnitude of the priestly sin of
omission, the failure to teach the law, is seen in its staggering
consequences: the collapse of the priesthood (vv. 4, 6c, e) and
the destruction of the nation (vv. 5c–6a). And the
preciousness of the law to Yahweh is underscored by its comparison to the children of the priest (v. 6d, e). On the tragic
meaning of *forget*, see comments at 2:13.

7–10. This paragraph builds upon the previous one: (1) the
likely antecedent of *they, their* and *them* (vv. 7–8, 10) is *children*
of the chief priest (v. 6); (2) the Hebrew pronouns revert to
the singular in verse 9, where the chief priest is again in view
(the LXX and Vulg. retain the singular while most English
versions – AV; RSV; NEB; JB; NASB; NIV – translate the pronouns
as plural as though either the singular *priest* stood for a company of priests or *people* is read as the antecedent of *them* in *I
will punish them . . . and requite them*; see below); and (3) on the
interpretation assumed here, verses 7–10 tell why and how
God *will forget* the priest's children (v. 6).

The increase described in verse 7 seems to be the numerical growth of the priesthood. Growth in numbers was matched by growth in sinfulness, since all priests were caught up in the sin of rejecting the law (v. 6). This multiplication of iniquity in the nation is evidently in proportion to the multiplication of the prosperity of the land in the reign of Jeroboam II. Instead of multiplying her devotion to God, Israel multiplies her self-reliant endeavours and, even worse, her dependence upon the Baals. The last line of the verse has provoked substantial comment. If we translate the Hebrew text unemended, the clause contains a threat of punishment stemming from the sin described. God is the speaker: 'I will change' (So LXX; Vulg.; AV; RSV; NEB; NASB; Mays; Jacob). Taking this tack, we understand 'glory' as either (1) the special duty and relationship of the priests to stand and serve before God (Jacob, p. 41), a relationship which they had clearly forfeited by their neglect of the knowledge of God (v. 6) or (2) the glory of Baal, described here sarcastically, since to Yahweh alone can true glory be ascribed (*cf.* Je. 2:11). If, however, we emend the verb to 'they have changed' (*cf.* Targ.; Syr.; JB; NIV; Wolff; Andersen; Jeremias) then *glory* refers to God (*cf.* Jer. 2:11) and *shame* (*cf.* also 4:18) to Baal. Since the unaltered text makes sense and continues a pattern in which threat of judgment is interleaved with accusation of sin (*cf.* vv. 6, 9–10), it seems better to stay with the reading, *I will change*. For lack of knowledge of him, God will transform the multiplication of the prosperity of the nation into its disgrace.

The priests' complicity in Israel's sin is nowhere stated more forcefully than in verse 8. The verbs *feed* (lit. 'eat;' *cf.* Hosea's use of Heb. *'kl* for enthusiastic consumption, frequently in contexts of a judgment that devours Israel, 2:10; 5:7; 8:14; 11:6; 13:8) and *are greedy for* (lit. 'lift his throat' in eagerness to swallow; *cf.* Dt. 24:15; Ps. 86:4; Je. 22:27) highlight the intensity of the priestly passion. So perverse had these anointed leaders become, that they craved *sin* (Heb. *ḥaṭṭā't*, 8:13; 9:9, borrows the language of hunting or war and means to 'miss the path or target') and *iniquity* (Heb. *'āwôn*, 5:5; 9:7; 12:8; 14:1, speaks of distorting or twisting oneself from the straight way, as a guide might deliberately lead a follower into trouble). *Feed* may literally describe the priests' custom of eating the sin-offerings; the Hebrew *ḥaṭṭā't* may describe either the sinful deed or the sacrifice offered to atone for it

(Lv. 6:25–26 [Heb. vv. 18–19]). They sated their appetites by encouraging *sin* and the consequent sin-offering.

The proverb, *like people, like priest,* in verse 9 announces the judgment on the priesthood which will be no more exempt from divine wrath than the people (*cf.* 1:2–9; 2:2–13; 4:1–3). Their *ways* (or 'paths') missed God's ways and their deeds turned perverse, as *sin* and *iniquity* proclaim (v. 8). The synonymous parallelism of verse 9b–c drives home the promise of suitable punishment, though in non-specific terms. For *punish* see at 1:4 and 2:13; for *requite* (Heb. *hēšîb*, lit. 'cause to return'), see 12:2, 14, where Yahweh is also the subject.

The announcement of general judgment is made specific in verse 10. The theme is frustration almost to the point of annihilation. The priest's voracious appetites will not be sated (*cf.* Mi. 6:14); the fornication will be doomed to sterility. *Multiply* is the word (Heb. *prṣ*) translated *break all bounds* in verse 2. The inability to multiply corrects the excessive increases which caused sin to abound (v. 7) and fulfills the grave promise: *I also will forget your children* (v. 6). The paragraph concludes as it began with an indictment as the reason for the announcement. *They have forsaken* shows that the priests have shared, even sponsored, the cardinal sin of the people (*cf.* 1:2; 2:13). With a number of translations (RSV; NEB; JB; NIV), we should read *harlotry* from verse 11 (*cf.* 1:2; 2:2, 3) as the object of *cherish* (Heb. *šmr*, lit. 'keep', 'guard', 'watch', a word that connotes 'practise with enthusiasm'; its customary objects in the law-codes are the divinely ordained statutes, *e.g.* Dt. 13:19; 15:5; 17:19; 32:46). The point completes the thought of verses 4–6: the knowledge and law of God have been replaced as objects of obedience by the harlotry of the cult.

ii. The corrupt religion (4:11–19). This section oscillates between the priests who have held centre stage in verses 4–10 (*cf.* vv. 13b–14 where the sons and daughters of the priests seem to be singled out) and the people who have willingly been led astray by the priests (*cf. my people,* v. 12; *a people,* v. 14; *Israel* and *Judah,* v. 15; *Ephraim,* v. 17). Since the corruption of the cult by acts of divination (v. 12), by idolatrous worship (vv. 12–13, 15, 17–19), by sexual promiscuity (vv. 13–14, 18) – is the subject matter, the priests are held culpable even when not directly addressed and are summoned back to the judgment bench in 5:1.

The speech is a series of accusations and contains no direct threats of punishment like those of 4:3, 5–6, 7, 9–10. Instead, the dire results are depicted as inevitable consequences of their foolish acts, in a manner not unlike that of Proverbs[1]: (1) their lust for the cult, symbolized by its *new wine*, robs them of *understanding* (lit. 'heart', v. 11; *cf.* on 2:15); (2) their idolatries at the shaded shrines brought the evil consequence – *therefore* – that their children acted immorally there (v. 13); (3) a people who lack insight can *come to ruin* on their own without outside intervention (v. 14); and (4) their worship itself will be a source of shame (v. 19).

Though verses 11–19 form a coherent unit, exposing the cult and its futility, they contain a variety of literary forms: (1) proverbs (vv. 11, 14e); (2) admonitions (vv. 15, 17b); (3) oath (v. 15e); (4) rhetorical question (v. 16b); (5) accusations addressed to the priests (vv. 13b–14), and to Israel (v. 15); and (6) accusations directed to someone else about Israel (vv. 12–13a, 16–19). The multiplicity of genres and the alternating forms of address suggest a courtroom scene where an indictment is being presented in turn to the accused and to whatever witnesses may be present.

11–14. Proverbial sayings at the beginning (v. 11) and ending (v. 14e) form an envelope that wraps these verses into a package[2]: *take away the understanding of my people* (reading the *'ammî* of v. 12 as the completion of v. 11 with BHS; LXX; NEB; NIV; Andersen; Wolff; Jeremias) is synonymous with *a people without understanding*. The first part states the cause – lust for the fruit of the vine (Heb. *tîrôš* crops up frequently in Hosea as a symbol of Yahweh's gifts credited to the Baals: 2:8, 9, 22; 7:14; 9:2) which the cultic autumn festival celebrated[3]; the latter part states the consequences – *shall come to ruin* (lit. 'be thrown away'; *cf.* Pr. 10:8, 10, the only other Old Testament occurrences).

---

[1]See D. A. Hubbard, 'Proverbs, Book of', *ISBE*, rev., III, p. 1019.

[2]On the envelope or inclusio in these verses, see J. R. Lundbom, 'Poetic Structure and Prophetic Rhetoric in Hosea', *VT*, 29, 1979, pp. 300–308.

[3]This interpretation follows the suggestions of Wolff (p. 72) that *harlotry* and *wine* be read as one Heb. word (*z⁽nûnîm* not *z⁽nût* as in MT) and attached to verse 10 as the direct object of 'cherish' (Heb. *lišmōr*). This leaves *new wine* as the sole subject of verse 11 which helps to account for the singular verb *takes away* (Heb. *yiqqaḥ*).

Within the envelope are three illustrations of Israel's dementedness. First, they seek revelation from wooden objects (v. 12). *Wood* could be a pillar (perhaps with phallic significance) or a sacred tree (*cf.* v. 13); *staff* might be smaller pieces of wood to be cast like dice and lots, or a larger rod to be spun and dropped to convey a message by the direction in which it landed – an act of rhabdomancy. In any case magic and even idolatry were involved and drew divine ire (Dt. 18:1–14), for they needed to *inquire* (Heb. *š'l;.cf.* Jdg. 1:1; 2 Sa. 2:1; Ezk. 21:26) of God who alone knew the future, who alone could give *oracles* (Heb. *ngd*). Such acts were rejections of true prophecy (*cf.* 9:7 for its explication).

Second, the Israelites are so engrossed in idolatry that they are under the sway, not of Yahweh whom *they have left* (Heb. preposition *mittaḥat* means 'from under the authority of' and is equivalent to *mē'aḥªrêy*, literally 'from [following] after' in 1:2), but of a spirit whose character causes them to wander wildly into acts of harlotry (v. 12c–d). *Spirit* comes close to describing demonic power and indicates how virtually inescapable Israel's harlotry with the Baals had become (*cf.* 4:19; 5:4). *Harlotry* dots this section of the book and links it tightly to the theme verse (1:2) and the descriptions of Gomer/Israel as harlot in 2:2–13; 3:1–2 (*cf.* 4:10, 12, 13, 14, 15, 18; 5:3, 4).

The first half of verse 13 gives the clearest description thus far of how and where the Israelites practised the cult. Their two prime activities were slaying and eating sacrifices (Heb. *zbḥ* is always used negatively by Hosea to signify the activities of the corrupt cult; *cf.* 4:14; 8:13; 11:2; 12:12; 13:2) and burning incense and other offerings (on Heb. *qṭr*, see 2:13; 11:2). The places for these exercises were the elevated sites that seemed closer to the heavens and were shaded by trees which Israel deemed sacred: *oak* (Heb. *'allôn*) may have symbolized the strength thought to be gained from such worship (*cf.* Is. 2:13; Am. 2:9); *poplar* (Heb. *libneh*) occurs only here (though perhaps also in 14:5) and in the curious account of Jabob's use of rods to increase the fertility of the flock (Gn. 30:37); *terebinth* (Heb. *'ēlâ*) cannot be given a precise botanical identification but seems to describe a large tree (see Ecclus. 24:6) to which the Old Testament frequently assigns a religious significance (*cf.* Gn. 35:4; Jdg. 6:11, 19; Is. 57:5; RSV translates as *oak* in all these passages; but *cf.* Is. 6:13 where *oak* and *terebinth* occur together). What all these trees had in common was good shade. Whether Hosea was mocking their practices with sarcasm we cannot be sure. In a hot land where large trees had long since been cut down for building materials, shade was precious (*cf.* 14:7). Yet it is hard to escape the feeling that Hosea is jeering at religious activity in sites whose only measurable benefit is the relief they offer from the sun.[1]

Third, one of the rude results (note the *therefore* of v. 13e) of the priests' infidelity to God was the promiscuous sexual conduct of their own daughters and daughters-in-law (the Heb. *kallâ*, 'bride', can describe both 'daughter' and 'daughter-in-law' who have preserved their virginity until the time of marriage; *cf.* Wolff, pp. 86–7).[2] The lascivious cult had caught them in its clutches, and, under the welcome shade of the trees just described, they engaged in illicit intercourse. For the same parallelism of 'harlotry' and 'adultery', see comments at 2:2.

In verse 14, God complains against the male members of the priestly clan who have thus set themselves up as wicked examples by slipping off apart (Heb. *prd*, 'to separate from') from the throngs to the shady glades where copulation with harlots and carousing with temple prostitutes seem a part of the prosperity of God's gifts to them. There they could enjoy the foods offered in sacrifice (so *zbḥ*, here and in 8:13; on *cult prostitutes* see Guideline three of introduction to 1:1 – 3:5). With the priests so lacking in spiritual understanding and insight (for Heb. *byn* and its use in Wisdom Literature, see Jb. 28:23; Pr. 1:2, 6; 8:5; 14:8), it is easy to understand how the people were unable to discern the real issues of their day and why they consequently were headed for certain disaster.

15. The focus on the people (v. 14e) leads to an address to the entire nation, both Israel and Judah, in a series of admonitions. The most straightforward way of reading a very difficult text is to follow the RSV, which centres attention on *Judah* and encourages that southern kingdom to stay away from the cultic centres and not to emulate Israel's bad example of physical and spiritual harlotry.[3] Amos' experiences at Bethel

---

[1] On the groves and trees, see King, p. 122.

[2] For comments on Wolff's theory that it is an initial act of intercourse in the sacred forest that Hosea describes, see Guideline three in the introduction to 1:1 – 3:5.

[3] Andersen (p. 343) reads the first part of verse 15 as a pair of oaths which

and his mention of the southern-most shrine at Beersheba (Am. 5:5; 7:13; 8:14) testify to the pilgrimages that brought southerners north and northerners south (Jacob, p. 43). *Judah* may add a sarcastic touch: the admonition to protect *Judah* from the contaminating guilt of Israel would be a needling reminder of the depths of Israel's cultic evil (Mays, p. 77). Moreover, *Judah*, not named in Hosea since 1:11, anticipates his key role in the next major section (5:8 – 7:16).

The imperatives – *enter not, nor go up, swear not* – are plural and may be addressed either to individuals in Judah (which is accompanied by a singular verb in v. 15a) or to residents in *both* kingdoms who are urged to abandon their customary cultic pilgrimages. *Enter* (Heb. *bô'*) is a standard verb for pilgrimage (Is. 1:12; Am. 4:4; 5:5; *cf.* Ho. 9:4,10); *go up* (Heb. *'lh*) is appropriate to Bethel's mountain site (see below); *swear* adds a new ingredient to Hosea's attack on the cult – Israel's custom of treating lightly the divine name by using it for oaths or covenant promises that they could not or did not intend to keep (*cf.* 4:2; Am. 8:14; Zp. 1:5). In denigrating these religious journeys, Hosea took a leaf from Amos for whom denunication of the shrines was a major mission (2:8; 3:14; 4:4–5; 5:4–5 [the closest parallel to Ho. 4:15]; 5:21–27; 7:9, 10–17; 8:3, 14; 9:1). And both Amos and Hosea challenged a cherished tradition in singling out *Gilgal* and *Bethel* for attack,[1] words that must have seemed the essence of heresy.

---

the people are forbidden to utter—oaths excusing Israel's harlotry and clearing Judah of guilt. The Hebrew surely admits of this interpretation, but its dramatic turn seems a bit unexpected. Wolff (p. 89) erases the reference to Judah and refers the entire verse to Israel. Emmerson (pp. 77–83) handles the Judah clause as an addition from Josiah's day and understands verse 15 as a set of commands barring Israel from the northern shrines, not because the shrines themselves are corrupt, but because Israel's harlotry disqualifies her from pilgrimages and the use of Yahweh's name in oaths.

[1]For Bethel, see W. Ewing, R. K. Harrison, *ISBE*, rev., I, pp. 465–467. For the view that Beth-aven in Ho. 5:8; Jos. 7:2; 18:12; 1 Sa. 13:5; 14:23 was a separate town from Bethel, whose name was derived from an original *bet 'awwan*, meaning 'House of Refuge', see E. A. Knauf, *Bib.*, 65, 1984, pp. 251–253.

Bethel (whose early name was Luz; Gn. 28:19), situated in the hill country about nineteen kilometres due north of Jerusalem and at an elevation of over 700 metres (its site has been identified as Tell Beitin and was excavated by W. F. Albright and J. Kelso between 1934 and 1957), loomed large in patriarchal history (Gn. 12:8; 13:3–4; 28:18–22; 35:1–15). Apparently conquered by Joshua along with Ai, Bethel was allotted to Benjamin (Jos. 18:22) but was situated on Benjamin's boundary with Ephraim (Jos. 18:13) and spent much of

To Hosea, seized by the pathos of a Lord who suffered over the disloyalty of the people, tradition itself had to be obliterated if righteousness was to be restored.

16–19. This section brings to a close the words of condemnation against the priests and the people whom they have misdirected. It adds little new information but summarizes with graphic language what has already been said about Ephraim's fanatical attachment to the idolatry (v. 17) and the drunken debauchery of the cult (v. 18). Like verse 11 and verse 14, it sketches the inevitably wretched consequences of Israel's comportment (v. 19).

The passage begins (v. 16) with similes drawn from animal-husbandry – Israel is like a headstrong cow (*cf.* 10:11) wilfully resisting her Master's orders (for *stubborn, cf.* Dt. 21:18) yet expecting to be treated like a pet *lamb.* Hosea mocks, with images of agricultural and wildlife, Israel's folly: She is a senseless dove (7:11), a wild ass (8:9), a heifer (10:11) that will

its history under Ephraimite control (1 Ch. 7:28). Its religious prominence continued under the judges (Jdg. 20:18) and Samuel (1 Sa. 7:15; 10:3). Jeroboam I erected a shrine at Bethel equipped with a priesthood to rival Jerusalem's, a different religious calendar, and a golden calf (1 Ki. 12:29–33), all of which drew the ire of the man of God who prophesied judgment on the shrine (1 Ki. ch. 13), which was destroyed during Josiah's reform a century after Hosea's ministry closed (2 Ki. 23:15–18). From Amos' pun, 'and Bethel shall come to nought' (Heb. *'āwen* 'trouble', 'sorrow', 'wickedness', and even 'idolatry', Ho. 12:1; Is. 41:29), Hosea coined the mocking name Beth-aven (*cf.* 5:8; 10:5, 8), where 'trouble-bringing idolatry' is substituted for the divine name that had graced Bethel since Jacob's day.

Gilgal's prominence dated from Joshua's conquest when the Israelites set up their base camp there after crossing the Jordan and entering Canaan (Jos. 4:19–20; *cf.* 5:13–15; 9:6; 10:6–7, 15, 43; 14:6 for its role in the assaults that subdued the land). Immediately it became Israel's most important sanctuary (Jos. 9:23, 27; 1 Sa. 10:8) and remained so until the ark was apparently moved to Bethel after the Moabite Eglon captured Gilgal (Jdg. 3:15–23). With the collapse of Shiloh (1 Sa. ch. 4), Gilgal returned to prominence as a spiritual centre where Samuel judged (1 Sa. 7:16), the people gathered (1 Sa. 10:8; 13:4, 7, 15–18; 15:10–33), Saul was made king (1 Sa 11:14–15), and David was hailed, after the quelling of Absalom's rebellion (2 Sa. 19:15, 40). The most likely site for Gilgal is about two kilometres north of Jericho and nine kilometres west of the Jordan near Khirbet el-Mefjer. See W. H. Brownlee, *ISBE*, rev., II, pp. 470–472. His discussion includes a description of cultic practices that may have been carried out at Gilgal. For Hosea, Gilgal's present corruption, thanks to the cult (12:11), was an extension of a rebellious past to be traced to the inauguration of the monarchy there under Saul (9:15). With Amos (5:5), he saw its destruction as the inevitable solution to its contamination (12:11; Heb. *gallîm*, 'stone heaps', is both a pun on Gilgal and a reminder of Joshua's pile of stones from the Jordan; Jos. 4:19–22).

be broken until like a trembling bird (11:11) she shall answer
at last God's call. The second half of verse 16 is best read as a
rhetorical question (RSV; NEB; JB; NASB; NIV; Andersen, p. 377,
interprets the clause as a statement in which shepherd or
'feed' has a sinister or sarcastic sense) which may have been
voiced in response to an unrecorded protest (*cf.* on v. 4) that
tried to turn aside Hosea's indictment with claims of Israel's
innocence and special favour with Yahweh (so Wolff, pp.
90–91). The rhetorical question is a common tool in Old
Testament debate and has the advantage of forcing the audience to produce the appropriate answer (*cf.* Am. 3:3–8; 6:12),
in this case, No! Anybody who knows anything about animals
must agree that a stubborn cow does not deserve the gentle
treatment of a harmless lamb. Resisting the yoke cannot be
rewarded by extra rations (for Israel's stubbornness, see Zc.
7:11–12). However much God would like to shepherd Israel
with his wisdom, it seems he must, because of her continual
intransigence, treat her as those dumb animals which will not
respond to their master.

Ephraim (v. 17), one of Hosea's favourite designations for
Israel, is used here for the first time. Technically, it describes
both the most influential tribe in the Northern Kingdom (*cf.*
Jos. 16:5–10 for the land originally allotted to the descendants
of this son of Joseph in Gn. 48:1–7) and the hill territory that
it occupied, which may have been Hosea's home. Used by
itself or in clear parallelism with Israel, it seems to stand for
the whole northern people (*cf.* 11:1, 3, 8, 9; 12:8); at other
times it more specifically defines the chief tribe (*e.g.* 13:1) or its
territory, especially when it is part of three-fold parallelism:
Ephraim, Israel, Judah (*e.g.* 6:10–11a; 11:12). Towards the
end of the book (*e.g.* 7:8–10; 12:1, 14; 13:1; 12; 14:8),
Ephraim becomes the most frequent name used of the people
and seems to describe the rump state centred in Samaria,
which alone retained a measure of independence when
Assyrian conquest gobbled up Gilead and other parts of the
Northern Kingdom (see on 7:8–10).

What is meant precisely by Ephraim's connection with
idolatry (*cf.* 2:8; 3:4) is hard to know. *Joined* (RSV; NASB; NIV)
may describe an 'ally' or 'partner' (Heb. *ḥbr* is 'band' in 6:9),
though this interpretation carries some linguistic problems
and would convey the idea of parity between Ephraim and the
idols rather than his captivity by them which is implied in

4:12, 19; 5:4. Andersen (p. 378) has called attention to a second set of meanings for Hebrew *ḥbr* which connote binding by tying or weaving and occur in contexts where magical spells or charms are in play (Dt. 18:11; Ps. 58:5 [Heb. v. 6]) That *Ephraim* is charmed or spellbound by *idols* (*cf.* 13:1, for the same word for idols) is precisely what is meant by *spirit* in 4:12, 19; 5:4.

Let him alone (v. 17b) is the logical response to the stubbornness and the enchantment. The command is plural and may be Hosea's aside to some faithful companions of his who were also baffled as to how to deal with a people charmed out of their wits (Wolff, p. 91). An alternate interpretation could address the command to the priests as a mandate for them to stop misleading the people. In fact the third masculine plurals in verses 18b–19 may bring the speech full circle to where it began in a controversy with the priesthood (see Andersen, p. 379) in the person of the chief priest (v. 4). Such a reading provides a transition to 5:1, where the priests are again called to attention.

NASB has captured the first half of the verse: 'Their liquor gone, they play the harlot continually' (an appropriate way to translate the reinforcement given the verb by the infinitive absolute in Heb.). The connection between drunkenness and sexual orgies is noted in Ezekiel 23:42. Fuelled and dazed by drink, they turned to the harlotry/idolatry that was their passion, as *love* (reinforced by repetition in Heb.) proclaims. Here as earlier (3:1) what Israel loves is shameful, or as Wolff (p. 91) has it 'the dishonour of the shameless', *i.e.* the same kind of dishonour (shame) in adoration of Baal that the priests have embraced in verse 7 (*cf.* NEB and JB which emend the text to conform to v. 7). This reading depends on attributing the final word in the clause to a Hebrew root derived from an Arabic word meaning to be 'indifferent about slander'. In the Old Testament the word has been proposed to interpret the consonants *mgn* (in Ps. 47:9 [Heb. v. 10]; Pr. 6:11; 24:34; Ho. 4:18) and translated 'insolent' or 'shameless' (*cf.* KB, *mgn II*, p. 494). Both NASB and NIV read the final Hebrew word as 'their rulers' (lit. 'shields') and make it the subject of the sentence: 'Their rulers dearly love shame' ('shameful ways', NIV). The force of these renderings is about the same: Baal worship is Israel's undeniable passion, a passion celebrated by nobody with more ardour than by the priests.

The interplay between 'her' and 'their' in verse 19 (obscured in RSV) seems best explained by interpreting the 'her', which is the object of *wrapped* as Israel/Ephraim, the stubborn cow, with which this paragraph began and the *their* of 'sacrifices' (or *altars*) as the priests, whose final lot will be total *shame* in the acts (or places) where they most ardently vented their passions. Two other interpretations need noting. Sexual innuendos may underlie a number of the words: *shame* can stand for female genitals (Je. 13:26; Na. 3:5); *spirit* may mean passion; *wings* is used of sheltering love (Ru. 3:9; Ezk. 16:8). The whole scene, then, would be an expansion of the descriptions of ritual intercourse in 4:13–14.[1] The puzzling feminine pronouns may be a cryptic reference to a nameless fertility goddess whose orgies have become the place of God's judgment.[2]

The context (*cf.* 4:12; 5:4) encourages the translation *spirit* not *wind* for Hebrew *rûaḥ*, which can mean either (for *wind*, *cf.* 8:7; 12:1, 13:15, none of which seems to have any bearing on 4:19). The modifying word *of harlotries* attached to *spirit* in the two references that precede (4:12) and follow (5:4) should be assumed here, just as 'of God' is assumed with *the knowledge* in verse 6 on the basis of verse 1. The way in which the *spirit of harlotries* is described in each passage is slightly different – *has led them astray* (v. 12), *is within them* (5:4), *has wrapped her* (Ephraim) in its *wings*, *i.e.* completely possessed and sheltered her (this translation seems the best solution even though spirit is a feminine noun and the Heb. verb *wrapped* looks masculine in form). Together, these expressions convey how Israel was held in the grasp of her idolatrous religion.

There seems to be no need to read *altars* instead of 'sacrifices' (with MT; Vulg.; AV; NEB; NASB; NIV). It is *sacrifices* that Hosea has specifically condemned in verse 13 (see there for comments on their significance in Hosea). Turned from the knowledge of God, priest and people, to their shame, were caught up in the empty worship of their idol-making.

iii. The culpable leadership (5:1–7). This passage both recapitulates and expands the basic themes of 4:4–19; it also

[1] A. Szabó, 'Textual Problems in Amos and Hosea', *VT*, 25, 1975, pp. 511–512.
[2] G. I. Emmerson, 'A Fertility Goddess in Hosea IV 17–19?', *VT*, 24, 1974, pp. 492–497. Andersen (p. 373), despite a very different structural analysis

closes the first block of Hosea's messages – *the covenant shattered* – since it summarizes the judgment on the cult in verse 7b and is followed in verse 8 by a complete change in grammar (note the imperatives), style (the battle warnings), and content (the threat of invasion to southern Ephraim).

The three-fold call to attention (v. 1) presumes a larger and more official audience than do the announcements of controversy to the people (4:1) and the priests (4:4). As in 4:4–19, different segments of the audience seem to be addressed at different times: the leaders in verses 1–2; the nation in verse 3; the priests in verses 4–7. Despite the presence of royalty (v. 1), the priests remain at centre stage: they are addressed first (in contrast to the sequence in Je. 2:26; 4:9; 8:1); the wrongs listed are all connected with the cult; the summarizing judgment in verse 7b is on the cult and a set feast; the final four verses seem to be addressed to the priest, as the nation's sins are paraded – sins for which the priests are largely accountable.

1–2. As is usual with clusters of Hebrew synonyms, the three verbs in this summons to hear serve to reinforce each other rather than to call attention to any nuances of difference among them (*cf.* Is. 28:23). *Priests* continues the emphasis begun in chapter 4, yet swings the attention from the chief priest (4:4–6) to the entire company who failed to enforce the covenant stipulations. *House of Israel* is most likely the entire Northern Kingdom, consisting of the clans of Ephraim, *i.e.* the inhabitants of Jordan's west bank and Israel, *i.e.* the families who lived east of Jordan in Gilead (*cf.* 5:3 for mention of both). It is possible that *house of Israel* (*cf.* 1:4, 6; 6:10; 11:12) embraces both kingdoms and includes Judah (5:5). *House of the king* probably includes the administrative bureaucracy along with the ruling family. The order of address sandwiches the nations as a whole between the two entities of leadership entrusted with its welfare. It is by no means held guiltless (*cf.* v. 3b), yet its behaviour and destiny are in the hands of the leadership whose ministries were strongly intertwined by the fact that royalty served as sponsors of the shrines and patrons of the priesthood (*cf.* Am. 7:13).

Judgment (Heb. *mišpāṭ*) is susceptible of two meanings. Wolff

---

from Emmerson's, posits the presence of a reference to a named idol 'Ignominy', based on a repointing of *'ōṭāh, her,* as *'awwātâ*.

(p. 98) reads it as 'justice' and hears in it an allusion to the leaders' responsibility to enforce justice (drawing on a purported parallel in Dt. 1:17). Andersen (pp. 384–385) is more probably right in finding in it a pronouncement of judgment, *i.e.* a 'verdict' which is spelled out in the rest of the passage. The declaration of judgment in verse 1 forms an inclusio, a favourite device in Hosea, with the last line of verse 2. Having ordered the leadership to attention (v. 1b–c), the Lord (1) directs the verdict of judgment to them (v. 1d), (2) indicts them for fostering corrupt shrines (vv. 1e–2a), and (3) promises to enforce the necessary discipline (v. 2b).

That the leadership more than the people is being put on notice is clear in the accusations of verses 1e–2a. *For* (Heb. *kî*) introduces the reason for the negative verdict of verse 1d. Entrapment in the cult seems to be the crime, as *snare* (*cf.* 9:8; Am. 3:5) and *net* (7:12) suggest. Bird hunting seems to be the background and points to the gullibility and vulnerability of the people. The fact that the enslavement was perpetrated in famous places made it only easier. *Mizpah*, which can mean watchtower, seems here to be a proper name. Probably, given Hosea's penchant for historic references, it is the Mizpah in Benjamin that served, along with Bethel and Gilgal (*cf.* 4:15), as a site for Samuel's annual circuit of judging (1 Sa. 7:5–11, 15–16) and even earlier had hosted Israel's judicial assemblies (*cf.* Jdg. chs. 20–21). Archaeological explorations have surfaced Astarte figurines, possible evidence of fertility religion in the 8th century BC.[1] An alternate venue of Mizpah has been sought in Gilead (Wolff, p. 98 n. 27). *Tabor* is the landmark mountain in north-central Palestine, just south of the Lebanon border.

The nature of the crimes of *Mizpah* and *Tabor* seems to be explained in verse 2a. Our approach to this difficult clause avoids the temptation to emend the text in order to continue the hunting metaphor a step further (by reading Heb. *šaḥᵃṭâ* 'slaughter' as *šaḥaṭ*, 'pit', *sēṭîm* 'wanderers' or 'rebels' as *šiṭṭîm*, Shittim, a place name, and *heʿmîqû* 'they made [or 'dug'] deep' [*cf.* 9:9] as *taʿᵃmîqû* and 'you will make deep'), as do Robinson and *BHS* (*cf.* Wolff, p. 94 and RSV for somewhat similar readings). As attractive as it is to find here a triple indictment to

---

[1]C. C. McCown and J. C. Wampler, *Tell en-nasbeh excavated under the direction of the late Wm. Frederic Bade* I (Berkeley, 1947), p. 8. See also King, p. 48.

match the triple address, such a reading both wrenches the text by emending at least two of the three words and violates Hosea's normal pattern of interpreting metaphors with more literal clauses at either the beginning or close of the figure of speech (*cf.* 5:15ab, cd; 7:3, 4–7ab, cd; 7;11ab, cd; 7:12ab, c). Unless verse 2a explains the metaphor, we stare vainly at the text to discern the precise nature of the crime. Consequently most modern versions (NEB; JB; NASB; NIV) have followed the LXX and the Vulgate in reading the clause as explanation of, not addition to, the metaphors. Andersen's translation (p. 380) follows NIV: 'The rebels (Heb. *śwṭ*, 'to wander' or 'revolt'; *cf.* Job 1:7; 2:2; Nu. 5:12) are deep in 'slaughter', and his interpretation, with considerable cogency, sees the crime as nothing less than child-sacrifice, on the basis of the use of 'slaughter' in Isaiah 57:5 and Ezekiel 16:21; 23:39; *cf.* Genesis 22:10 – Abraham and Isaac!

It is this ensnaring iniquity that warrants God's chastening discipline in verse 2b. Discipline or correction (Heb. *mûsār*, a favourite word in Proverbs; *cf.* 4:13; 5:23; 13:1; 15:33) can be used of strict punishment (*cf.* Je. 30:14). It may also be a reminder that, short of the final judgment, Yahweh's wrath has a corrective as well as a punitive motive (*cf.* 2:6–7; 3:4; Am. 4:6–11; Heb. 12:3–11).

3–4. These verses are framed by another envelope pattern: *I* (Yahweh; *cf.* v. 2) *know* [you], *Ephraim* (see below for vocative) in verse 3a is both paralleled by and contrasted with *and they know not Yahweh* in verse 4c. The ignorance and rejection which mark Israel's and Ephraim's (again the east and west districts of the kingdom) relations to God are more than matched by Yahweh's full acquaintance with their harlotry/idolatry. Our interpretation follows Andersen's suggestion (p. 390) that both halves of verse 3 should be read as addresses to Ephraim and Israel, and the pronoun 'you' should be implied as the object of 'I know', in order to provide a parallel to the address in verse 3b: *you have played the harlot, Ephraim.* The verb forms describing Israel's open sin (*not hid*) and consequent ritual and moral impurity (*defiled*) should be read as participles. Verse 3 thus understood reads:

> I myself know you, Ephraim,
> and you, Israel, are not hidden from me;
> for now you have played the harlot, Ephraim,
> you, Israel, are defiled.

Having addressed Yahweh's indictment directly to the accused in verse 3, the prophet seems in verse 4 to expand it in a statement pointed at some other part of the audience, perhaps the priests who were summoned in verse 1. The plural pronouns *they*, *their*, *them* probably described Ephraim and Israel together, the whole Northern Kingdom, whose *deeds* – a catch-all word used to sum up all manner of iniquity, but especially their spiritual fornication with the Baals (*cf.* 4:9) – do not permit them to take the only decision that will please God: to *return* (*cf.* 2:7; 3:5). The explanation of the failure is the captivating presence of the demonic power (*spirit*) of their idolatrous activities that has led them in exactly the opposite direction of the covenant obedience which knowing Yahweh entails. For Hosea so to speak to the priests about the people is a shocking condemnation of the religious leaders, whose divinely ordered task it was to make sure that the people were schooled in the knowledge of God (*cf.* 4:6).

5–7. The prophet continues to speak about the people to the priests, without addressing them specifically. The semilegal tone persists: *testifies* (lit. 'will answer', v. 5) means to give testimony in response to interrogation in court (*cf.* 7:10); the accused is Israel, the entire people, hailed into court to bear witness against itself; sentence is passed (shall *stumble*; *cf.* the judgment on prophet and priest, 4:5) not only on Ephraim and Israel but on *Judah* as well, further evidence that the whole people is in view, north and south; part of the judgment is divine 'withdrawal' (lit. 'removal' as one might remove clothes; *cf.* Dt. 25:9–10) from the cult (v. 6), the very place where they had hoped to find Yahweh (*cf.* 5:15 for another expression of divine withdrawal); treachery/infidelity (*dealt faithlessly*; Heb. *bgd*; *cf.* 6:7) is listed as the last crime and the summation of them all (v. 7). The final sentence, the necessary verdict and chastisement (*cf.* vv. 1–2), is introduced by *now* = 'therefore'.

The beginning charge (*the pride of Israel*, v. 5) is self-reliance, failure to depend on God utterly. The concluding charge (v. 7) sums up their spiritual treason (*cf.* 6:7), evidenced in the *alien children*, religiously and literally bastards, produced by the illicit unions that Hosea flailed in 4:13–14. In between, the focus is on the futility of the cult and its myriads of sacrifices which are symbolized in the two words *flocks* (*i.e.* small cattle like sheep and goats) and *herds* (*i.e.* large cattle like cows and oxen). Judgment by frustration is what was prescribed for Gomer/Israel in 2:7, and here it does not produce a penitent return. The frustration turns calamitous in the closing clause (v. 7c), when God will devastate *their fields* (which should be read as sole object of the verb) and thus put the Baals to shame in their impotence and strip Israel of the crops that clothed and fed her (*cf.* 2:9, 12). 'Them', *i.e.* the Israelites or the *alien children* (v. 7b), should be deleted because the Hebrew *m* can more readily be explained as an emphatic appendage to the verb (so-called enclitic *mem*) than as the third masculine plural suffix (so Andersen, p. 396). If Yahweh is the subject, *new moon* should be read as a point of time, 'at the new moon', a meaning that could be conveyed by the simple addition of the vowel *a* to the word. Rather than the joyful feast of new beginnings (*cf.* 2:11), the new moon will become the time of the end. *New moon* may point to the time and setting of the convocation addressed by Hosea in 5:1–7.

c. The politics run amok (5:8 – 7:16)

This section (whose beginning is signalled in the cluster of imperatives, 5:8, and whose ending is marked in the summary note of judgment in 7:16, followed by a new imperative in 8:1) is a composition pieced together with a variety of speeches whose *contents* centre in the political ups-and-downs of the Northern Kingdom's relations with Judah (5:8 – 6:11a), its vacillations as to who should be its chief ally, whether Egypt or Assyria (5:13; 7:8–16), and its dynastic instability (6:11b – 7:7, 16). This political chaos is portrayed in a variety of *literary forms*:

(1) judgment speech in the guise of battle alarms (5:8–11);
(2) similes of Yahweh's wrath (5:12–15);
(3) song of partial penitence (6:1–3);
(4) divine complaint – fickleness (6:4–6);
(5) illustrations of fickleness (6:7–11a);
(6) divine complaint – deceitfulness (6:11b – 7:2);
(7) judgment speech in an extended metaphor of baking (7:3–7);
(8) judgment speech in a double metaphor of inedible bread (7:8–10);
(9) judgment speech in a double metaphor of bird trapping (7:11–12);

(10) judgment speech in a double divine complaint –
rebellion (7:13–16).

Hosea plays the theme of judgment in so many variations
that we gain the impression that he will spare nothing to
confront Israel with their crimes and urge them to true
repentance.

Without losing sight of his major theme of cultic corruption
(6:6, 10; 7:14) Hosea introduces fresh evidence: (1) Israel and
Judah have become involved in some altercation for which
both are held culpable (5:8–15); (2) Assyria enters Hosea's
picture for the first time not as a threat to invade but as
temptation for Israel to court (5:13; 7:8–12); (3) Egypt
appears not in nostalgia for the Exodus (*cf.* 2:15) but as an
alternative to Assyria as political bed-fellow (7:11, 16); (4)
Israel is heard to sing a song of return to God (*cf.* 2:7) which
God painfully rejects (6:1–6); (5) the poignancy of the
wounded Lover so clearly developed in chapters 1–3 and
softly echoed in 4:16 becomes prominent again in the
complaints of God, who pits his acts of grace against Israel's
persistent rebellion (6:4–6; 6:11b – 7:2, 11–16); (6) to the list
of cultic abuses are added the crimes of murder and political
insurrection (6:7–11a; 7:3–7); and (7) the prophet as instrument of divine activity is singled out (6:5; *cf.* 9:8; 12:10, 13).

While breaking this new ground, Hosea continually recalls
what he has said in the previous speeches (4:1–3, 4–19; 5:1–7)
and never allows the experiences of chapters 1–3 to be
forgotten: (1) priests, people and rulers all get attention,
almost as though the summons of 5:1 were still in play; (2)
seeking him (5:15; *cf.* 2:7; 3:5; 5:6), knowing him (6:3, 6; *cf.*
2:8, 20; 4:1, 6; 5:4), returning to him (6:1; 7:10; *cf.* 2:7; 3:5;
5:4) and practising covenant love (6:4, 6; *cf.* 2:19; 4:1) are
again of crucial importance; (3) Judah's rebellion and judgment, along with Israel's, are once more in view (5:10–12; 6:4,
10–11a); (4) Ephraim's harlotry and Israel's defilement are a
constant (6:10; *cf.* 5:3); (5) drunkenness still befuddles their
understanding (5:11; 7:5; *cf.* 4:18); and (6) they who have
snared innocent victims in the crude sacrifices of the shrines
will themselves be trapped by Yahweh (7:12; *cf.* 5:1–2). How
intricately the pattern of new themes and familiar ones is
woven by the poet-artist! Such subtlety makes tentative most
of the decisions about the length of the individual paragraphs,

and scholars have struggled to explicate their historical background, but we cannot escape the pathos of their concerns!

Additional Note: Possible historical backgrounds

If we are correct in spotting here (5:8 – 7:16) clues to a struggle between Judah and Israel (5:8–11) as well as increased Assyrian prominence (5:13; 7:8–9, 11) and a metaphorical account of insurrection against Israel's ruling household (7:3–7), then it is likely that these speeches stem from the latter part of Hosea's ministry, sometime after 733 BC. The setting usually, though not universally, pictured as background is the Syro-Ephraimite war sketched in 2 Kings 16:1–9 (2 Ch. 28:5–7) and alluded to in Isaiah 7:1 – 8:22 and, perhaps, Micah 7:7–20.[1] Only a rough outline of that encounter, when Rezin of Damascus and Pekah of Samaria engaged Ahaz of Judah in battle, can be reconstructed.[2]

The beginnings of the conflict date from Tiglath-pileser's first western incursion in 738 BC, when he conquered Hamath in Syria and made it an Assyrian province. The relative peace and freedom which the western states had enjoyed for more than a half century was brought into jeopardy. Court records of Tiglath-pileser III name Menahem of Israel and Rezin (Rasyan) of Syria among those who accepted the first stage of Assyrian vassalage by paying tribute, while retaining political freedom and remaining in power. Menahem raised his tribute by taxing Israel's 60,000 landowners some 50 shekels per head (2 Kings 15:19–20). The initial invasion was followed by four years of respite, while the Assyrians protected their own northern and southern flanks. When the Great King marched west again, this time to Gaza in Philistia in 734 BC, Pekah had assassinated Pekahiah, Menahem's son and successor, and seized the throne of Israel (2 Ki. 15:25). The coup that thrust Pekah to power seems to have been motivated by an anti-Assyrian sentiment, embittered by the harsh payments of

[1]For a possible Northern provenance of Mi. 7:7–20, see J. T. Willis, *VT* Supp. 26, 1974, pp. 64–76; also D. R. Hillers, *Micah*, Hermeneia (Philadelphia: Fortress Press, 1984), pp. 89–91.
[2]For such reconstructions, which draw on inscriptions of Tiglath-pileser III (e.g. *ANET*, pp. 282–284) as well as the biblical accounts, see Donner pp. 243–254; Bright, pp. 269–276; M. E. W. Thompson, *Situation and Theology: OT*

annual tribute and emboldened by the fact that in the years 737–735 BC the Assyrians made no show of military might in Syria and Palestine.

Pekah took immediate steps to implement his anti-Assyrian policy by joining forces with Rezin of Damascus, who dreamed of fashioning a Greater Syria and smarted under Assyrian taxation, to form the Syro-Ephraimite coalition. How much the two kings counted on Egyptian help in their bolt from Assyrian vassalage we can only guess. The fact that Tiglath-pileser made Gaza the target of his 734 BC campaign may hint that Egypt was waiting in the wings and that the Assyrian emperor had to display his strength near the Egyptian border to keep Egypt at bay. Hosea's mention of Egypt as both a potential ally (7:11) and a place where Israel's fall will be greeted by derision (7:16) may be clues to a foreign policy in which Ephraim's king banked on Egypt for aid against Assyria.

But between Israel-Syria and Egypt lay Judah, which had thus far escaped Assyrian vassalage, though spending the past half century in the shadow of the more lustrous kings of Damascus and Samaria. If the west were to be consolidated and the routes from the south kept open to Egyptian access, Judah had to become part of the coalition. This Ahaz refused to do, and that refusal, as Pekah and Rezin saw it, left them no choice but to march against Jerusalem, depose Ahaz, and set their puppet, Ben-Tabeel, on Judah's throne (Is. 7:1–2, 6). Ahaz found no recourse but to implore Tiglath-pileser for help and to accept first-stage vassalage by sending tribute to Assyria in support of his plea (2 Ki. 16:7–8).

First, Assyrian troops, in 733 BC, subdued Israel, including Gilead, Galilee and all the land of Naphtali, taking captive the cream of the citizenry and deporting it to Assyria (2 Ki. 15:29). Then they ravaged Damascus in 732 BC, killed Rezin its king and shipped its leadership to Kir (2 Ki. 16:9; *cf.* Am. 1:5; 9:7) – all of this, apparently, in response to Ahaz's desperate overture. For both kingdoms of the coalition, the results were disastrous: the bulk of Israel was divided into Assyrian provinces and locked into the third stage of vassalage, totally under Assyrian dominance, the elite members of society

---

Interpretations of the Syro-Ephraimite War (Sheffield: The Almond Press, 1982), pp. 104–114; Miller and Hayes, pp. 314–339.

removed and an Assyrian governor and bureaucracy put in their place; Ephraim only, the hill country around Samaria, retained for a brief moment the semi-independence of first-stage vassalage and then were clapped into the second stage, with Pekah's demise by assassination and Hoshea's appointment to the throne as lackey of the Assyrians (2 Ki. 15:30; 17:1–3).[1] Damascus, so strategically located between the desert and the mountains of Lebanon, was a prize catch for the Assyrians who used it as an outpost for commercial and military activities for the next century or so.

Hosea's words in 5:8 – 7:16 seem to flow from a period shortly after the events of 733 BC when the wounds of the ill-fated war were just beginning to heal. His attention alternates between Israel's folly (5:11, 13) and Judah's greed (5:10). The battle alarms (5:8) combine with the accusation that Judah's princes are *like those who remove the landmark* (5:10) to suggest a land grab on Judah's part. The troops are pictured as marching north from Gibeah through Ramah to Bethel (Beth-aven) as though trying to extend Judah's borders by trimming Ephraim's. As good an explanation as any is that Judah took advantage of Israel's struggles with Tiglath-pileser at the close of the Syro-Ephraimite war to enlarge her *Lebensraum*. The overthrow of Pekah by Hoshea (732 BC), perhaps with Assyrian help since Tiglath-pileser's annals claim that the Great King elevated Hoshea to the throne after the Israelites had slain Pekah, may be the event of conspiracy described in 6:7 – 7:7, although the passage may remember Pekah's coup against Pekahiah (2 Ki. 15:25). In either case, priestly complicity made the deed all the more dastardly according to Hosea's interpretation.[2]

i. Folly and greed in foreign affairs (5:8–15). This passage, cryptically terse, seems to divide into three parts: (1)

---

[1]For a summary of what each stage of Assyrian vassalage entailed, see Miller and Hayes, pp. 320–322.

[2]This reconstruction roughly follows those of M. E. W. Thompson, *Situation and Theology*, Bright, and N. K. Gottwald, *All the Kingdoms of the Earth* (New York: Evanston; London: Harper & Row, 1964), pp. 148–162. Opinions differ widely as to the motives of the various parties and the extent to which Egypt played a part. The most controversial historical question turns on the sequence of events: did the Syro-Ephraimite war precede or follow Tiglath-pileser's campaign to Philistia in 734 BC? We have agreed with Thompson, Bright and

verses 8–9 are a formal and dramatic announcement of judgment, which begins with battle alarms that warn of a northward march through the cities of Benjamin toward the territory of Ephraim, and ends with an official declaration to Israel's tribes that the warning is to be believed; (2) verses 10–11 comprise a judgment speech directed first towards Judah for trying to extend their borders, then towards Ephraim for pursuing something filthy; and (3) verses 12–15 contain similes of divine judgment designed to rock both Judah and Israel out of their foolish reliance on Assyria for security and prosperity. The judgment, severe though it be, is designed not to annihilate the two kingdoms but to drive them to repentance as *until* in verse 15b clearly indicates. The fact that verse 15 concludes with a verb marks the close of the literary unit and clears the way for the song of penitence with which 6:1 begins.

8–9. The scene shifts without warning from cult (4:4 – 5:7) to battlefield. In the role of watchman (*cf.* 9:8; 8:1), the prophet shouts the battle alarm, calls for both kinds of trumpets – ram's horn (*cf.* Jos. ch.6; 2 Sa. 2:28; 20:22; Am. 3:6) and silver bugle (*cf.* Nu. 10:2) – to sound the danger signal, summoning all sentinels to lift the cry of warning (*cf.* Jos. ch. 6:5). These alarms may be a link to the priestly indictments of 4:4 – 5:7, since it was probably members of the priestly caste, perhaps army chaplains, whose duty it was to warn of danger (*cf.* Je. 6:1). They who had failed to proclaim the law (4:6) now had to herald the consequent destruction.

The three towns mentioned lie in a line that stretches almost due north from Jerusalem. They are listed in a sequence that suggests an invasion from the south: *Gibeah* (*cf.* on 9:9; 10:9; Jdg. 19:12–16, the sordid story to which Hosea alludes; *cf.* also Gibeah's connections with Saul, 1 Sa. 10:10), modern *Tel-el-Fûl*, is five kilometres, *Ramah* (*cf.* Samuel's family home, 1 Sa. 1:1a) modern *er-Ram*, eight kilometres, and *Bethel/Beth-aven* (*cf.* on 4:15), modern *Beitin*, eighteen kilometres north of Jerusalem. The immediate context (v. 10) suggests that the invaders are the military leaders (so *princes* should be understood) of Judah. If the theory, first posited by A. Alt, adopted by Wolff (pp. 111–12) and refined by M. E. W. Thompson, is

Gottwald that the war preceded the Assyrian invasion and prompted it. Donner and Herrmann place the Philistine campaign before the war.

correct, the occasion is the Syro-Ephraimite war (see Additional Note on 'Possible historical backgrounds', p. 118), when Ahaz of Judah apparently took advantage of Samaria's preoccupation with the Assyrian troops of Tiglath-pileser to try to retake the portions of Benjamin that Jehoash of Israel had wrested from Judah three generations earlier (2 Ki. 14:8–14).[1] No wonder all of *Benjamin* was put on guard with the brief cry, 'Behind you' (RSV/mg. *cf.* Jdg. 5:14), as though the threat were from the rear.

The outcome of the battle, deleterious for Ephraim, is announced in verse 9. Ephraim, the once proud territory, now reduced to a remnant by Tiglath-pileser's incursions, is due for complete desolation at a time when the divine judge presses his charges and exacts his penalties – a time to be known officially as a 'day of accusation' or 'chastisement' (*punishment*), a phrase used only here (*cf.* 2 Ki. 19:3; Ps. 149:7; Is. 37:3 for other uses of the Heb. word). The formal nature of the sentence is underscored by the declaration of certitude in which God vouches for the reliability (*what is sure*) of the judgment – perhaps another link to the preceding section (*cf.* 4:1; 5:1). *Israel* in verse 9 must refer to the entire nation and, thus, links the judgment speech to Ephraim with the one to Judah that follows (v. 10).

10–11. These verses describe the sins of the two kingdoms and prepare the way for the stinging blows of divine judgment inflicted in verses 12–15. Judah's crime seems to have been the land-grab implied in the battle language of verse 8. With a zeal born of frustration and opportunism, they marched north to snatch back their own territory and, apparently, much more. Moving boundary markers to expand, by force or deceit, one's own allotted holdings, was an intolerable offence in ancient Israel (Dt. 27:17). The punishment, an outpouring of divine wrath, shows how deeply God cared that the rights of others be regarded. It also shows that instruments of Yahweh's anger, as Judah well may have been, are not exempt from that anger, especially when the judgment they execute is carried out in reckless, ruthless ways (*cf.* Is. 10:5–19).

With characteristic even-handedness (*cf.* on 1:6–7; 4:15; 5:5, 12–13; 6:10–11a), God describes Ephraim's fate. It is

---

[1]A. Alt. in *Neue Kirchliche Zeitschrift* 30, 1919, pp. 537–568; Thompson, *Situation and Theology*, p. 67.

oppression and fragmentation at the hands of the Assyrians and, to a lesser degree, the military leaders of Judah. The words *oppressed* and *crushed* are descriptive of the social injustice of which Ephraim was guilty (Am. 4:1). God points explicitly to the cause of the judgment: the ardent, pressing pursuit of stinking filth (Heb. *ṣāw* from *ṣw'* which means to 'stink' and has produced a derivative word 'excrement' (*cf.* Is. 28:10, 13). Andersen (pp. 399, 410) understands the term to be the name of a deity, Filth, but the context, which centres on political relations with Assyria, suggests that the 'filth' was either their ill-fated alliance with pagan Aramaeans or their ambivalent dealings with Assyria.

12–15. The remarkable conclusion to this section pictures God as a carrier of pestilences (v. 12) and an inflicter of fierce damage (v. 14). The sequence of divine judgment is noteworthy: (1) Ephraim and Judah are chastened with a purulent disease because of their civil war (v. 12); (2) they turn not to God but to Assyria for healing – and in vain (v. 13); (3) God's response to their entanglements is even more ferocious – he tears them beyond repair and drags them away from all rescue (v. 14); and (4) then, as a *lion* retires to his lair, he withdraws (*cf.* on 5:6) to wait for their distress to prod them to repentance (v. 15). God is surprisingly quick to take personal responsibility for the military damages inflicted on the two kingdoms by Assyria and the Syro-Ephraimite war (v. 12). He is the source of the debilitating infections described in the similes, of 'pus' (a meaning that suits the context in verse 13a, better than *moth*) and 'ulceration' (the *rot* here affects the physical body; *cf.* Hab. 3:16; Pr. 12:4, where it attacks bones; for illness and putrefaction as judgment for rebellion, see Is. 1:5–6).

The parallelism in the naming of Ephraim and Judah in verses 12, 13 and 14 should be carried over to verse 13b: *Ephraim went to Assyria and* [Judah] *sent to the Great King.* Clear references, these are, to the acceptance of vassal status by both kingdoms – probably Ahaz's begging of Assyrian help against the Samaria-Damascus coalition and Hoshea's puppet-like subservience after the death of Pekah. *Went* or 'walked' implies not exile but submissive courting and *sent* probably assumes an object like 'tribute'. By merely redividing two Hebrew words (*melek yārēb*, a king that will contend) we obtain the title *Great King*, a label attested in at least one Aramaic inscription;[1] and well-known in Assyrian documents (Andersen, p. 414). We thus avoid the difficulties of identifying an unknown King Jereb mentioned in the LXX (*cf.* NASB). If the Hebrew word division must stand, then 'patron king' is a possible meaning.[2] The *wound* of *Judah* helps us interpret verse 12: it is the most specific word used and depicts an infected and oozing sore. Until Lister's discovery of antiseptics such wounds were often fatal. Certainly Assyria had no adequate balm. Great kings in antiquity were often thought to have access to magical or miraculous powers. But Assyria's distinguished monarch had no panacea for Ephraim's and Judah's ailments. The pronouns *you* and *your* must embrace both kingdoms.

No distinction should be sought between *lion* and *young lion* in verse 14. They are synonyms that reinforce each other and help to shape the general picture of ferocity (*cf.* Am. 5:19). Hosea's use of leonine similes may convey either restoration (11:10–11) or judgment (13:7–8, a passage that also uses the key verb of v. 14 – *rend*). The repetition of the pronoun *I* is calculated to clear any doubt from the hearers' minds as to the agent of judgment and hence to emphasize its magnitude, inescapability and purpose. That purpose becomes plain in verse 15. The judgment of the divine Lion is meant to prompt repentance and to cause a sincere seeking of God outside of the corrupt cult (Heb. *bqš* appears frequently in Wisdom Literature where the cult is not in view, *cf.* Jb. 7:21; 8:5; 24:5; Pss. 63:1; 78:34; Pr. 1:28; 7:15; 8:7).

ii. Song of feeble penitence (6:1–3). This is the call to return to God that the priests ought to have led. God himself may be quoting their words, as he did Israel's in 2:7. The cohortative form 'let us' argues against the view that the song is Hosea's own plea to return. Nowhere else does the prophet use this means of addressing the people. The verbal echoes of 5:12–15 are several: (1) *come* (Heb. *hlk*) recalls both Ephraim's going to Assyria (v. 13) and Yahweh's retreat to his lair (vv. 14–15); (2) *has torn* corresponds to the threat to tear in verse 14; (3) *may heal us* promises what Assyria could not do (v. 13);

---

[1] J. A. Fitzmyer, *The Aramaic Inscriptions of Sefîre*, Biblica et Orientalia 19 (Rome: Pontifical Biblical Institute, 1967), p. 61.
[2] *Cf.* E. M. Good, 'Hosea 5.8 – 6.6: An Alternative to Alt', *JBL*, 85, 1966, pp. 277–78; H. L. Ginsburg, *Encyclopedia Judaica*, 8, cols. 1010 –24.

(4) *before him* (v. 2) parallels *my face* (v. 15); and (5) *dawn* (v. 2) is the same root as the second verb to *seek* in verse 15. These similarities imply that the song was crafted to meet God's terms of 5:15. Moreover, the prominent play given to 'returning to' (v. 1) and 'knowing God' (v. 3) claims that the priests are now urging the people to make up for what was lacking in covenant loyalty (4:1, 6; 5:4).

Yet none of this is enough. The crucial requirement of 'admitting their guilt' (v. 15) has been omitted. They have faced their woundedness (v. 2; *cf.* 5:12–13) but not their waywardness. Healing is sought, even resurrection, but no specific sin is mentioned. This absence of repentance and failure to confess sins by name contrast sharply with Hosea's closing song of penitence (14:1–3). And God's complaint (vv. 4–5) seems to indicate his dismissal of the song as inadequate, whereas Israel's final song is followed by Yahweh's promise of love and healing and then by his own love song (14:4–7). The second and third lines of verse 1 should be read as concessive clauses, each beginning with 'although' (a perfectly acceptable meaning of Heb. *kî*), since God's tearing and smiting are obstacles to the return (Andersen, p. 418). Israel's confidence in God's help rests not in the judgment he has rendered but the rescue he has offered (5:15, see Jb. 5:18; Ezk. 30:21).

The wounding is unto death (v. 2). The duration mentioned is the period of time after which decomposition of the body sets in (*cf.* Jon. 2:1; Jn. 11:39). The verbs *revive us* (*cf.* 1 Sa. 2:6), and *raise us up* (*cf.* Is. 26:19) are frequent expressions for resuscitation and resurrection. Such language anticipates the clearer accounts of national resurrection after death in exile or through persecution found in Ezekiel chapter 37 and Daniel 12:1–2. Hosea 6:2 may have been part of what Paul alluded to in his resurrection argument (1 Cor. 15:4): 'that he was raised on the third day in accordance with the scriptures', although we have no direct record of apostolic or patristic use of this proof-text before Tertullian (Wolff, p. 118). If recovery from sickness not revival from death (so Wolff, p. 117) is the meaning, the time-frame seems trivial. A three-day illness, especially in antiquity, would have been no big thing. The consequence of the longed-for national resurrection is a life lived in Yahweh's presence, where joy is available to the people (Ps. 16:11) and praise to Yahweh is their constant response (Pss. 6:5; 30:9; 88:10–12). It is just possible that the first word of verse 3 should be attached to the end of verse 2 as a second statement of consequence: 'and we shall know [him]' (*BHS*; Andersen, p. 422).[1] The clause would add a climax to verse 2 akin to that of 2:20.

The song (v. 3) calls for a pursuit (*press on*; Heb. *rdp*) of the knowledge of God to make up for what has been so desperately lacking (*cf.* 4:1, 6; 5:4) and to displace both the passionate pursuit of the Baals (2:7) and the frustrating chase after political stability (12:1). The pursuers are confident that their quest will be successful, because they count – in reversal of God's withdrawal in 5:15 – on divine intervention, which, though the precise meaning is obscure, seems to be expressed in the double image of the regularity of the *dawn* (*cf.* Mal. 4:2) and the refreshment of the *spring rains* (*cf.* on Joel 2:23). The latter figure may be important to Hosea for whom one form of judgment was drought (*cf.* 2:12; 5:7; 7:14; 9:2; 14:7).

iii. Divine complaint of fickleness (6:4–6). Were Israel's contrition genuine, we should expect a salvation-promise (*cf.* 14:4). Hope that the song (vv. 1–3) would avail is dashed by Yahweh's complaint against both Ephraim and Judah (*cf.* 5:10–14): the similes of Yahweh's intervention (v. 3) are more than matched by other similes of Israel's violation of covenant responsibility – vanishing *cloud* and evaporating *dew* (v. 4). Talk of covenant loyalty, of hunting down the knowledge of God (v. 3), is cheap. When the winds of promiscuity blow, when the sun of competition blazes, Ephraim and Judah behave alike: they fail to treat each other or their fellow citizens with the covenant (*steadfast*) *love* that Yahweh has shown to them (see on 2:19). In a land that depended on predictable rain and persistent dew, the figures carry impressive power. The poignant questions of verse 4 are a major link in a chain of complaints that end at 11:8–9.

Therefore (v. 5) serves to explain the judgments that have already been inflicted (the first two verbs are *past* tense) through God's agents, the prophets, who have faithfully and forcefully conveyed the destructive words of Yahweh's *mouth*. The link between the prophets and their Lord is so intimate that their utterances of judgment constitute the very acts of 'hewing' or 'hacking' and 'slaying' that Israel's sin warranted.

[1]Gordis, pp. 114–115.

Hosea's words are general enough to embrace a whole line of prophets from Moses and Samuel (*cf.* on ch. 12), through Elijah and Elisha, to Amos and Hosea. The close resemblance between verse 6 and Samuel's indictment of Saul (1 Sa. 15:22) suggests that Israel's first prophet-judge may be in view. The Hebrew suffix *them*, attached to the verb *I have slain*, should be understood as the object of *I have hewn* as well, as most versions have noted. This brief summary of the history of judgment shows that the fickleness of Ephraim and Judah is no new thing but has been the object of prophetic assault through the centuries. The final clause (v. 5c) seems to threaten a continuation of the pattern of judgment. The Hebrew words should be redivided so that the final *k* of 'your judgments' should be attached to *light*, leaving a consonantal text that can be read *my judgment as the light* (or 'sun', *cf.* Jdg. 5:31; Hab. 3:4; Andersen, p. 429) *will go forth*. The clause obviously plays off *his going forth is sure as the dawn* in verse 3. The tone is ironic: in her feeble song of penitence Israel had banked on the dependability of God's healing; 'what is really as dependable as daybreak', Yahweh countered, 'is my judgment.'

As verse 5 echoes verse 3, so verse 6 expands on verse 4. It is the importance to Yahweh of *steadfast* (covenant) *love* and *knowledge of God* that explains why (note *for*, Heb. *kî* at the beginning of v. 6) his judgment is so severe. Once again the cult comes into full view. In 5:6 Hosea pictured the quest for divine approval through animal offerings as vain. Here he tells us why: the quest was not accompanied by the essential components of loyalty to God's covenant grace and obedience to his covenant demands (see on 2:19–20; 4:1, 6). The sacrifices themselves were not evil, but they were measurably less important (so the Heb. *min, rather than*, NIV, connotes) than the covenant obedience which Yahweh desired and in which he took delight (*desire*; Heb. *ḥpṣ* alludes to acceptable sacrifices in Ps. 51:17; Is. 1:11; Mal. 1:10). Any other view of sacrifices turns them into magical acts which try to manipulate Yahweh and, accordingly, are spurned by him. Every segment of the society is culpable (6:10–11a). Judah has attacked Ephraim (5:10). Ephraim and Judah both have courted Assyrian favour (5:13). The priests have disrupted social stability by murderous conspiracies which violated the terms of Yahweh's covenant (6:7–9).

127

iv. Illustration of covenant infidelity (6:7–11a). Two basic questions rise from these verses: (1) do they describe three separate crimes, one at each site mentioned (so Wolff, pp. 121–122), or a series of episodes in one connected event that touched all three places (so Andersen, pp. 435–436)?, and (2) who are the antecedents of the pronoun *they* (v. 7) and the subjects of the verbs of mayhem? The second question seems easier to answer: the *priests*, who have been targets of the prophet's attention since 4:4 (in singular) and 4:7 (in plural; *cf.* 5:1), who were responsible for the practice of empty sacrifice condemned in 6:6, and who are specifically mentioned in 6:9. As for the first question, the descriptions are so terse as to be virtually unintelligible unless there is some connection among them. The abbreviated style does suggest that the event was contemporary not ancient, since Hosea seems to take for granted that his hearers know what he means and since no episodes in Israel's earlier recorded history suit these circumstances (Wolff, p. 121; *cf.* our ignorance of what really happened in 5:1b–2).

Virtually all interpreters (NASB; NIV are exceptions; with the Vulg. they retain 'like Adam') read Adam (v. 7) as a place name, emending the 'like' (Heb. *k*) to *at* (Heb. *b*, shaped much like *k* in later scripts). Adam is located near the Jordan in Joshua 3:16 (*cf.* perhaps Ps. 78:60b, translated 'among men' in RSV) and is usually identified as *Tell ed-Damye* at the mouth of the river Jabbok (Wolff, p. 121). Andersen's (p. 436) understanding of the geography implied in verses 7–9 is helpful: the murderous event centred in the city of Adam, which is further identified as a town in *Gilead*, located on the road to *Shechem*, *i.e.* near the point where travellers and pilgrims crossed the Jordan on the way to *Shechem* and points west or north.

This compacted scheme of geography is matched by a compressed account of the wicked act: (1) the deed is introduced as a covenant-transgression committed *at Adam* (*there*), an act also branded as deceit or treachery against Yahweh (v. 7; *cf.* 5:7, where the word, Heb. *bgd*, has the more specific meaning of marital infidelity); this verse links the deed to verse 6 and shows how drastic was the violation of *hesed* and the lack of knowledge of God; (2) both the locale and corruption of Adam are specified in verse 8 – 'a *city* in *Gilead* (assuming an original locative case ending on Gilead), occupied by people who perform evil deeds (*evildoers* which may be an expression for adulterers as in Pr. 30:20 or for political fools as in Is. 31:2, a passage which may shed light on Hosea's meaning) and *tracked with* evidences of *blood*'; (3) the malefactors are exposed as a gang (lit. 'band') of *priests* (v. 9) who are further labelled as gangsters (lit. *robbers* or 'kidnappers'; *cf.* 7:1, where the term is parallel to *thief*), who wait in ambush and whose specific crime is branded *murder* committed on the road to *Shechem*; and (4) their wickedness is summarized at the end of verse 9 as altogether 'indecent' (Wolff, p. 122), *villainy* (RSV), 'appalling behaviour, indeed' (JB) – a clause that evaluates decisively the transgressing of covenant and treachery of verse 7 and the working of wickedness of verse 8.[1]

The cluster of indictments may reflect a regular pattern of brigandage in which travellers were assaulted and robbed by priests. More likely it encapsulates a momentous event in which priests collaborated in a conspiracy, perhaps against the royal family. Gilead was remembered as the launching site for at least one such plot: in his *coup d'état* against Pekahiah, Pekah was joined by 'fifty men of the Gileadites' (2 Ki. 15:25). If we are correct in reading 5:8 – 7:16 as Hosea's reflections on the Syro-Ephraimite war and events surrounding it, this may be as good an explanation of 6:7–9 as we are likely to find. In that case, it is possible that 7:3–7, with its puzzling metaphor of the baker's oven, is a parallel account of the same event, seen from the standpoint of the conspiracy's dénouement in Samaria. Such a reading enhances the unity of this entire section of the book and assembles into an intelligible pattern segments which are discouragingly baffling if left separate. The fact that the priests were both subservient to royalty and dependent upon their patronage for support made them ready candidates to sponsor rebellion. Hosea's pages are tracked with evidence that the rejection of divine law left the priests open to all manner of corruption, not excluding murder (4:2; 5:2; 7:7).

[1] See Nicholson, pp. 179–186, for a discussion of Ho. 6:7 concluding that: (1) the *covenant* was not an international treaty (against L. Perlitt, *Bundestheologie im Alten Testament*, WMANT, 36 [Neukirchen-Vluyn, 1969], pp. 139–152) nor a pact between the king and the citizens of the Northern Kingdom (against G. Fohrer, 'Der Vertrag zwischen König und Volk in Israel', *ZAW*, 71, 1959, pp. 1–22) but the bond between Yahweh and Israel; and (2) that the crimes were neither memories of wicked deeds in the distant past nor acts of cultic infidelity but 'violent acts committed in the course of political upheavals ... in the time of Hosea' (p. 186).

The divine Complainer brings this section to a close (vv. 10–11a) with a summary of the crimes of the nation. *House of Israel* should be understood to embrace all three major components of the land: *Ephraim*, the scrap of territory around Samaria, not yet entirely under Assyria's boot; *Israel* chiefly the east bank of Jordan that had already succumbed to full vassalage; and *Judah*, which under Ahaz had yielded to Assyria's sway by begging for help against the Syro-Ephraimite invasion. God serves as witness (*I have seen*, v. 10; *cf.* Ec. 3:10, 16; 4:1 *etc.*) to the 'horror' of their *harlotry* (*cf.* Je. 5:30; 18:13 for similar expressions depicting the results of false leadership by priests and prophets).

Harlotry, which centres in *Ephraim* and spreads its defilement to *Israel* (*cf.* 5:3), seems to have a broader meaning here than in the contexts which have focused on the Baal worship at the cultic shrines. The setting of verse 10 suggests that the political insecurity which has led the leaders to cast their lot with Assyria and to foment revolution against Samaria, their own capital, is also an expression of *harlotry*, a failure to trust God for protection and to respect the laws intended to keep society stable (*cf.* v. 6).

The inclusion of *Judah* (v. 11a) provides the announcement of judgment – *harvest* here must carry that meaning as in Matthew 13:24–30, 39 – not only for *Judah* but for *Ephraim* and *Israel* who are indicted but not threatened with punishment. The parallelism of the three clauses,

> *Ephraim's harlotry is there,*
> *Israel is defiled.*
> *For you also, O Judah, a harvest is appointed.*

can readily be interpreted to say that all three have shared in the infidelity of political corruption. In 5:10–14 and 6:4, *Ephraim* and *Judah* are mentioned together as agents free enough to take foolish political initiatives; east bank *Israel*, shackled to Assyria, enjoyed no such freedom but was contaminated by Ephraim's harlotry. Together the three will share the appointed judgment.

v. Divine complaint of deceitfulness (6:11b – 7:2). Again (*cf.* 6:4) the gracious divine intent collides with the realities of Ephraim's rebellion. God's longing to show mercy is expressed in the desire to return Israel, his battered and beleaguered people (5:10–14), *i.e.* the entire land (*cf.* on 1:9 – 2:1; 2:23; 4:1, 6, 8, 12) to a robust state of social, spiritual and material health: *restore the fortunes* is a familiar prophetic way of expressing this (*cf.* on Joel 3:1); *heal* is one of Hosea's favourite terms for the reversal of Israel's immorality and consequent suffering in judgment (5:13; 6:1; 11:3; 14:4). The two clauses – 6:11b and 7:1a – are parallel and should be read together (*cf.* RSV; NEB; NIV) despite the unfortunate chapter division that separates them (Vulg.; AV; JB; NASB).

The gracious intention embraces the entire nation, but it is blocked by the sinful conduct that centres in *Ephraim*. The crimes are voiced in general terms first – 'iniquity' (*corruption*; Heb. *ʿāwôn*; *cf.* 4:8; 5:5; 8:13; 9:7, 9; 12:9; 13:12; 14:1–2) and *wicked deeds*, one of the most comprehensive terms in Hosea's well-stocked vocabulary of sin, embracing both harmful acts (Heb. *rāʿôt*, lit. 'evils', and their destructive consequences, 7:2, 3; 9:15; 10:15). More specifically the indictment points back to the murder and looting by the priests in 6:7–9, as the similarities in wording indicate: (1) 'doers of evil' (6:8) is virtually synonymous with 'doers of fraud' or 'falseness' (7:1; Heb. *pōʿălê ʾāwen* and *pāʿălû šāqer*); and (2) *robbers* (6:9) is the plural of the singular word translated collectively *bandits* in 7:1 (Heb. *gᵉdûdîm; gᵉdûd*). The iniquity of Ephraim and the evil deeds of Samaria are, in short, the violent activities of the priests, who are the subject of *they deal falsely* (7:1) and *they do not consider* (7:2). God wants to restore the nation. What keeps him from it? The wickedness of one segment, Ephraim and its corrupt capital. What corrupts Ephraim and Samaria? The criminal actions of one group within that region, the priests who ought to have been exemplars and teachers of covenant righteousness (*cf.* 4:4–6).

The priests' passion for crime and power so warped their judgment that they behaved as though God no longer held them accountable for their conduct. Being masters of deceit (6:7; 7:1), they had no difficulty deceiving themselves. *Consider* (7:2) is literally 'say to their heart', a clause that recalls how addled the *heart*, *i.e.* the capability of making sound choices, had become in the excesses of the cult (*cf.* 4:11). The magnitude of this priestly error is underscored by the use of: (1) *all* – nothing they have done will escape divine attention; and (2) *evil works* (*cf.* 'evil deeds', the same Heb. word in 7:1) –

131

the term is general enough to capture the manifold forms of their wickedness; and (3) 'I have remembered' (Heb. *zkr*, 2:17; 8:13; 9:9) – a verb that connotes a vivid re-experiencing of the evil acts.

As a result, they are hemmed in by their own conduct, encircled (*encompass*) as a captive army by the troops of their own wickedness. And the Lord, whom they had systematically ignored, is at hand to see for himself the damage which their activities have inflicted on them. These verses, which describe evil as both encompassing Israel and witnessed by God (*revealed* in 7:1; *cf.* on 2:10; *before my face*; *cf.* Jb. 26:6; Ps. 38:9; Pr. 15:11), seem to combine two biblical pictures of judgment: sin spawns its own consequences – 'Be sure your sin will find you out' (Nu. 32:23); sin is judged by God personally – 'I, even I, will rend and go away' (Ho. 5:14). There is, of course, no essential conflict between these views, since God is the author of order in the creation, and part of that order is a pattern of retribution and reward.

vi. Judgment simile of the heated oven (7:3-7). Four interpretative clues may help decipher this difficult passage. First, the priests remain the subject of the action, as they have, since 4:4 and 6:7 (*cf.* 6:9). *They, their* and *them* point uniformly to the priests who stood at the centre of the conspiracy.

Second, the more literal statements (vv. 3, 5, 7b–d) that frame and anchor the simile hold keys to its interpretation. They picture (1) a new *king* and his court (*princes made glad* by the wicked *treachery* of the priests who toppled the old king, v. 3); (2) a coronation *day* debauched by drunkenness that left the courtiers addled and the king tricked into partnership with those who *mocked* his authority (v. 5); and (3) a pattern of ruthlessness that consumed ruler after ruler with none of the conspirators seeking Yahweh's will or help (v. 7b–d).

Third, the chief component in the simile, the *oven* (vv. 4, 6, 7), describes the priests as inflamed by disloyalty (*adulterers* they are called in v. 4, practitioners of political as well as religious infidelity; *cf.* Je. 9:2) and by passion for power (vv. 6–7a). The identity of the *baker* is harder to determine (vv. 4, 6). In the latter verse his presence is obscured by the tendency of commentators and versions to repoint the Hebrew word to read 'their anger' (but see Andersen, pp. 447, 449–454). Both references to the baker's work suggest an idleness, a sleeping

132

at the switch, that contributes to the conspiracy against the king. If the idleness is passive neglect, then the baker probably depicts a chief court official whose task was to assure the security of the king; if the idleness is maliciously intended, the baker may be identified as the chief priest (see on 4:4) who used his position to trick the king into trusting him, when all the while treason was his goal. These verses are obscure and ambiguous enough to keep any interpretation somewhat tentative.

Fourth, there is a movement in the passage from royal joy (v. 3) to royal collapse (v. 7), made understandable by the role of the *wine* (v. 5) which contributed to and symbolized the pagan abandonment which made conspiracy possible. Furthermore, the movement begins with a specific instance – one *king* made *glad* by the faithless priests (v. 3) – and concludes with a broad generalization – *all their kings have fallen* (v. 7), as though the extended simile describes one instance to which there were many parallels: Shallum's conspiracy against Zechariah who had reigned six months (2 Ki. 15:8–12); Menahem's against Shallum after only one month (2 Ki. 15:13–15); Pekah's overthrow of Pekahiah after two years (2 Ki. 15:23–26); and Hoshea's coup against Pekah after eight years of solo reign (2 Ki. 15:30). Pekah is sometimes credited with twelve years of partial reign in Gilead, while Menahem and Pekahiah ruled in Samaria – *c.* 752–740 BC.[1] The single episode with which the passage begins (v. 3) is usually identified with one of these last two revolts. The generalization at the close (v. 7) suggests that the priestly participation in dynastic destruction was more an ingrained habit than a solitary lapse.

3. Though the royal court was addressed in 5:1, along with the priests and people, the *king* of Israel gains the centre of Hosea's attention here for the first time – in a context that highlights priestly *wickedness* (a catch word which connects v. 3 with vv. 1–2) and *treachery* (which picks up the *deal falsely* note of verse 1 but with a different Heb. word) along with 'royal naiveté'. If the Adam-Gilead-Shechem plot of 6:7–10 and the conspiracy of 7:3–7 are the same episode, then Pekahiah was the victim and Pekah, together with the priests, the culprit (2 Ki. 15:25); if the two accounts depict separate events, then

[1] Dates of kings here and elsewhere are taken from E. R. Thiele, *A Chronology of the Hebrew Kings* (Grand Rapids: Zondervan, 1977), pp. 76–78.

it is the evils and treachery done by the priests to Pekah that brings joy to the heart of Hoshea and his court (2 Ki. 15:30). Paucity of evidence makes sure identification is impossible. In any case, the whole scene of 7:3–7 plays priestly guile against royal gullibility. And nobody wins.

The *princes* (Heb. *śārîm*; see on 3:4; 5:10), first mentioned here will play an on-going role in the prophet's indictments (*cf.* 7:16; 8:4, 10; 9:15; 13:10), partly because they were the king's lackeys who implemented his foolish foreign policies and partly because they may have doubled as military commanders who executed the futile battle strategies condemned by Hosea (10:13–15; 13:9–11; see comments for the textual problems in the latter passage). The wicked folly of the court helps to put in perspective Hosea's earlier prophecies both of disciplinary judgment (3:4) and restoration (3:5). A royal coterie that found their joy in the heinous falsehood of the priestly leader needed to be set on the shelf and replaced by a king after God's own heart.[1]

4. The priestly political treachery is underscored by *adulterers* (*cf.* Ephraim's *harlotry* in 6:10). Their passions burned towards goals that violated the covenant that was theirs to uphold. The *oven* and *baker* similes make this clear. The baker's negligent watch of the oven, so that its *fire* kept blazing while the dough was rising, led to an intolerable result: the one who should have guarded the king left him defenceless, ready to be scorched by the red-hot oven of conspiracy.

5. The similes are temporarily suspended while the prophet reaches back to the literal relation of king to priests outlined in verse 3. The setting seems to be a festival, the birthday or more likely the coronation anniversary of the king. In concert with the other clauses (vv. 3, 7), the subject of the main verb, 'they made sick' (a causative form in Heb.), must be the priests, who also are called *mockers* or *scorners*, a term descriptive of their derisive attitude towards royalty, an attitude whose sting Hosea himself must have felt more than once (*cf.* Is. 28:14 where kings are called 'scoffers'). Who else would have jeered, 'the prophet is a fool, the man of the spirit is mad' (9:7)? With the chief officers (*princes*) down, addled into

---

[1] The suggestion (*BHS*) that *make glad* should be emended to 'anoint' by transposing the first two Heb. letters can be laid aside, in the light of the scene of debauched revelry sketched in verse 5.

drunken lethargy by the *heat of wine*, the *king*, himself deprived of sound judgment by the festivities, clasped his *hand* (*i.e.* in common cause and warm fellowship) with those of the priestly conspirators. All this may suggest that the *princes* are the negligent bakers, asleep by their cups, while the fires of potential rebellion rage. Their king is left vulnerable and may readily be added to the list of those royal sons who *have fallen*, never to rise again (v. 7).

6. The *oven* imagery is resumed and brought to a climax in a flaming blaze of fire. The priests remain the subjects of the plot. The difficult verse may be construed like this:

> When they [the priests] drew near,
>   their heart was [hot] as the oven.
> In their ambush all through the night
>   their baker slept till morning.
> It [their heart] was burning like a fire of flame.

'They drew near' (rejecting the emendation of 'drew near', Heb. *qrb*, to 'burn', Heb. *qdh*; *cf*. LXX; RSV; NEB; Wolff) hints at their execution of their assassination plot. The sentence should begin with 'when', a translation of Hebrew *kî* equally acceptable and better suited to the context. By now their *hearts*, fired with their evil choices, are at full furnace temperature. While they spent the night in a posture of *intrigue* (lit. 'ambush'; *cf*. Jdg. 16:2 and the Gazans' conspiracy against Samson), *their baker* (reading MT with Vulg.; AV; Andersen; against most versions, which change the pointing of the Heb. to read 'anger' or the like) lies asleep till morning. Their inebriation left their sovereign at the mercy of the plotters, whose *heart* must be the implied subject of 'it was burning like a fire of flame' (*cf*. Andersen, pp. 447–461, for the reading I have followed and adapted). A close prophetic parallel to the scene of drunken officialdom is found in Isaiah 28:1–4, 7–13.

7. For the third time (*cf*. vv. 4, 6) the *oven* figure describes the ambitious passions of the priests, called *all of them* as in verse 4. But here they have broken out in animal-like fury that *devoured* (lit. 'have eaten'; *cf*. at 2:12; 5:7) 'their judges'. Judges (*rulers*) is an appropriate term to describe the *kings* whose responsibility was to enforce justice, to render sound verdicts (*cf*. 5:1), and to seek God's help in times of emergency by leading the people to rely on him as did Israel's judges of old.

But it is more likely that in this passage 'judges' is synonymous with *princes*, the courtiers whose task was to carry out the king's righteous commands and thereby enforce the covenant. They who had failed to protect the king, either religiously or physically, themselves became victims of the coups (*cf.* another mention of their demise in 7:16). *Their kings* reinforces the reading of the Targum in verse 5. These are kings put in place by conspiratorial bands who come close to owning them. Neither God nor the prophet has any sense of loyalty to such monarchs (*cf.* 8:4). *Fallen* is almost an understatement: four assassinations in twelve years – a row of tombs that memorialized the failure of royalty to provide peace, security or stability.

Yet – and this is the indictment to which the entire passage has been building since 5:8 – none of the priestly leaders *calls* to Yahweh for any real solution. Every other expedient has been tried: military invasion (5:8–12), foreign intrigue (5:13), sham repentance (6:1–3) and murderous conspiracy (6:7–9; 7:3–7). God, who has not spoken directly since 7:2, now voices both his pain and wrath at such monumental insult. What has a people come to when its religious leaders bank on a chain of wicked, incompetent men to provide salvation and then murder them when they fail? 'The supreme sin', this has been called: 'they have tried to go on their own without Yahweh'.[1]

vii. Judgment metaphor of the inedible bread (7:8–10).

The text still hovers under the shadow of the Syro-Ephraimite War, although Judah is no longer in view, and Ephraim is the focus of attention (vv. 8, 11). Even more noticeable is the absence of the priests who appeared on the scene at 4:4 and have had the centre-stage most of the time since. They will not reappear by name until 10:5 (and even then will be branded *idolatrous priests* [Heb. *kᵉmārîm*] not regular priests, *kōhᵉnîm*), though their potential frustration when deprivation and exile halt their festive services is described in 9:4–6. The exit of the priests, their hands bloodied from their plot against the crown, triggers a switch in content from Ephraim's internal confusion to their ambivalence and compromise in foreign affairs. So stupid seems their behaviour that Hosea caricatures it in a whole string of cartoons: half-baked bread (v. 8),

[1] M. E. W. Thompson, *Situation and Theology*, p. 72.

mouldy bread (v. 9), senseless dove (v. 11), loose-strung bow (v. 16), futile farming (8:7), useless pot (8:8), wild ass (8:9), and, shepherd of the wind (12:1). By choosing everyday experiences or objects that people would chuckle at, the prophet has more than made his point that Israel's foreign policies run counter to common sense, not to speak of divine revelation.

8. We assume that Hosea used *Ephraim* to describe the Northern Kingdom because the rest of Israel had already been reduced to Assyrian vassalage. Only the hilly enclave around Samaria, part of the old tribal territory of Joseph's son Ephraim, retained any semblance of political freedom (see Additional Note on 'Possible historical backgrounds', p. 118, and comments on 6:7–11a). The rump-state of Ephraim, then, had mixed itself with the nations, especially Aram, Egypt and Assyria (vv. 11, 16; *cf.* the description of this at 5:13) in such a way that its unique identity as God's people was obscured. Though God may echo the baking simile of verses 3–7 by a hint that Ephraim is the oil stirred in the foreign flour, it is more likely that the metaphor actually begins in the second line. The function of the first, more literal, clause is to make clear the meaning of the metaphor. The same pattern is followed in verse 9, while in verse 11 the order is reversed: the simile takes the lead and the interpretation follows.

Bread-baking provides the background of verse 8b as it did in verses 3–7, but here the point is made from the loaf (*cake*) not the oven. The flat disk of dough (shaped like pita-bread) was clapped onto the side of the oven and left unturned by the baker. The result was inedible raw dough on one side, scorched crust on the other. It may not be pushing the imagery beyond its bounds to say that Ephraim's side that was turned towards the nations was badly burnt, while the other side – the unpalatably weak commitment to Yahweh – was underdone.

9. Ephraim's stupidity is stated even more blatantly. 'He himself did not know' that: (1) his agricultural and economic *strength* was being eaten up by tribute paid to *aliens* ('foreigners', a term used in 5:7 to describe the bastard children produced by the fornication of the cult), as the priests had devoured Ephraim's judges (v. 7); and (2) his whole way of life had turned rotten with mould that grows its repulsive *gray hairs* on over-aged food. This interpretation (see Andersen, pp. 467–468) has the advantage of preserving the culinary metaphor and of avoiding the question of why gray hairs would be viewed negatively here, when biblical people usually saw them as a badge of blessing (Pr. 20:29). Wolff (p. 126) reads gray hair as a synonym for fright. The verb describing the onset of grayness (Heb. *zrq*) is usually translated 'sprinkle' but more likely is derived from one of two Arabic roots meaning either 'to become white/bright' or 'to creep/steal upon'.[1] The latter seems more appropriate to the context, where Ephraim's shameful ignorance is stressed (*cf. not know* at 2:8). Drunkenness (v. 5) may have helped to dull their perception (*cf.* 4:11).

10. The prophet's summary accusation becomes blunt in this verse, the first line of which is echoed verbatim from 5:5 (see comments), while the last two lines restate the familiar emphases on Israel's failure to *return* (see on 3:5; 5:4; 6:1) and *seek* (see on 3:5; 5:6) the Lord, here called *Yahweh their God*. This longer name (*cf.* 1:7; 3:5; 12:9; 13:4; 14:1) reminds people to whom their allegiance is owed. Lack of proper response to their God is a dominant theme of this entire section:

> and none of them calls upon me (v. 7),
> and he knows it not (v. 9 twice),
> nor do they seek him for all this (v. 10),
> but they speak lies against me (v. 13),
> they do not cry to me from the heart (v. 14),
> they rebel against me (v. 14),
> yet they devise evil against me (v. 15).

No wonder that God has to keep turning up the volume of his judgment, a judgment implied in *for* (or 'in') *all this*, until it reaches an intensity that captures Israel's attention. Only after the judgment has reached the terrifying magnitude of destruction of the entire kingdom and the exile of its people will the seeking and the returning take place (3:5; 11:10; 14:1–2).

viii. Judgment-simile of the senseless dove (7:11–12). Though the figure changes, from culinary language to that of

[1] For the former *cf.* KB, following G. R. Driver; for the latter, J. Blau, *VT*, 5, 1955, p. 341.

ornithology and hunting, the message remains the same: Ephraim's stupidity in banking on foreign relations for security and stability. The ambivalence that sent them flitting from Mesopotamia to the Nile in search of an ally could only be called 'scatter-brained', whether from fear, gullibility (the Heb. *pth*, translated *silly*, means readily seduced; *cf.* on 2:14) or both (for foolish of heart, see Dt. 11:16). *Without sense* is literally 'without heart', *i.e.* without power and judgment to make sound choices, readily influenced by irrational factors (*cf.* on *heart* at 4:11). Their *calling* to Egypt stands in contrast to their failure to call on God (v. 7), while their journeying (*going*) to Assyria has prevented them from returning to him (v. 10). Wolff (p. 127) argues for the Syro-Ephraimite setting for these verses and dates their message at 733 BC (see Additional Note on 'Possible historical backgrounds', p. 118).

The picture of inedible food (vv. 8–9), suggested a judgment that was a matter of cause and effect: stupid conduct brought dire results (*cf.* Gal. 6:7). In verse 12, however, Yahweh, speaking personally as in verse 7, threatens his direct intervention. If Ephraim will be the dove, Yahweh will be the crafty hunter. If Ephraim will make treaty with the nations, so declares the Lord, 'I will chastise them according to the report of their treaties' (see Andersen's translations, p. 461).

The last line of verse 12 probably gives the literal explanation of the hunting metaphor, though its precise meaning is puzzling. Many commentators (with Wolff, p. 107) emend the last word to 'their evils' (Heb. *rā'ātām* for MT *'adātām*) and read the verb as *chastise* or 'discipline' (Heb. *ysr*; *cf.* 5:2). This understanding makes the line convey a general threat, picks up the word *evils* that was predominant earlier (vv. 1, 2, 3), and repeats the emphasis on judgment as discipline from 5:2. Andersen's interpretation (p. 471) features the treaty-making context suggested by 5:13 and 7:11. Reading 'their covenant' for MT's 'their congregation' (Heb. *'ēdûṭām* from *'wd* for *'adātām* from *y'd*), he stresses that Ephraim's rebellion against God took the specific form of treaty-making with the nations, a crime directly condemned in 12:1, where Hosea returned to the theme that dominates 7:8–16.

ix. Double divine complaint of rebellion (7:13–16). Verses 13 and 15 bear the marks of divine complaints and are part of a sequence of complaints begun at 4:16, reaching a climax at

11:8–9 (*cf.* on 6:4–5; 6:11b – 7:2). They make clear that training, strengthening and rescuing were what God had in mind, while wandering, lying (v. 13) and rebelling (v. 14) marked Israel's way. The stupid foreign policies remain the theme of this section (note that Egypt closes this section in v. 16, as Assyria helped to begin it in 5:13), and continue to be a personal affront to God. Words like 'strayed from *me*', 'rebelled against *me*', 'speak lies against *me*' (v. 13), 'do not cry to *me*', 'rebel against *me*' (v. 14), 'devise evil against *me*' (v. 15) pound this point home.

13. The threats of judgment in the form of *woe* (*cf.* Nu. 21:29; Is. 3:9; Je. 13:27; Ezk. 16:23; Ho. 9:12, where *woe* is directed to others and not to oneself and, hence, implies a 'denunciation', BDB, p. 17) and *destruction* (Heb. *šōḏ*; *cf.* 12:2; Am. 3:10; 5:9), with their exclamatory force, show God bent on judgment. The case against Ephraim and Judah has been built up, charge on charge and accusation on accusation, until the evidence is overwhelming. The wicked skirmishes between north and south (5:8–12), the foolish overtures to Assyria (5:13), the empty ploy of penitence (6:1–3), the priestly plots of violence (6:7–10; 7:3–7), Ephraim's stupid political ambivalence (7:8–12) – these have left Yahweh no recourse but to announce the advent of his judgment, but he does so with great pain and no joy.

Israel's ungrateful conduct is summed up in three words: (1) *strayed* or better 'fled' (Heb. *ndd*; *cf.* Je. 4:25) indicates a deliberate and desperate attempt to elude Yahweh's sovereignty; (2) *rebelled* (Heb. *pš*ʿ) can describe political revolution, military mutiny, juvenile delinquency (1 Ki. 12:19; Is. 1:2), breach of human decency (Am. 1:3, 6, 9, 11, 13; 2:1), as well as opposition to the stipulations of God's covenant (*cf.* Ho. 8:1; 14:9; Am. 2:4, 6; 4:4); and (3) *speak lies* (Heb. *kᵉzāḇîm*, 'falsehoods'; *cf.* 11:12) underscores the deceitfulness that marks Israel's conduct (*cf. dealt faithlessly*, 5:7; *deal falsely*, 7:1; *treacherous bow*, 7:16). It may have at root Ephraim's idolatry (*cf.* Am. 2:4, where *lies* mean idols), the ultimate lie about God; from that lie stem the others – false penitence (6:1–3), belief that their domestic stability depends on their own contrivance (6:7–10; 7:3–7), and conviction that God cannot defend them against their enemies (7:8–11). The poignancy of this divine complaint resides in the contrast between Yahweh's desire to rescue (Heb. *pdh* 'ransom', 'redeem by payment of price') and

Israel's rejection of his every attempt so to do. The contrast is reinforced in Hebrew by the explicit use of the pronouns *I* and *they* for emphasis: 'I, on my part . . . but they, on their part . . .'. When next Yahweh speaks of rescue, it is in a tragic rhetorical question whose expected answer is No: *shall I ransom them from the hand of Sheol?* (13:14).

14. Insincere prayer to Yahweh – their 'crying out' to him is perfectly proper (*cf.* 8:2; Joel 1:14), but their *heart*, the focus of wilful choice and full commitment (*cf.* v. 11, where their 'heart' [*sense*] is missing), is not in it (*cf.* 6:1–3) – is matched by other religious activity carried on at a fever pitch: *they wail* in mourning or despair (*cf.* Is. 14:31; Je. 4:8; Joel 1:15, 11, 13; Am. 8:3) as part of a cultic exercise, perhaps in lament for the death of Baal, symbolized by a prolonged season of drought and aggravated by the devastation brought to their crops by ravaging invaders (*cf.* v. 9). The cultic setting of their wailing is clearly suggested: (1) in *beds* or 'couches', places of reclining for fertility orgies at the hilltop shrines (*cf.* Mi. 2:1); (2) in the reference to *grain and wine* (*cf.* on 2:8, 9, 22; *cf.* especially 4:11 where *new wine* takes away the *heart*), the chief symbols of Baal's blessing and the gifts of the cult offered to Baal or Yahweh (*cf.* Joel 1:10); and (3) in the ritual acts of self-laceration used to reinforce their prayers (*cf.* 1 Ki. 18:28; Je. 16:6; the law forbade such disfigurement, Dt. 14:1); the reading 'slash' or *gash* is suggested by the LXX (*cf.* RSV; NEB; JB) and entails reading the verb from a Hebrew root *gdd* rather than MT's *grr*, a readily understood scribal error, given how closely *r* and *d* resemble each other in most stages of the Hebrew alphabet.

The final line, *they rebel against me*, is better read 'they turn away from me', reading preposition *b* to describe separation, 'from'; *cf.* NEB; NASB; NIV; *cf.* Am. 6:7 for Hebrew root *swr*, 'to turn away', a key word for apostasy in Isaiah (30:11) and Jeremiah (5:23; 6:28; 17:5). It serves as a summary to describe the unrelenting waywardness not only of verses 13–14 but of the whole section beginning at 5:8.

15. The second divine complaint looks at Israel's past (*cf.* 11:3) as the first had looked at their present (v. 13). The language here turns parental: God's grief is compounded by the fact that he worked diligently to *train* Israel by discipline (Heb. root *ysr*, see at 5:2; 7:12) to have spiritual and moral strength – *strengthened their arms* must mean much more here than physical fitness – yet they used any craftiness acquired, including their powers to reckon and plot (*devise* translates Heb. *ḥšb* in the intensive stem which means 'to count', Lv. 25:27, 50, 52, or to 'set out plans', Na. 1:9), to do him harm by violating his will. *Evil* (Heb. *rā'*) is an all-encompassing word for 'painful wrong': it can mean crimes that people commit (*cf.* 7:1, 3) or the harm done to them as a result of the crimes (*cf.* Am. 3:6). When God is the target of such disloyalty, the two meanings merge: human sin inflicts incredible hurt on him whom Hosea pictures as Husband and Parent. The tight link between verses 14 and 15 is sealed with a word-play: the apostasy of verse 14 is expressed by the Heb. *swr*; the gracious divine training of verse 15 (*cf.* Dt. 8:5; Heb. 12:11) by the root *ysr*. The pun reminds us that in Israel's behaviour God got the exact opposite of what he had every right to expect.

16. The only solution to this pattern of apostasy is a 'return' (*cf.* on 3:5; 6:1), yet Ephraim's return (*turn*) like all else they do in these chapters is exactly the wrong thing. The obscurity of the first line has prompted a variety of renderings, but the context makes clear that Ephraim is being accused of wrong: he is as unreliable as a 'slack' or 'faulty' *bow* (Ps. 78:57). The Heb. *'al* which ends the line is the puzzle. One solution has been to amend it to 'Baal': *they turn to Baal* (RSV; JB). Another reads it as 'Most High' and applies it to Yahweh: 'they return but not to the most high' (AV; NIV). A third, and perhaps better, alternative interprets *lō' 'āl* as No-god, an appropriate epithet for *Ba'al* (*cf.*8:6) or any other Canaanite deity (*cf.* Dt. 32:17, 21). This rendering, which Andersen (p. 477) reached by equating *'āl* with *'elî* and *'elyôn*, speaks of exalted or elevated deity. Such an interpretation has the support of the LXX which translates the clause, 'they returned to nothing' (*cf.* also Jeremias' 'zur Ohnmacht', 'to the powerless one', p. 91).

The death (*shall fall*) of the *princes* at the sword-point serves as a complement to their destructive role in the collapse of the monarchy (7:3–7). What they let happen to their kings – *all their kings have fallen* – will happen to them, not necessarily in palace intrigue but in open warfare, when the nation they have courted will strike them down, thanks to the *insolence* with which their *tongue* greeted God's prophetic call upon their lives (5:10, 12–14; 6:5; 9:8). *Egypt* (*cf.* v. 11), watching Ephraim's pro-Assyria policy reduced to shambles, will have the last laugh (*derision; cf.* Ezk. 23:32; 34:7; 36:4) at political opportunists. For Hosea, who treasured the rich grace manifested in the Exodus (13:4–5) and who longed for Israel's new answer which would signal a new Exodus (2:14–15), letting the last word of this substantial section (5:8 – 7:16) go to *Egypt* must have been painful indeed.

d. The cult ripe for destruction (8:1 – 9:9)

This is the third of the four sets of speeches that comprise the messages of 4:1 – 11:11. It divides readily into two parts – 8:1–14; 9:1–9: (1) both parts begin with warnings expressed in imperatives (8:1; 9:1); (2) both open with general indictments about disloyalty to Yahweh (8:1–3; 9:1–3) and close with general announcements of judgment (8:14; 9:9b); (3) both make the perversion of the cult their central indictment and its destruction their primary threat (8:4c–6, 11–13; 9:1–6); and (4) both contain the summary announcement of judgment:

> he will remember their iniquity,
> and (he) will punish their sins (8:13; 9:9b).

If 8:1 – 9:9 return our attention to the cult (*cf.* 4:1 – 5:7), they do not allow us to forget the other expressions of covenantal disloyalty which were prominent in 5:8 – 7:16: (1) the dynastic roulette, which deposed a cluster of kings (8:4, 10; *cf.* 6:7–10; 7:3–7); (2) the spineless foreign policy which wavered between Assyria and Egypt as prime ally (8:9–10; 9:6; *cf.* 5:13; 7:8–12); (3) the hollow hope in military might (8:14; *cf.* 7:16); (4) the pivotal role of the priests in Israel's defection (9:5–9; *cf.* 6:7–10; 7:1–7, 14, 16a); and (5) the emptiness of Israel's professions of loyalty (8:2; 9:1–6; *cf.* 6:4–6). So close is the tie between 8:1–14, at least, and 5:8 – 7:16 that the one may be called a shorter parallel version of the other, as 5:1–7 was seen as a briefer account of 4:4–19 (so Jeremias, p. 103).

This section reaches back even further, to the cultic descriptions of 2:2–13, and resumes the assault on the fertility cult by recalling the use of the divine gifts of silver and gold (8:4; *cf.* 2:8),·the paying of hire for illicit companionship (8:9–10; 9:1; *cf.* 2:12), and the devastation of the crops which were thought to be the fruit of Baal's largess (9:1–5; *cf.* 2:12). As firm a barrier as is the line between chapters 1–3 and chapters 4–14, it does not divide the book into water-tight compartments. Rather, it is regularly perforated by verbal and thematic cords that bind Hosea's work together in a remarkable unity of language and message.[1]

i. Broken law (8:1–3). Despite the uncertainty of our understanding of verse 1a, it seems quite clear that these verses are a judgment speech whose accusation centres in the violation of the covenant stipulations (v. 1b) and whose announcement of judgment heralds Israel's pursuit by an enemy (v. 3b). If the traditional understanding of verse 1a is adopted – the *vulture* symbolizing an invading army – then the passage is an envelope:

> announcement of judgment by enemy invasion, v. 1a
> indictment for broken covenant, v. 1b
> expansion of indictment, v. 2
> summary of indictment, v. 3a
> announcement of judgment by enemy pursuit, v. 3b.

One key to the structure of these verses is the role played by *because* (Heb. *ya'an*) in verse 1b. Andersen (pp. 486–489) has argued compellingly for reading *because* as the lead clause in a sentence whose main clause is not found until verse 3. For reasons to be mentioned below, we shall take Andersen's main point on the use of *because* without adopting his readings of verses 1–3 *in toto*:

> Because they have transgressed my covenant
> and against my instruction they have rebelled –
> [though] to me they keep crying out, 'My God,

---

[1]Again the variety of literary forms is impressive: (1) a call to alarm (8:1–3); (2) a brief cry of complaint—how long (8:5c–6a); (3) wisdom sayings (8:7); (4) hyperbole (8:12); (5) formulaic announcement of judgment (8:14); (6) parody of a salvation speech (9:1); (7) rhetorical questions (9:5); (8) quotation of popular opinion about the prophet (9:7b); (9) allusion to history of past crimes (9:9). All of these are woven together to form a two-part (8:1–14; 9:1–9) judgment speech in which the typical elements of indictment (8:1b–3a, 4–6a, 7–9, 11–13a, 14a; 9:1, 7b–9a) and announcement (8:1a, 3b, 6b, 10, 13b, 14b; 9:2–7a, 9b) are subtly interwoven; indictment dominates chapter 8, where Yahweh is chief speaker; announcement is emphasized in 9:1–9, where Yahweh is spoken of in the third person singular and the prophet seems to be the herald of the judgment.

> we know you, we Israel' –
> Israel has rejected good
> An enemy will start pursuing him.

The *covenant* stands at the heart of these words: (1) to set the tone, it is mentioned first in the indictment (*cf.* 6:7); (2) it is implied in the *law* ('instruction;' Heb. *tôrâ*; *cf.* 4:6) which has the covenant story and demands as its centre (on *transgressed*, 'rebelled', see at 7:13); (3) the strong cry (*cf.* 7:14, where the cry has no heart) *we know you*, connotes a profession of covenant loyalty consistent with Hosea's use of the word *know* (Heb. *yd'*; *cf.* 2:20; 4:1, 6; 5:4; 6:3, 6); (4) the *good spurned* by Israel – an antithetical way of describing the same attitude expressed in 'they devised evil against me' (7:15) – in the main affirmation of this passage may be an expression of covenant amity[1]; and (5) the threat of enemy pursuit is precisely the form of judgment that a broken treaty (covenant) would warrant – the sovereign's protection is withdrawn and the rebellious vassal is left open to hostile assault.

The identity of the *enemy* (v. 3b) is not stated. Consistency would suggest that *enemy* and *vulture* (v. 1a; *cf.* Hab. 1:8; La. 4:19 for the devouring, swiftness of the *vulture* or 'eagle' – Heb. *nšr* can mean either) must describe the same entity.[2] The absence of verbs in verse 1a so compresses the language that we can do little more than guess at its full meaning. It seems to be a call to the prophet to sound an alarm to the people, as a sentry would blow a ram's-horn trumpet (*cf.* 5:8; Am. 3:6, though the verb 'blow' is lacking in v. 1a). Though modern versions use *lips*, the literal Hebrew word is 'palate' which often occurs in parallel with 'lips' or 'mouth' (Pr. 5:3; 8:7; Song 5:16; 7:10). The cause for the alarm is stated in the next phrase: '[something] like the *vulture* [*is*] *over the house of Yahweh.*' A line of interpretation as old as the Targum sees the vulture-enemy as *Assyria*. The context would appear to support this: *e.g.* the violence that fells the princes in 7:16; the swallowing up of Israel by foreigners in 8:7–8; the specific mention of Assyria in 8:9; the military defeat and exile implied in 8:14 and 9:5–6. For *vulture* as a figure of both

---

[1] W. L. Moran, 'A Note on the Treaty Terminology of the Sefir, Stelas', *JNES*, 22, (1963), pp. 173–176.

[2] For detailed discussion of vultures in the Middle East, see W. Brownlee, *Ezekiel 1–19*, WBC, 28 (Waco: Word Books, 1986), pp. 261–265.

Babylonian and Egyptian aggression, see Ezekiel's allegory (17:1–24). This interpretation may be reinforced by the word-play between *enemy* (v. 3) and *lovers* (v. 9; Heb. *'ôyēḇ*, and *'ōhēḇ*): the *lovers* (allies) whom Israel courted have turned on her and will devour her as a *vulture* would consume a carcass.[1] The site of such gorging is the *house* of *Yahweh* (v. 1a) which is not likely to mean the temple of Jerusalem or a Baalized shrine (unless the phrase is utterly sarcastic) but rather to embrace the whole land of Israel (*cf.* 9:3–4), which God gave his people.

ii. Illicit rulers and doomed idols (8:4–6). The general indictment of verses 1–3 now becomes more specific. Its first target is the *monarchy* (v. 4ab), sustained only by cruel ambition and changed only by violent treachery (2 Ki. 14:23 – 17:2; Ho. 7:3–7). His will was not sought nor his approval courted (for 'know' meaning 'care for' or 'approve', see Ps. 1:6) in any of these dynastic changes. The rulers and hence all their chief officials (*princes*; *cf.* 7:3, 16) were chosen by criteria that had nothing to do with God's purposes for his people. The contrast between this process of arbitrary selection and God's choice of David by the hand of Samuel is striking (1 Sa. 16:1–13).

The second target of indictment is the *idols* that flourished in the cult (vv. 4c–6; *cf.* 2:8 for *silver and gold*). The whole religious enterprise which had degenerated to calf-worship (*cf.* 10:5–6; 13:2) was doomed to destruction (vv. 4d, 6d). Though the prohibition of idolatry in covenant law (Ex. 20:3–6; Lv. 19:4) was certainly in view (*cf.* v. 1), it is the *folly* of the idolators not their disobedience to law that draws Hosea's attention here (*cf.* Is. 40:18–20; 41:29; 42:8, 17; 44:9–20; Hab. 2:18–19). Can anything be more foolish than to worship what we outrank, a no-god (*cf.* 7:16), our creation not our Creator? Like any other fabricated material, an idol shaped of wood and clad with precious metal (*idol* is the subject of 'destroyed' or 'cut off' not the people, v. 4d) can be cut up

[1] For a different and very plausible interpretation that reads *nešer*, 'vulture' as *naśśār* or *naśśār* from an Arabic word meaning 'herald', see Grace I. Emmerson, *VT*, 25, 1975, pp. 700–710. By such a reading she posits a cultic-covenantal setting for the whole passage, whose opening words she gives as: 'Set the trumpet to your lips as a herald [making a proclamation] against the house of the Lord.' This rendering comes out about where traditional emendations do, which read *vulture* as 'watchman' (*cf.* JB).

(v. 4d) or shattered to bits (v. 6d; *cf*. Ex. 32:20). Samaria's *calf* was in all probability situated at Bethel, housed at the royal shrine (*cf*. 1 Ki. 12:28–30 for its construction by Jeroboam I and Am. 7:13 for its importance to Jeroboam II). Hosea clearly links the calf of Bethel with the citizens of Samaria, when he describes their mourning at its departure (10:5–6).

The logical subject of 'he spurned' (v. 5) is God, yet the switch from third to first person in the next line, *my anger*, is a bit abrupt, unless we assume that the latter is a direct quotation introduced by an implied 'saying' (*cf*. NASB). Is is also possible to read *my anger* as the subject of both clauses: 'my anger has spurned your calf, O Samaria, and burned against them.'[1] Such readings alleviate the need to emend the verb to *I spurned* (RSV), 'spurn' (impv.; *cf*. NIV), or 'was spurned' (*cf*. Mays). Andersen (p. 482) with some plausibility, connects the last line of verse 4 with the first clause of verse 5: 'So that it will be cut off he rejects the calf of Samaria.'

The spurning is God's response to Samaria's spurning of his covenant (v. 3) and the transferring of their loyalty from Yahweh to the *calf* that symbolized for them the fertility of Baal. These Samaritans, who are the subjects of the verbs in verse 4, must be the *them* against whom God's *anger burned* (*cf*. Is. 5:25 for this wrath, which in Isaiah is coupled with God's outstretched hand, ready to smite in judgment; *cf*. 9:12, 17, 21; 10:4). That burning wrath, not forgiving love, is Yahweh's disposition here is due both to the lack of Israel's penitence and to the intensity of their sin. The honour of the jealous God has been crudely compromised in the calf-cult (*cf*. Ex. 32:10, 11, 19 where Yahweh and Moses both burn with anger at the sight of the golden calf), and his entire countenance (*anger* and 'nose' are the same Heb. word, *'ap*) has been set aflame with a righteous blaze that only Israel's full return will quench (11:9; 14:4). The second half of verse 5 is a complaint (*cf*. Ps. 4:2; 6:3). *How long*? does not raise a chronological question but laments that Israel's lack of purity (*cf*. Gn. 20:5; Pss. 26:6; 73:13, where the Heb. word describes innocent hands, clean of guilt) has become a permanent practice.

The first phrase of verse 6, literally 'for (or indeed) from Israel', seems to connect with verse 5, but its precise meaning is so difficult that, again, the text has promoted numerous

[1] J. R. Lundbom, *VT*, 25, 1975, pp. 228–30.

emendations. Wolff's translation (p. 132), 'But they are from Israel!' may be as close as we can come. Yet even so, the meaning is ambiguous. The tone could be poignant: Yes, they seem incapable of purity, but they are from Israel and may return (so Wolff, p. 141); or it could be sarcastic: But they are from Israel, with its dark history of rebellion, and will not return.

iii. Fruitless foreign alliances (8:7–10). The threat of judgment continues with a different literary form, a three-part proverb (v. 7). The proverb serves to change the pace and to create suspense. Its cause and effect argument – you reap what you sow and worse (*cf.* Gal. 6:7–8) – is not immediately obvious to the reader. Not until the mention of *Assyria* in verse 9, is it plain that Hosea is here resuming the themes treated in the previous set of speeches (*cf.* 5:13; 7:8–16) – the dangers of foreign alliances, which will prove not only fruitless (v. 7ab) but downright destructive (vv. 7c–8a).

The literary art of the proverb is seen in (1) the assonance of the first line – *they sow* is Heb. *yizrāʿû* (in which we hear echoes of Jezreel's name; *cf.* 1:4–5, 11; 2:22) and *they reap* is *yiqṣōrû;* (2) the rhyme of the second line – *grain* is *ṣemaḥ*, and *meal* ('flour') is *qemaḥ*; and (3) the progression in the three lines – bad sowing leads to even worse reaping (7a), grain that manages to grow at all produces little that is edible (7b), and the little that is edible will be wolfed down by strangers, who raid the field (7c). The force of this chain-like argument – a form of *sorites* (*cf.* Joel 1:4) – is both to highlight Israel's folly and to show how sweeping will be its consequences (for an interpretation of v. 7 as *curse* not proverb, see Andersen, p. 497).

Wind (v. 7) is a figure of fickleness and futility (*cf.* 12:1, where foolish foreign policy is again in view; Jb. 7:7; Pr. 11:29; Ec. 1:14, 17). *Whirlwind* or 'storm' (see Stuart, p. 127) speaks of increased destruction (*cf.* Ps. 83:15; Jb. 29:20–23 for the terrors of wind-caused disasters); the consequence not only matches the folly, it outdoes it. *Aliens* (*cf.* on 5:7; 7:9; 8:13) are foreigners who owned no land and therefore had to forage on the property of others to survive. Marauding bedouin were a constant threat to settled farmers in the ancient Middle East. The word anticipates the international thrust of this indictment, a thrust that becomes increasingly clear with the mention of the nations (*gôyîm*) in verse 8 and then of Assyria in verse 9.

Swallowed (v. 8a; *devour*, RSV, v. 7c) links the proverb to the beginnings of its interpretation and makes a sarcastic joke: Israel is not only the foolish, fruitless farmer but also the crop which the Gentiles, the nations outside the covenant, especially Assyria and Egypt, gobble up. 'Now' (v. 8; RSV *already*) rather than denoting time, probably indicates that Israel's absorption among the nations is the consequence of the folly (*cf.* 5:7 and comments on similar usage). *Useless vessel* (v. 8, lit. 'without value'; Je. 22:28; 48:38) describes a broken pot or a shattered weapon, another graphic metaphor of Israel's stupid impotence (*cf.* 7:8, 11; 8:9). *Gone up* (v. 9) is a reminder that Israelites reached *Assyria* by marching north to Damascus and then to the Euphrates whose channel they followed to the east, since the desert made a direct eastward journey hazardous. *Assyria* again plays its double role in Hosea (*cf.* on 5:13): tempting Israel to break the covenant with God and standing ready to inflict the consequent judgment, parts of which Galilee and Gilead experienced at the time of the Syro-Ephraimite war in 733 BC (see Additional Note on 'Possible historical backgrounds', p. 118).

The description of *Ephraim* as *wild ass* (or possibly 'zebra' v. 9; there is a pun intended; *'pr*, the first three consonants of Ephraim, need only slight shifting to remind us of *pr'*, the consonants in *wild ass*; *cf.* 13:15; 14:8 for other puns on Ephraim) should be read as the beginning of a separate sentence, contrary to MT and most versions. The image portrays not stupidity as did the hopping dove in 7:11 but a loneliness conveyed by the participle *wandering* (*cf.* Is. 14:31; Ps. 102:7), by the particle *lô* which here means 'by himself', and by the natural habitat of the *wild ass* as described in Job (39:5–8) as 'steppe' and 'saltland'. The remainder of the sentence which has *Ephraim* hiring *lovers* (*cf.* 2:12) points to the picture of a people so lonely, so cut off from covenant roots, that they are no longer attractive (*cf. useless vessel* in v. 8) and now have to pay others to give them the attention they crave (*cf.* Na. 3:4 for the sharp portrait of Nineveh as treacherous whore). This is precisely Jeremiah's later picture of Judah's lust:

> a wild ass used to the wilderness,
> in her heat sniffing the wind!
> Who can restrain her lust? (Je. 2:24).

149

Given Hosea's sensitivity to Israel's patriarchal history, *wild ass* may also be an allusion to Ishmael who was so named (Gn. 16:12).

Verse 10 builds on verse 9 in a fashion similar to the progression spelled out in verse 7: Israel in its lustful solitude may hire allies (v. 9b) but such hiring (the verb is repeated; it seems to derive from a root *tnh* and is connected with the nouns for hire used in 2:14; 9:11 – *'etnâ* and *'etnān*) does no good, because Ephraim's destiny is in the hands of God, whose intention is to *gather* up his people, *i.e.* to muster them for judgment as the use of the root *qbṣ* (*gather*) in 9:6 suggests (*cf.* Joel 3:2; Zp. 3:8).

A glance at the various translations shows how troublesome is the text of verse 10b. The passage seems to contain a threat of judgment, and that rules out the interpretation that finds in the words a description of a sacral procession where idol-deities are borne aloft: 'they will cease entirely from carrying the image of the king of princes' (Jacob, p. 60; see Am. 5:26 for the possibility of such a procession in Israel's religious life). A second reading comes closer to the severe threat required: 'that will soon put a stop to their anointing kings and leaders' (JB; *cf.* NEB). Though such a reading can cite the LXX as authority it does involve emending *burden* (Heb. *maśśā'*) to *anoint* (Heb. *mᵉśôaḥ*; *cf.* BHS) and thrusts the theme of 8:4 suddenly into this context. The third way of dealing with the text finds in it an announcement of the continued pain that Israel will bear under the burden of the tribute (*i.e.* the hire to her lovers, vv. 9–10) which they are forced to pay the Assyrian king and court (*cf.* 5:13, where the Assyrian ruler is called the Great King; here the *princes* [Heb. *śārîm*] may reflect the Akkadian word *šarrāni*, 'Kings', in an attempt to reconstruct the well-known royal title, 'King of Kings'. Wolff's reading (p. 133) is as good as any: 'so that they soon writhe under the burden of the officials' king'). They have a habit of dependency on foreign support which they can no longer afford. The proverb of sowing and reaping with which this section began will more than come true in Ephraim's experience.

iv. Empty religious enthusiasm (8:11–14).

Attention shifts back to the cult (*cf.* 7:14–16; 8:4–6), but this time the emphasis is on altars and sacrifices (*cf.* 4:8, 10, 13, 14, 19; 5:6) not on prayer rituals (7:14–16) or calf-worship (8:4–6). One thread that connects these verses is the motif of multiplication, (see on 4:7) displayed in the repetition of the Hebrew roots *rbh* or *rbb*: multiplied altars (v. 11), multiplied laws (v. 12), multiplied fortress-cities (v. 14). The first and last are symbols of the incredible energy that Israel poured into religious expression and self-defence; the second speaks of God's frustration with the fact that no super-abundance of laws could curb Israel's zeal to pursue their wrong-headed ways.

Perhaps we should find a connection between these foolish excesses and the proverb which sets the tone of verses 7–10, where everything Israel did turned to ashes: crops were foolishly sown; harvests were unproductive; what did grow was devoured by strangers; Israel struggled to pay Assyria a prostitute's hire only to be whisked away by Yahweh before the purchased favours could be enjoyed. In verses 11–14 the frustration continues: multiplying of altars leads to multiplying of sin (v. 11); abundant ritual results in divine displeasure (v. 13); frenzied building activities merely stock-pile fuel for the fire (v. 14).

Tracing this thematic unity helps us to understand the place of verse 14. It adds evidence to the initial charge of broken covenant and transgressed law (8:1). It also highlights from a different angle the follies of the monarchy (8:4), which was responsible for the personal aggrandizement and social exploitation expressed in the showy architecture which Amos had also decried (3:15; 5:11; 6:4, 11; *cf.* Je. 22:13–17). Moreover, the word *eat* (or 'devour'; Heb. *'kl*; *cf.* on 2:12; 4:8, 10; 5:7; 7:7) serves as a catchword tying together Israel's insatiable appetite for the flesh roasted in the sacrifices with the insatiable fire of judgment that will literally *devour* the strongholds of the Israelite cities (vv. 13–14). Finally, verse 14 makes explicit and concrete the more general announcements of judgment in verse 13 – the form of Israel's punishment is *fire upon his cities*. Of the several ways in which verse 11 has been interpreted, the most likely is that of the pun captured in the NIV:

> Though Ephraim built many altars for sin offerings,
> These have become [for him] altars for sinning.

This reading entails emending (by a change in vowel pointing only) the first occurrence of *for sinning* (RSV) to a causative verb stem in Hebrew that is used both for making a sin-offering (*e.g.* Ex. 29:36; Lv. 9:15) and for cleansing from sin or uncleanness (Nu. 19:19; Ps. 51:7 – *purge* in RSV; Nyberg, followed by Jacob, p. 60, seems first to have suggested this pun, based on the different pointings of the identical consonants). The point is that Israel's intentions have boomeranged. The zeal for the altars was a means of dealing with sin to find forgiveness; instead it became a way of increasing the sins.[1]

As is typical of this part of the book, the indictments of sin and announcements of judgment are punctuated by divine complaint (v. 12; *cf.* on 7:13–16). The verse is poignant, sarcastic and hyperbolic all at once. It deliberately exaggerates God's law-giving activity to show the magnitude of Israel's sin of rejecting the law. More law is not the answer when every piece of instruction is rejected (*cf.* on 4:6; 8:1). The poignancy has God at the end of his patience; all the normal remedies for setting people straight have failed. The sarcasm comes in the perverse response of Israel; what should have been treasured as familiar and precious was viewed as *strange*, foreign, alien (*cf.* on v. 7, where the same root *zr* occurs). A one hundred and eighty degree error this was – Assyria who should have been considered foreign was courted with a prostitute's pay (vv. 9–10), but the laws of Yahweh written (note the emphasis on writing as the way of preserving and transmitting the divine Word) for Israel's guidance and blessing were gainsaid as alien, even pagan, and worthless.[2] Both the syntax and the vocabulary of verse 13 are difficult, especially the first two words, which seem literally to read 'sacrifices of my lovers', though the word for 'lovers' is not the normal Hebrew *'hb* (*cf.* v. 9) and has also been connected with a root meaning 'give' or 'bring', in the sense of offering a sacrifice (note NASB, 'My sacrificial gifts'; NIV, 'They offer sacrifices given to me'). Andersen (p. 510) raises the possibility that 'my loved ones' may allude to child sacrifice (*cf.* on 5:2). The cited response of God seems too weak, however, for such pagan conduct: *but*

[1] Andersen's translation (p. 501) takes an entirely different tack, reading the root *rbh* as connoting arrogance in vv. 11–12. Yet he neglects the clear enveloping catchword (Heb. *hirbâ*) which links v. 11 and v. 14. Both occurrences of the same form must surely mean the same thing.

[2] Phillips, p. 223, cites this text as evidence that Israel's prophets already in Hosea's day had 'a clear complex of written law accredited to Yahweh, to which appeal could be made'.

Yahweh has no delight (cf. 1 Sa. 15:22–23) *in them.* The parallelism and sarcasm evident in verse 11 seem to shape the tone of verse 13. The paraphrase in JB may not be too wide of the mark:

> They love sacrificing: right, let them sacrifice!
> They love meat; right, let them eat it!

This involves reading the difficult *habhābay* as derived from *'hb* or a root *hb* akin to it and carrying its force over to the word 'meat' (or *flesh*) as its second direct object along with 'sacrificing'. These clauses are another way of stressing that lust and greed were more important motivations to Israel's festive worship than obedience or adoration (*cf.* on 4:8, 10, for the role of eating in Israel's sacrificial system). For a people whose standard diet was cereal and vegetable, the savoury, fragrant meat of the sacrifices was mouth-watering beyond resistance.

The two verbs of judgment, *remember (cf.* on 7:2) and *punish* (lit. 'visit'; *cf.* on 1:4) show how personally God is involved in reckoning with Israel's paganized worship, no matter what secondary means he may use to inflict the judgment. For *sins* (*ḥaṭṭā'*) and *iniquity* (*'āwôn*), *cf.* on 4:8. Part of the punishment is a *return to Egypt*. One could read this as a political comment: they will return to their policy of seeking Egypt's support in their quest for independence from Assyria (*cf.* on 7:11). More likely it represents a *return* to the captivity that they knew in Egypt, wherever that captivity may be. This prophecy of *return* anticipates the ampler form in 9:3 and 11:5, where failure to return to God (*cf.* on 3:5) requires a return to slavery either along the Nile or beside the Tigris. The threat of fire in verse 14 confirms the notion that it is invasion/exile, not a return to foreign politicking, that forms the judgment. Israel's 'forgetting' in verse 14 (*cf.* on 2:13; 13:6) stands in clear contrast to God's 'remembering' and is a continuation of the long-term pattern of wilful ignorance (*cf.* 5:4) which is all the more pathetic in the light of their cry in verse 2:

> My God, we Israel know thee.

What they have forgotten specifically in this accusation is who made them a nation. With Psalm 100:3, Hosea uses *Maker* not in the sense of creator, but in the sense of initiator of the covenant, implementer of the Exodus, giver of the law, provider of the land, protector of the people.

The spiritual crimes that accompanied the massive building projects in both kingdoms (note that *Judah* reappears by name for the first time since 6:11, where his judgment was also announced) were several: (1) *palaces* ('great houses') speak of preoccupation with wealth and power; they are evidences that Israel's nobility succumbed to the temptation to behave like their rich and landed gentile neighbours, without regard to their special status before God (*cf.* Je. 22:13–17); (2) Judah's *fortified cities* (NIV's 'towns' is better, given their size) speak of the false reliance on self-protection and military might (*cf.* 10:14; 11:6) which Judah (and Israel) substituted for trust in God (*cf.* Ps. 127:1); Sennacherib claimed to have taken forty-six such Judean towns just three decades after Hosea spoke these words; and (3) the means used for building such lavish enterprises were themselves unjust – unfair taxation, profit from crooked businesses, and slave labour. The close similarity between Hosea 8:14 and Amos' doleful refrain reminds us of the common pool of themes and forms from which the prophets drank (*cf.* Am. 1:4ff).

v. Frustrated cultic festivals (9:1–9). A new set of commands (v. 1) marks the opening of this section and a summary announcement of divine judgment signals its close (v. 9). The tone of the entire passage is threat of judgment by an exile (v. 3) which will make their religious festivities impossible (vv. 4–5). In the *land* that belongs to Yahweh (v. 3), their feasts have become pagan activities (*cf. like the peoples*, v. 1). Now they will be dispatched among these pagan peoples (vv. 3, 6), where singing Yahweh's song will be only a tearful memory (Ps. 137). The threat of exile has been sounded before (7:16; 8:13). Here for the first time it is amplified by a disclosure of its monumental consequences for Israel's treasured calendar of worship.

We can assume that Hosea's audience remains about the same as in 8:1–14, where Samaria is addressed specifically (vv. 5–6). This is confirmed by the references to *Ephraim* (9:3, 8), which refers to the region around Samaria which yet had a measure of freedom under Assyrian vassalage (see Additional Note on 'Possible historical background', p. 118). *Israel* (v. 1) may indicate that citizens from the Assyrian-dominated sections of Galilee and Gilead had made the pilgrimage to Bethel (or less likely to Samaria) for the harvest celebrations which became the occasion for Hosea's doom-laden declarations. This denunciation touched Ephraim's rawest nerve. The autumn harvest festival was a sacrament of life for them, a symbol of their expectations of survival, a proof of the soundness of their religious zeal. The more bountiful the crops – the grain for a year's supply of bread (v. 1), the must (grape juice v. 2) for a year's stock of wine, the olives whose oil supplied their food, light, hygiene and medication – the more affirmed was Israel in the rightness of their religion. If Yahweh allowed their apostasy to be accompanied by material prosperity, they would only dig themselves more deeply into their pagan habits. Intervention was necessary; Yahweh's chosen means was exile. So went Hosea's message.

And Israel's reaction was predictably fiery. It took the form of an *ad hominem* attack on the prophet himself (v. 7). The citation of the people's (or the priests') exclamation gives a clue to the disputational tone that permeates this passage (*cf*. 4:4 for another clear instance of argument between prophet and audience). Wolff (p. 152) may be right in assuming that the prophet was interrupted after verse 1 with protests that called attention to the plentiful harvest as evidence of divine blessing. After all, the *threshing floors* and *wine vats* were full. Hosea's answer was the grim prophecy of verse 2, further explained by the clear word of exile in verse 3. The argumentative tone is amplified by the rhetorical questions (v. 5) that force Israel to answer, 'Nothing', and thus confirm Hosea's threat that all festivities will cease, once the people are translated to foreign soil. It is probably the debate-like nature of these speeches that accounts for the switches in person from direct address (second person, vv. 1, 5) to indirect (third person, vv. 2–4) in reference to Israel. But it is possible to hear the second person passages as addressed to the *priests* (*cf*. their prominent role in 4:4–5:7) and the third person to the *people*, a pattern suggested already at 5:1–7. Throughout 9:1–9 the interplay is between prophet, people and perhaps priest; God neither speaks nor is addressed – in contrast to the vocal role he played in 4:4 – 8:14 and will play again in 9:10ff. Hosea's more assertive tack in 9:1–9 helps to account for the direct assault on him at verse 7.

1–2. The negative imperatives 'do not *rejoice*' (*cf.* Is. 9:3, for
a picture of jubilation at harvest time) and 'do not *exult* (*cf.* Is.
41:16 for exultation over an even more impressive harvest)
fell like rain on Israel's parade of celebration.[1] They not only
dampened the worshippers' exuberance, but they threatened
their salvation. The very words of joy that were often part of
salvation promises, introductions to magnificent announcements of good news (*cf.* Is. 25:9; 66:10; Mt. 5:12), now spelled
their devastation.

Indeed, *the peoples*, *i.e.* the heathen nations like Egypt and
Assyria (v. 3), may be able to continue their joyful orgies in
fertility cults but Israel, whose special history had taught them
better, were no longer going to join them. Their paganizing
practices had reached their nadir: they were not worship but
harlotry (*cf.* on 1:2; 2:2, 5, 12). The crops were now the wages
of a prostitute (*cf.* on 8:9–10, where Israel pays such wages to
Assyria). Andersen's suggestion is worth noting (p. 523) that
loved may mean *made love* in parallel to *played the harlot*. *Hire*
would then be an accusative of reference: 'in regard to' or 'in
exchange for *hire*'. 'Grain' (*cf.* on 2:8–9; 7:14), the final word
in verse 1, not translated in RSV or NIV but included in *threshing
floor*, may be in apposition to *hire* and explain the nature of the
harlot's pay. Though Baal is not dignified by any mention
here, all that was said about the Canaanite fertility god earlier
(*cf.* 2:13) is applicable to this accusation: he was thought to be
the source of Israel's material blessing and that blessing was
thought to be generated by ritual prostitution with priests and
priestesses at the shrines, which here are connected with
threshing floors. In addition to the private threshing areas
which individuals or small groups of farmers may have used,
there seem to have been public, more commercial, threshing
areas larger in size, with firmer floors and better access to the
chaff-carrying winds. Examples of these are in Judah, the
floor that belonged to Araunah, where David erected an altar
(2 Sa. 24:18–23) and Solomon would build the Temple (1 Ch.
22:1), and in Israel, the gate of Samaria, where Ahab and
Jehoshaphat held court with Israel's prophets (I Ki. 22:10).

---

[1]Technically neither word is imperative in Heb., but both seem to be negative commands: the first is jussive, negated by *'al*; the second is probably
infinitive absolute to be read as jussive in light of its parallel; the MT *'el*, 'unto',
should be read as *'al*, although Jb. 3:22 may show that MT's 'unto joy' is a
possible reading.

Both indicate some sacral use of threshing floors, which at harvest celebrations offered the tangible signs of divine blessings in the crops and adequate room for festive gatherings. Sexual activity may have accompanied such feasts even in Israel's early days (*cf.* Jdg. 21:16–24; Ru. 3:6–14).

The threat of judgment against the corrupt feasts is heard in verse 2. The symbols of her prosperity – the *threshing floor* and *wine-vat* (a double-level hollowed space where grapes are pressed in the upper trough and juice collected in the lower) – would no longer supply her food. The *new wine* (see on 2:9) would *fail* ('deceive' her into depending on it and then run out, *cf.* Hab. 3:17), and she would be unable to rejoice now (the MT feminine pronoun should be retained and not emended to *them*; it marks Israel as a *harlot*, v. 1; Wolff, p. 149).

3–4. The chain of explanation continues with the prediction of exile not crop failure (*cf.* 2:9, 12) as the means of the food shortage. Exile follows on the heels of invasion, and each stage is disastrous: in invasion enemy troops devour the food supply; in exile the victims are removed from any access to their goods and any opportunity to produce more. The *land of the Lord* (v. 3) is a stern reminder that the territory occupied by Israel was God's to give as a token of his grace, God's to bless as a sign of his covenant fidelity, and God's to take back as an act of his judgment (see on 8:1).

The *return to Egypt* (see 8:13) alludes to exile in Assyria as a reversal, because of her uncleanness, of God's promise to her. Previously, Israel was branded *unclean* for her sexual promiscuity and political treachery (5:3; 6:10). Now the theme of *eating* introduced in 8:13 is expanded, and the whore finds herself condemned to live where no law of food selection and preparation is possible. For the priests, who sought to maintain the distinctions between the sacred and the profane (Lv. 10:8–11), even when they had violated the covenant (*cf.* 4:4–6; 6:7–10), a diet of unclean food was a fate tantamount to death (*cf.* Am. 7:17).

The exile's further toll is the absence of libations of poured-out *wine* (v. 4; *cf.* Ex. 29:38–41; Lv. 23:13; Nu. 15:1–12) and 'offerings' of slain animals (*cf.* on 4:13, 19; 5:6).[1] The next

---

[1] Heb. *'rb* means either to 'offer' as its Ugaritic use in parallel to 'sacrifice' suggests or 'to be pleasing', in which case *their sacrifices* would be the subject not the object of the clause; *cf.* Je. 6:20.

clause should be read, 'indeed (reading Heb. *kî*, for *kᵉ* 'as'), the *bread* (or 'food' *i.e.* what they would eat of their sacrifices) of *mourners* (or *'idols'*; *cf.* Andersen, pp. 526–27) belongs to them'. Its connection with death, according to the laws of cleanness, renders all those who eat it unclean (*cf.* Nu. 5:1–2). Assyria's paganism is death-dealing in its contagion. Such food (*bread*), whatever the intentions of the worshipper, means nothing to God. It is for the 'gullet' (*hunger*) only (*cf.* 4:8). The whole exercise was so defiling that no Israelite (which is the subject of *come*, not *bread*) could return to the holy land, here described, in keeping with the sacral context, as the *house of Yahweh, i.e.* the *land of Yahweh* (v. 3) and Israel's homeland (*cf.* 8:1; 9:15).

5–6. The rhetorical questions (v. 5) serve to clinch the argument: no significant festal activity will be possible in the contaminated environment of exile. *Appointed festival* (*cf.* 2:11) and *feast of Yahweh* are probably synonymous terms depicting the autumn festival, which seems to be the setting for this entire passage (*cf.* 1 Sa. 1:3, 19–20; 1 Ki. 8:2; 12:32).

More is said about the exile's impact in verse 6: (1) those who try to flee destruction at the hands of ravaging Assyrians to find refuge in Egypt will not find respite but will be collected (*cf.* 'I will gather them up' in 8:10) and buried in *Memphis* (a city in northern Egypt just twenty kilometres or so south of the Delta), with its huge graveyard and ancient pyramids; and (2) their cultic paraphernalia will be abandoned as they flee and are overrun by briars (*nettles*) and *thorns* – including their *precious* idols overlaid with *silver* (*cf.* 2:8; 8:4, for special value of silver) and *their tents* set up as temporary shelters at the shrines.

7–9. Hosea removes all uncertainty about the time of judgment. It is now, it has already *come* – the tenses are past. Its character is divine 'visitation' (*i.e. punishment*; *cf.* on 1:4; 8:13; 9:9); Yahweh marches with Tiglath-pileser's Assyrians. The carving up of the land that has begun (*cf.* note at 5:8 – 7:16) is God's work. Its character is also 'just retribution' ('complete payment'; Heb. *šillum*; *cf.* Is. 34:8; Mi. 7:3).

The third line of verse 7 should probably be read as an admonition not a prediction: 'Let Israel know [this]!' So understood, it serves both to reinforce the judgment threat and set the stage for Israel's *ad hominem* reaction to Hosea's message in verse 7c–d. Beyond that, it mockingly echoes

158

Israel's cry in 8:2 *My God, we Israel know thee.* Israel purports to know Yahweh but does not. Let them know assuredly, then, that judgment is coming and is here.

The announcement of judgment cues a sharp response from Hosea's opposition – a response which Hosea cites, in order to refute it. The whole picture of exile had seemed so absurd that they labelled the prophet *a fool* (*i.e.* blabbering mindlessly; *cf.* Pr. 10:8) and even *mad* or 'crazy' (*i.e.* cooing endlessly; *cf.* 2 Ki. 9:11; Je. 29:26). The synonym for *prophet* here is *man of the spirit*, which was intended as an insult not a compliment (despite the role of the spirit in the line of Israel's great prophets – Elijah, *cf.* 1 Ki. 18:12; Micaiah, *cf.* 1 Ki. 22:21; Elisha, *cf.* 2 Ki. 2:9), especially since Hosea uses *spirit* to describe the almost demonic way in which the Israelites were captured and controlled by their harlotrous worship (4:12, 19; 5:4). Out of his head, chattering senselessly, prompted neither by wisdom nor the divine word – so ran the popular estimate of the prophet. That these words are the public reaction to Hosea not his indictment of the false prophets (*cf.* 4:5; Mi. 3:5–8; Je. 23:9–32) seems clear from the context, where they stand in opposition to verse 8, and from the fact that virtually everything Hosea says about prophets supports their divinely sponsored task (6:5; 9:8; 12:13).

The last phrases of verse 7 seem *not* to be part of Israel's criticism (yet see Andersen, p. 515), but a succinct explanation of what motivates it: the Israelites say what they do to Hosea because their *iniquity* (*cf.* on 8:13) is too great to face and consequently their *hatred* ('hostility'; *maśṭēmâ* is used in the Qumran scrolls and the Book of Jubilees to describe the work of the enemies of God, including Satan; KB Suppl., p. 169, v. 8) is 'abundant' (both nouns are modified by words that suggest the motif of multiplication – Heb. *rb*; *cf.* at 4:7; 8:11). As is typical of our human behaviour, when we cannot acknowledge our guilt we may react towards our accusers with anger. Hosea's critics answered sharply not because they thought he was wrong but because, deep down, they knew he was right.

Hosea's refutation (v. 8) lays out the prophet's true role: a *watchman of Ephraim* (*cf.* Je. 6:17; Ezk. 3:17; 33:2, 6, 7, who pick up this term from Hosea). Given the alerts the prophet has already sounded (5:8; 8:1), the title is well-chosen. He has spotted the impending disaster, thanks to divine revelation, and has relayed the warning to God's people. 'With my God' follows the MT without the need to repoint it to *people of my God* (RSV; NEB) and emphasizes that the *watchman* does only what he should when he does it as God's agent even in God's presence. There may be a hint here of the prophet's participation in the divine council where he hears first-hand Yahweh's word (*cf.* 1 Ki. ch. 22; Is. ch. 6; Je. ch. 23). The tragedy is compounded by the fact that the *watchman* cannot give full attention to the dangers that loom before the people. He has to watch his own step. Israel's bird-traps are laid for him (*cf.* on 5:1; 7:12) and the land, here called *the house of his God* (*cf.* 8:1; 9:4, 15), is full of *hatred* (*cf.* v. 7) towards him. He, Yahweh's prosecuting attorney – note the timing of the verdict in verse 7 and the content of it in verse 9 – is a marked man.

Along with the motif of multiplication, Hosea knows a motif of *deepening* in verse 9 (*cf.* 5:2), in which the description of Israel's corrupting activity (Heb. *šḥt*) is intensified by its coupling with the verb 'made deep' (Heb. *hēʿmîq*). Here what is deepened is the harm done by Israel's misconduct which reaches rock bottom in the rejection of the prophet who seeks to point the way out of the unfathomed pit. The historical parallel, summarized in *as in the days of Gibeah*, serves four purposes: (1) it underscores the ancient precedents that underline Israel's present conduct; the depth of the rebellion is evidenced by its affinities with events four centuries earlier; such crime is in their genes; (2) it compares the present spiritual chaos to what may be the most sordid scene in the Old Testament: the gang-rape and sex-murder of the Levite's concubine at the hands of Gibeah's lewd citizens (Jdg. chs. 19–21; for *Gibeah*, see at 5:8; 10:9); (3) it recalls a number of details which tie in with the language and setting of 9:1–9: *a.* the old man who abandons the concubine to the Benjaminites of Gibeah was raised in *Ephraim* (Jdg. 19:16, 25; *cf.* Ho. 9:3, 8); *b. Mizpah*, *i.e.* 'watchtower', whose meaning is closely associated with *watchman* plays a key role (Jdg. 20:1, 3; *cf.* Ho. 9:8); *c. Bethel*, the probable setting for Hosea's speeches in 9:1–9 is a centre of activity in the story (Jdg. 20:26; 21:2); *d.* a pivotal part of the story's message is the *inescapability of judgment* for the men of Gibeah (Jdg. 20:29–48; *cf.* Ho. 9:9); *e.* the story concludes with a ribald dance in the vineyard at the 'yearly feast of Yahweh' at Shiloh (Jdg. 21:19; *cf.* Ho. 9:1–2 and the comments about sexually oriented activities as part of the autumn harvest festival); and *f.* the summary verse of Judges 21:25 could well describe Hosea's day with its dynastic instability (*cf.* 8:4) that left basic laws unenforced (*cf.* 4:2–3); and (4) as Wolff (p. 158) has suggested, Hosea may have counted the Levites as his allies in the struggle with the established priesthood and thus valued this story partly for the way it described the maltreatment which Levites some- times endured. All this is a theme to which Hosea will return (10:9).

The final summary of judgment repeats the middle lines of 8:13. It assumes that more than enough reasons have been listed to warrant such punishment. And particularly it interp- rets *as in the days of Gibeah* as the crowning argument, with which the prosecution rests its case.

e. The calling unfulfilled (9:10 – 11:11)

The fourth set of speeches in the section of Hosea's messages, begun at 4:1, adds little new in content to what precedes it but takes such a fresh tack in developing the themes that it is one of the most poignant and powerful sections in the book. Its four main divisions are signalled in metaphors that describe Israel's past relationship with God:

> Grapes in the wilderness, 9:10–17;
> Luxuriant vine, 10:1–10;
> Trained heifer, 10:11–15;
> Beloved child, 11:1–11.

In each division, the tone of nostalgia is mixed with shock at Israel's apostasy. The literary result of this mixture is a *tragic reversal*, a grave comparison between the fruitful intimacy that once was and the barren apostasy that now is. And the implication constantly drawn in each division is the necessity and finality of judgment. So clear are Israel's shortcomings from the Redeemer's plan that relatively little space is given to their elaboration. Instead, announcements of judgment are the dominant literary form, until the closing verses of chapter 11.

The first three divisions are dotted with *agricultural imagery* that seems to link them with 8:1 – 9:9, with its notes of vain sowing and reaping (8:7) and nettles and thorns as agents of desolation (9:6): Israel's pristine innocence is likened to grapes and figs (9:10); part of Ephraim's judgment is a withered root that can support no fruit (9:16); Israel is a fruitful vine, whose produce is put to bad use (10:1); Israel's justice has become wild, poisonous weeds (10:4); divine judgment takes the form of thorn and thistle on the once busy altars (10:8; *cf.* 9:6); Ephraim used to be a pet heifer tenderly trained by Yahweh (10:11); her present lot, however, is to *plow* (10:11); relief can come only if Irasel will change its pattern and sow the right seed (10:12); in the meantime the whole agricultural cycle has miscarried – wrong ploughing, wrong reaping, wrong eating (10:13; *cf.* 8:7). One implication of this imagery is to picture *Yahweh as farmer*, tender with the crops and flocks, eager for their produce, frustrated by the failure, drastic in his means of correcting the problems.

Familiar *themes* make brief appearances: (1) the appeal to Israel's history of sin as explanation of her conduct and argument for her judgment – Baal-Peor (9:10; *cf.* Nu. 25:1–9), Gilgal (9:15; *cf.* 1 Sa. 11:14–15), Bethel (called Aven in 10:8; *cf.* on 4:15), Gibeah (10:9; *cf.* on 9:8), Admah and Zeboiim (11:8; *cf.* Gn. 10:19; 14:1–17; Dt. 29:23); (2) the motif of multiplication in which Israel's material abundance and religious excess lead to uncountable transgressions (10:1, 13; *cf.* 4:7; 8:11, 12, 14); (3) the unkept covenant (10:4; *cf.* 6:7; 8:1); (4) the pernicious idolatry (10:5–6; *cf.* 8:4–6); (5) the futility of military might (10:13–14; 11:6; *cf.* 7:16; 8:14); (6) the cessation of the monarchy (10:15; *cf.* 3:4; 7:7, 16); (7) the adoration of Baal as the grantor of fertility (11:1; *cf.* 2:13); and (8) exile as the predominant form of judgment (10:6; 11:5; *cf.* 9:3, 6).

The section begins at 9:10 with a tender reminiscence of Israel's past with God as speaker, *I found Israel*. The prevalence of divine speech (9:10–13, 15–16; 10:10–11; 11:1–9, 11) contrasts with the absence of it in 9:1–9 and is another clue to the unity of the section. Its close is marked by the climactic way that the divine complaint moves to a crescendo in God's decision not to make judgment the ultimate experience of Israel (11:9) but to issue the call for return and restoration: 'but I will make them dwell in their homes' (11:11). Not since 3:5 has this note been sounded with such force and clarity. It brings to a culmination the book's second long journey from judgment to hope. The formula 'oracle of Yahweh' (11:11), used for the first time since 2:21, puts a full stop to the promise of salvation and clears the stage for the third and final section of the book which will both repeat and complete the journey from judgment to hope, which is the plot of the divine story as Hosea has experienced it.

i. Grapes in the wilderness (9:10–17). This brief section takes its title from the simile with which it begins. It needs to be divided into five short sub-sections:

An *accusation* based on Israel's failed potential early in their history – verse 10;

An *announcement* of judgment in a chain-link argument that threatens literal extinction of Ephraim's descendants – verses 11–12;

An *expansion* of the announcement which culminates in a prayer curse on Ephraim's reproductivity – verses 13–14;

An *announcement* of judgment in exile with an accusation that centres in Gilgal where Saul was first crowned king (1 Sa. 11:14–15) – verse 15;

An *announcement* that sums up what has been said about Ephraim's double judgment of fruitlessness and exile – verses 16–17.

This capsule account of Israel's history captures its tragedy: it began with God's delight in Israel's potential for fruitfulness (v. 10a–b); it soon turned sour in their seduction by Baal (v. 10c–d); it lost all hope of fruitfulness by counting for fertility on a no-god (vv. 11–14); it forfeited the fine land in which it was called to produce fruit for Yahweh because it chose to substitute human rule for God's hegemony (v. 15); its pristine fruitfulness gave way to permanent barrenness (v. 16); its rejection of the divine Host (*cf.* Ps. 23:5–6) condemned it to be no longer planted and cultivated but to wander wild among the heathen nations (v. 17).

10. Though Yahweh speaks here of *your fathers*, the tone of verses 10–17 becomes increasingly reflective, and Israel is described in the third person in the rest of the passage. It is as though the reminder of the splendid past is too heavy a subject for either the speaker or the listeners to cope with directly, so Yahweh and the prophet (vv. 14, 17) talk about them and not to them.

Grapes speak of refreshment, of possibilities of wine or raisins (*cf.* 3:1) which preserve the fruit beyond its growing season (Dt. 32:14). *Wilderness* as the site of the vineyard connotes both God's joyful surprise at finding such delight in an unlikely place and his provision for Israel in that desolate setting. Beyond that, *wilderness* suggests the Exodus honeymoon that Hosea both remembers and anticipates (2:14–15). *Fig tree* also pictures delight, especially in the emphasis on *first* (*i.e.* not only early but choice; *cf.* Mi. 7:1) *fruit* and *first season*. Waiting all winter and spring is difficult but waiting for the five or six years necessary for a tree to bear delectable fruit can not help but put an edge to the farmer's appetite when the first ripe figs appear. So God recalls his delight at his new covenant relation with Israel's ancestors (for grape vine and fig tree as symbols of security and prosperity, *cf.* Mi. 4:4). Both vine and fig tree are familiar metaphors of *Israel*, especially in contexts that call for judgment (for vine, see Ps. 80; Is. ch. 5; Je. 6:9; for fig tree see Jesus' sign-act in Mk. 11:12–14, 20–21 and the sign of the fig tree in Mk. 13:28).

Baal-peor holds a prominent place in Israel's geography of shame (Nu. 25:1–5; Dt. 4:4; Ps. 106:28). Originally the title of the Baal venerated at Peor (*cf.* Jos. 22:17) – a mountain in Moab from which Balaam, at Balak's behest, was supposed to curse Israel (Nu. 23:27–28) – *Baal-peor* came later to mean the name of both the place and the deity. The name has become a byword for Israel's gullibility and waywardness and for the fragility of the covenant relation with Yahweh.

Consecrated themselves means to vow their loyalty; it suggests a deliberate ritual act by which Israel identified themselves with Baal. 'And the people ate [the sacrifices] and bowed down to their gods' – acts that the text of Numbers described as a 'yoke' to Baal of Peor (Nu. 25:2–3). Hosea's verb (Heb. *nzr*) brings to mind the intense dedication of the Nazirite vow (*cf.* Nu. ch. 6; Jdg. 13:5, 7, for the nature of this vow; *cf.* Am. 2:11–12). 'Shame' (NASB) really stands for *Baal* (*cf.* RSV), which may have been in the original text and then removed at an early stage (*cf.* discussion of 2:13, 16–17) in fulfilment of the divine promise-command to remove the very names of the Baals from Israel's vocabulary. Biblical faith saw the Baal-peor episode as far more than a casual dalliance. It shook the structure

of the covenant to its very foundations and for a reason that
Hosea explains: the character of the one whom we worship
rubs off on us. The abominable imposter who purported to
love Israel (the Heb. verb form for *love* is active not passive;
thus, as Andersen has noted [p. 536], it is the Baal's love for
them not theirs for Baal that is featured) has infected them
with his *detestable* qualities (for the Heb. word *šiqqûṣ*, *cf*. Je. 4:1;
7:30; 13:27; 32:34; Ezk. 5:11; 7:20; 11:21; 20:30; 37:23). The
Hebrew language is hard-pressed to come up with a more
degrading term to describe the depths to which Israel's initial
and continued contact with Baal had lowered them.

11–12. The judgment announced here is appropriate to
that failure: the fruit that *Ephraim* cares most about – the
future generation, which will assure their continuity, will be
cut off. *Ephraim* is not the subject of verse 11, but is a hanging
nominative: 'As for Ephraim . . .' (*cf*. NASB). Their *glory* is the
subject and refers here neither to Yahweh's presence (*cf*. Ezk.
ch. 8) nor to Baal's, in whose false promises Israel gloried (*cf*.
on 4:7), but to Ephraim's progeny, all hope of which will *fly
away* like a frightened *bird* (*cf*. Pr. 23:4–5). The three compact
phrases – *no* (literally 'from' which can also mean 'without')
birth, no pregnancy (lit. 'womb'), *no conception* – define what is
meant by the disappearance of *glory*. They run in inverse
order to the facts of life. So sterile, so fruitless, is Ephraim's
future that none of the steps necessary for national survival
will occur – not birth, not even pregnancy, no, not even
conception. The chain-like argument of what sounds like a
curse (*cf*. on 8:7, where the argument and the point are very
similar) is capped by the further announcement that if any
babies do slip through the net and Ephraimites (note switch to
plural verb to include all individual families) try to raise them,
God will see to it that *none* (lit. 'without a human being'; *cf*. Is.
6:11) will survive (v. 12; *cf*. v. 16 where Yahweh's intervention
is made even more plain). The *bird* simile may connect verses
11–12 with verse 10, since birds are among the great enemies
of fruit crops and can ruin the productivity of both vine and
fig tree.

To seal this threat, God adds a brief *woe* (*cf*. on 7:13; Am.
5:18; 6:1) which contains no mention of the crime – verse 10
has taken care of that – but announces the grief in store for
Israel, as God withdraws his love and grace by *departing from
them*. The threat to be active in depriving them of children

165

(v. 12a) and to withdraw (MT root *šwr*, 'to depart'; *cf.* Song 4:8, where *šwr* means 'to descend') from them are one and the same act. It is Yahweh's vital presence that makes possible the cycles of life; for him to withdraw is a sentence of death.

13–14. The picture of Ephraim's annihilation by the loss of their children is amplified in these verses. Most commentators and translations read the first line of verse 13 in one of four ways. Some follow the LXX and its imagery of the hunt: 'Ephraim, as I have seen, has made his sons a hunter's prey' (Mays, p. 131; *cf.* Wolff, p. 160; NEB; JB); the reference is an allusion to the risks of war against the Assyrians during the Syro-Ephraimite conflict. That death-dealing folly will be compounded by the further *slaughter* encountered in judgment (v. 13b). Others read the troublesome Hebrew word *lᵉṣôr* as the Phoenician city Tyre: 'Ephraim, as I have seen, is planted in a pleasant meadow like Tyre' (NASB; *cf.* Vulg.; NIV); the emphasis then is on the contrast between what Ephraim has been (*cf.* v. 10) and what he will become, as his *sons* are slaughtered. Some ancient readings like Theodotion and the Akhmimic (Coptic) speak of Ephraim as planted on a *rock* (Heb. *lswr*) and thus coin another image of barrenness, *i.e.* stony, unproductive soil (*cf.* Wolff, pp. 160–61). As good a solution as any is Jeremias' rendering (p. 119) based on suggestions of Hitzig and Rudolph to read the *lᵉṣôr* as 'a *palm tree* (Arabic and late Heb. *ṣawr*) planted in a meadow'; this would be a symbol of God's past care and oversight of Ephraim and set up the bold contrast with the *slaughter* (lit. the 'slayer', *i.e.* the Assyrian army) that awaits them.

Happily, all the words of verse 14 are clear. So is its genre – a prayer of the prophet to God. Even the suspense added by the delay in stating the object of the verb *give* is a well-understood poetic device (*cf.* Ps. 29:1). What is hard to know is the prophet's intention. Is he 'urging Yahweh to proceed with the extreme penalties' (Andersen, p. 544)? Perhaps. We have no hint elsewhere that Hosea shies away from the terrors of judgment. On the other hand, what he prays for is not the march of ravaging armies or the swinging of their swords but the cessation of birth and infant nurture. For this reason, many interpreters (Wolff, p. 166; Jeremias, p. 123; Mays, pp. 134–135) have read the prayer as *intercessory* after the fashion of Amos (7:2, 5) or Isaiah, who cried 'How long?', when the judgment was announced (6:11). They have read it as a tragic prayer for barrenness, stillbirth, or death in infancy as less grim alternatives than death by military *slaughter* (*cf.* Jb. 3:11–19; Lk. 23:29). Whichever tone we hear in the prayer, it is clear that Hosea does not back away from the need for judgment. And even his prayer is couched in language appropriate to a people who have looked not to God but to Baal for vital *wombs* and nourishing *breasts*.

15. God again speaks, reaching back into history (*cf.* Gibeah, 9:9; Baal-peor, 9:10) to show the continuity of Israel's present crimes with those of their fathers. *Gilgal* is targeted as the centre where *all their evil* (*cf.* on 7:2) was concentrated. Of the three monumental events associated with that town just north of Jericho (*cf.* on 4:15) – Joshua's entry to Canaan (Jos. 4:19–20), the operation of the calf-shrine by Israel's kings (*cf.* 4:15; Am. 4:4, 5:5), the inauguration (1 Sa. 11:15) and rejection of Saul's monarchy by Samuel (1 Sa. 15:12–26) – it is probably the last that Hosea has in mind. The context suggests that the monarchy is viewed as the heart of Israel's evils: kings established the Baal cult (1 Ki. 12:28–30); kings promulgated the foreign policy which resulted in the *slaughter* (v. 13); *princes*, the court officials (*cf.* 7:3, 5, 16; 8:4), are specifically mentioned as the leaders of rebellion (v. 15; note the pun in Heb. between *śārîm*, *princes*, and *sōrerîm*, *rebels*). This may be Hosea's sharpest blow against the monarchy; its very birth began to incur God's hatred.

The grounds for that hatred have so mounted with the *wickedness* ('evil'; Heb. *rōaʿ*) *of their deeds* (*cf.* 7:2 for *deeds*) that he is about to expel them (Heb. *grš*) from his *house*, *i.e.* from his land (*cf.* on 8:1; 9:4). There is a quiet irony about Yahweh's threat, *I will drive them out*, since it echoes the promises given to Israel at the Exodus and conquest (Ex. 23:29–30; 33:2; Jos. 24:18; Jdg. 2:3; 6:9) and reverses them. The Canaanites were driven out so that Israel could enjoy God's gift of the land; now the Israelites were to be driven out because of their assimilation to Canaanite practices. Another use of 'expel' or *drive out* may be salient here; it is found in the account of Abraham's expulsion of Hagar, his slave-wife and mother of his son Ishmael (Ge. 21:10). There may be a hint that Yahweh, an aggrieved husband, is banishing his faithless wife (*cf.* on 9:1–3). Yet another metaphor possibly implied in God's ejection of Israel from *my house* is that of an offended Host, who has offered impeccably generous hospitality to his guest only to have the guest prove ungrateful, abusive and disloyal (*cf.* Ps. 23:5–6 for a picture of Yahweh as Host).

The expulsion signals the withdrawal of God's love and the threat never to restore it. The relationship announced in the Exodus (Ho. 11:1) and continued even through the periods of apostasy in the land of Canaan (*cf.* 3:1) is to be broken off. The full weight of the threat expressed in Not-pitied's name (1:6) is now to descend on the nation. The reason suggested for the timing is the 'rebellion' (Heb. *srr*; *cf.* 'stubborn' in 5:16) of the *princes.* The whole cadre of political leaders whose task was to enforce the covenant and see that God's will was done had turned against him along with the priests (*cf.* 4:4–6; 5:1–7; 6:7–10). All hope for significant reformation had disappeared when the leaders now served in the ranks of Yahweh's foes.

16–17. God returns to the devastation of Ephraim's lineage (*cf.* vv. 11–13) in verse 16, while the prophet, who had voiced his frightful prayer for infertility (v. 14), adds in summary and conclusion his personal words of judgment. The horticultural language of verses 10 and 13 is brought to its fateful climax in the picture of *Ephraim* as a tree struck with an axe which has severed its *root* and thus made bearing *fruit* impossible. Again, God reverses the historic meaning of Ephraim's name which spoke of the fruitfulness (Heb. root *prh*) promised by God to Jacob (Ge. 48:3–6) and by Jacob to Joseph (Ge. 49:22). Hosea enjoyed punning on Ephraim's name both as a sign of judgment (*cf.* here and 8:9) and restoration (*cf.* 14:8).

God's role in the infanticide, plainly stated in verse 12, is described with even more intensity in his threat to kill any children who are brought to birth; 'treasured' ('cherished', NIV; 'precious', NASB) or *beloved* (RSV) is the same word used to described Israel's silver idols in 9:6. Having treasured what is worthless, they will now lose what is of matchless value. If the hints of Israel's practice of child-sacrifice, a custom well documented among ancient near-eastern religions, are correctly understood (*cf.* at 5:2), God's judgment may have been a gesture both to condemn it and to forestall it. The children belonged to him; he would go to any length to prevent their consecration to the gods of Canaan. As blood-chilling as this passage is, it serves, perhaps as forcefully as any in Scripture, to remind us of the zeal with which the Lord hates sin and the length to which he will go to purge his people of it. After all, he did not spare even his own Son (Rom. 8:32) when our sin had to be judged and our forgiveness achieved.

My God (v. 17) captures both the prophet's intimate relationship with Yahweh and the people's distance from Yahweh (*cf.* 8:2; 9:8). The verb 'reject' (*cast them off*) recalls the encounter with the priests in 4:6, but, more than that, it harks back to Samuel's denunciation of Saul:

> Because you have rejected the word of the Lord
> he has also rejected you from being king (1 Sa. 15:23).

The tie with Saul's story is strengthened when Hosea's reason for the rejection is stated: 'for they have not *hearkened* to him'. The root of Saul's sin was refusal to *hear* Yahweh's voice (Heb. *šm'* is used in Ho. 9:17 and 1 Sa. 15:22). When we remember that Saul's rejection took place at Gilgal (*cf.* on v. 15), we have further evidence for the interpretation given above that *all their evil* (v. 15) refers to the establishment of the monarchy and the abuses that flowed from it.

The final announcement (v. 17b) sums up the themes of rootlessness (v. 16) and exile (v. 3); Israel's lot was to become *wanderers among the nations*. They had already *wandered* from him (7:13) by seeking help from Egypt and Assyria; now wandering among the *nations* (*cf.* 7:8), whose pagan practices they had aped (9:1), was to become their way of life (*cf. wild ass wandering alone*; 8:9). From the time of Hosea's threat until the present the vast majority of Israel's daughters and sons have listed *Diaspora* as their address.

ii. A luxuriant vine (10:1–10). The picture of the vine (v. 1) extends the agricultural imagery (*cf.* above at 9:10–17) begun at 9:10: the grapes discovered in the wilderness have become the spreading, sprawling *vine* planted in Canaan. But the vaunted fertility of that land Israel has abused. What might have been only a temporary defection – their courtship with Baal at Peor (9:10) – has become a permanent obsession expressed in a fleet of *altars* and a legion of *pillars*.

The unholy alliance of monarchy and calf-cult will bring both to a shattering end. The passage rings with *announcements of judgment*, with only verses 1–2a and 4 spelling out the indictments that call for judgment. *Israel*, the whole Northern Kingdom, is the chief subject of the threat (vv. 1, 6, 8, 9), though *Samaria* is singled out for special attention as the capital city (vv. 5, 7) and *Ephraim*, the narrow mountainous confines around the capital not yet fully dominated by Assyria is mentioned once (v. 6). The prophet, not God, is the apparent speaker until verse 10, when Yahweh speaks directly. Israel is spoken *about* not *to* until verse 9, where he is openly addressed. The passage, whose beginning is clearly marked by the new metaphor describing Israel, may be divided into three sections:

Announcement of destruction of the shrines and the treacherous monarchy that sponsored them (verses 1– 4);

Announcement of devastation of Bethel and the deportation of its calf-idol (verses 5–8);

Announcement of judgment of Gibeah for its sins past and present (verses 9–10).

The decision as to whether to divide chapter 10 at verse 10, as we have, or at verse 8, as do numbers of commentators, is somewhat arbitrary. We have taken our clue from the key metaphors at 9:10; 10:1; 10:10; 11:1 and divided the text at those points. The argument for including the Gibeah section (10:9–10) with 10:11–15 is based largely on the switch to direct address of Israel by Yahweh in the first person. But there are no clear clues in the content itself to link verses 9–10 more tightly with verses 11–15 than with verses 1–8 (but see Stuart, p. 167, for the suggestion that the two threats of war [vv. 9–10, 14 –15] are an inclusio that tie vv.9–10 to 11–15). If our division is correct, 10:1–10 pivots on two geographical foci – *Bethel* (called Beth-aven or Aven; *cf.* on 4:15) and *Gibeah* (*cf.* on 9:9) – just as the prior section, 9:10–17, turned on the events at *Baal-peor* (9:10) and *Gilgal* (9:15). Hosea is keen on naming time and place in his documentation of Israel's history of sin. His conviction seems to be that Israel will understand neither the genesis of their rebellion nor its gravity unless they will see themselves as extensions of their past.

1– 4. The picture of abundant fruit contrasts sharply with the prophecy of barrenness with which the previous section closed (*cf.* 9:16). *Luxuriant* is probably the best rendering of the difficult Heb. *bôqēq*, which may be a participle cognate to

170

an Arabic root meaning to 'branch off' or 'spread'. The major difference is the meaning of *fruit*: in 9:16 it means physical progeny, the key to survival; in 10:1 it means material and agricultural prosperity. If we adopt Andersen's suggestions (p. 547) that *luxuriant* should be read as a verb, 'made luxuriant,' whose subject is Yahweh, and that Yahweh is also the subject of the following verb to be translated 'made it yield' (Heb. *šwh* usually means 'put' or 'place'; but no emendation of *šwh* has been agreed on [see KB, pp. 915, 954 for emendation to *śgh* as in Ps. 92:13; 73:12], and *śwh* [perhaps related to an Arabic word 'to ripen'; *cf.* Jeremias, p. 126] should probably be viewed as a synonym of the more familiar word for 'grow' or 'bear fruit', *'śh* [*cf.* 9:16]), then what we have is a picture of God and Israel utterly at cross-purposes. Yahweh's abundant grace is wantonly squandered (v. 1b):

> As God multiplied Israel's fruits
> Israel multiplied (*cf.* 8:11) [their pillars] at their altars.
> As Yahweh multiplied good to His land.
> Israel made the pillars better.[1]

The motif of *multiplication* (*cf.* at 4:7; 8:11) is expanded here in two ways: (1) God is featured as the one who took the initiative in multiplying Israel's blessings; Israel's response was to pervert them; and (2) a motif of *improvement* based on the Hebrew root *tb*, 'good' (*cf.* on 3:5) is used to embellish the passage by showing that, while Yahweh outdid himself in working for the betterment of the land, all of that excess bounty was poured by Israel into the adornment and decoration of the *pillars* whose purpose by Hosea's time had become largely pagan (*cf.* on 3:4).

The picture of Israel as God's *vine*, planted, cultivated and protected to bear the fruit of his righteousness and justice has been discussed at 9:10. It remains here to point out that Jesus' imagery of his relationship to the Father and to the church (Jn. ch. 15) assumes the background of passages like Hosea 10:1: the Father is the Grower; the church is the branches, the fruitful extension of Jesus' life and ministry, commissioned to

---

[1]This reading assumes Yahweh is also the subject of the infinitive construct *rôb* which serves as the verb and has two objects: *fruit* and, in the following line, *good*. It also assumes that the focus of Israel's activity was the building of *pillars* at the altars, not the building of the altars themselves (see Andersen, p. 551).

bear the fruit of *love*; Jesus is the vine, the renewed Israel through whom the purposes of God, violated in older Israel's failure to keep faith with their calling, are totally fulfilled.

In verse 2 Hosea adds the word *false* (Heb. *ḥlq*) to his inventory of terms for Israel's treachery and deceit (4:2; 5:7; 6:7; 7:1,13,16; 10:13; 12:1). The literal force is 'slick', 'smooth', 'slippery', and its meaning is illustrated in the picture of the psalmist's treacherous comrade whose 'speech was *smoother* than butter, yet war was in his heart' (Ps. 55:21). For *heart*, see at 4:11. The *false heart*, whose workings will be amplified in verse 4, underscores the depths of the sin – not accidental but premeditated. And what follows is God's verdict: *now* (*i.e.* 'consequently'; *cf.* on 5:7; 8:13) *they must bear their guilt* (*cf.* on 4:15; 5:15; 13:1, 16). God's name is rightly supplied by most translations as the subject of the verbs in verse 2b, because the pronoun *he* (*hû'* in Heb.) is virtually a proper name for deity, used in later Jewish literature as one substitute for the inexpressible divine name (*cf.* Jacob, p. 74, for documentation in the Qumran literature). *Break down* is often used in cultic contexts for the breaking of animals' necks (Ex. 13:13; 34:20; Dt. 21:4, 6; Is. 66:3). Perhaps the word implies that the horns or other decorative items are snapped off the *altars* in judgment (*cf.* Wolff, p. 174; *cf.* also on Am. 3:14). The synonym *destroy* is a favourite of Hosea's (*cf.* 7:13; 9:6; 10:14). Neither the pattern of multiplication nor improvement (*cf.* on v. 1) could spare the cultic paraphernalia once God's verdict was rendered.

For now (Heb. *kî 'attâ*) connects verse 3 with verses 1–2: 'In the light of this fearsome destruction of the cultic equipment (which will be part of the Assyrians' final assault on Samaria; *cf.* verses 5–8), *they will say, "We have no* [longer any] *king."*' The king is dead, in effect, as helpless as any other prisoner of war. And there is no use saying, 'Long live the new king' because without God's help he too would be powerless. And God's help is available only to those who *fear* – reverence, trust, obey – him. Israel knows himself to be disqualified to meet this condition and is left able only to utter the rhetorical question whose single answer is 'nothing!' This is Hosea's only use of this most common word for *fear* (Heb. *yr'*) but the same thought – in a positive context of return to Yahweh and a truly helpful king – is found in 3:5. This interpretation presupposes that verse 3 anticipates Israel's devastation at the collapse of Samaria, not their situation during Hosea's speeches when a king yet sat in Samaria's palace. Andersen's reading (p. 553) of *king* as '(divine) king' and therefore synonymous with Yahweh seems to introduce a complexity to the context beyond what is warranted. It also deprives us of the possible clue to future repentance and return that may be found in Israel's acknowledgment that without God's blessing their kings were impotent (*cf.* 8:4).

The *false heart* of verse 2 is further described in verse 4 as evidence for the absence of fear of Yahweh among the Israelites. Any pretence to loyalty is hollow talk; they swear to be faithful to the *covenant* with fingers crossed (*cf.* 6:7; 8:1; for the formula 'cutting a covenant' used here, *cf.* on 2:18) in *empty oaths* (*cf.* on 4:2 for such meaningless swearing). This interpretation assumes that verse 4 is *not* the answer to the rhetorical question in verse 3 but describes the deceitful behaviour of the nation, or what is left of it. The subject is *'they'* of the people not *'he'* of the king (*cf.* Mays, p. 140; Jeremias p. 129, for the contrary view). *Covenant* here is not primarily the covenant with Yahweh (*cf.* 6:7; 8:1) but a pact or treaty, either between king and people (so Mays, p. 140; Wolff, p. 175; *cf.* 2 Sa. 3:21; 5:3), or between the people and their alleged allies (*cf.* 12:1). In either case a violation of God's covenant may be implied because the covenant between king and people compromised Yahweh's role in the theocracy, while the international treaties were ratified by oaths to false gods. The result of such verbal duplicity is that the whole pattern of regulating the rights of the citizenry (*mišpāṭ* here as in 2:19, must mean 'justice' rather than 'judgment' *cf.* Wolff, p. 170; Jeremias, p. 126; Mays, p. 138) has gone awry and can no more nourish the people in righteousness than could *poisonous weeds* springing up (Heb. *prḥ* is used negatively here, perhaps to prepare for the positive contrast when Yahweh sings his love song in 14:5, 7; *cf.* Song 6:11; 7:13) in the *furrows of the fields* that have been ploughed to plant grain (*cf.* 12:11 for Hosea's other use of *furrows of the field*). Hosea's language on justice turned to poison may reflect Amos' (*cf.* 6:12).

5–8. The centre of attention here is on the deportation to *Assyria* of Bethel's calf-god. King gone, calf gone, shrines in rubble, the people are bereft of hope and purpose. Their suicidal cries (v. 8) echo through the *hills* and *mountains* where once rang the sighs and shrieks of their sexual orgies,

(4:11–14), the pleas of their masochistic magic (7:14), the hymns of their misplaced gratitude (2:8).

In coping with the difficulties in the Hebrew text of verse 5, it seems best to combine a number of scholarly suggestions which will make sense of the text with minimal emendations: (1) the first main verb is plural and should have as its subject the people as a whole, who were the *they* of *they utter* in verse 4; with Andersen (p. 555) we may link it to a root 'to stir up' (Heb. *gwr* II in BDB, p. 158, which cites uses, *e.g.* in Is. 54:15 and Ps. 56:7; *cf.* also *grh* in Pr. 15:18; 28:25; 29:22) and translate it 'they were alarmed' or 'excited'; (2) the objects of the verb are found before and after it and refer to the same thing – the *calf*, named first in what is probably a 'plural of majesty', employed by the people to show veneration for deity (another spelling would make it an abstract noun, *'eḡlût*, literally 'calf-stuff'; *cf.* Jeremias, p. 127), and then the *Inhabitant of Samaria*, a mock-honorific title for the idol, whose permanent residence is in immediate jeopardy of change; (3) the verb *shall mourn* has two subjects, *its people* (*i.e.* Beth-aven's) and the *idol-priests* (Heb. *kᵉmārîm*; *cf.* 2 Ki. 23:5; Zp. 1:4), whose livelihood and identity are at stake in the deportation; (4) these two groups are also the subject of the verb *yāḡîlû*, which here means not 'rejoice' (unless the intent is bitingly sarcastic) but 'be in distress' (*cf.* Andersen, pp. 556–567, for an account of the polarity of the word, which describes gyrating dancing motions which may interpret either joy or pain; *cf.* Ps. 2:11; for Hosea's positive use of *gyl*, see 9:1); (5) *its glory* must refer to Beth-aven's calf, *glory* being used to describe its worshipper's esteem (*cf.* on 4:7); and (6) the verb 'has gone into exile' (RSV, *has departed*) prepares us for the literal description of the calf's removal in verse 6; this is the only time Hosea uses the standard verb *glh* to describe the pending dislocation.

The resultant translation reads like this:

For the calf of Beth-aven they are in turmoil, for the Dweller of Samaria.
Indeed, its [Beth-aven's] people mourned over it, and its idol-priests over it.
They were distressed over its [Beth-aven's] Glory, for it [the Glory] has gone into exile away from it [Beth-aven].

The reasons for Israel's dismay are described more fully in

verse 6. The place of exile is pin-pointed as *Assyria* (*cf.* 5:13; 7:11; 8:9; 9:3); the purpose of the deportation is stated as a 'gift' (*i.e. tribute*; *cf. oil* as tribute to Egypt in 12:1) to the *great king*, *i.e.* the king of Assyria (see on 5:13), who would be identified as Shalmaneser V at the time of the assault on Samaria and as Sargon II at the ultimate collapse (*cf.* 2 Ki. 17:3–6). The grammar of the first line of verse 6 is a bit awkward. *It*, *i.e.* the idol, is thrust into prominence at the beginning in a form that marks it as direct object. Yet the verb *shall be carried* is passive and hence would not ordinarily take an object. The syntax, strange as it is, is probably intentional. The calf-idol is highlighted for what it is – a thing, an object, a detestable artifact (*cf.* 8:5–6). It has to be carried. What kind of deity is that? The contrast between the passive 'itness' of the idol and the active personhood of God (*cf.* the emphatic *he* as proper name in v. 2) has been drawn in bold colours.

The result of all this is the unbridled *shame* of the whole Northern Kingdom – both *Ephraim* and *Israel*. As Hosea has more than once reminded them, the calf-god has no value beyond the material wealth of which it was fabricated (2:8; 8:5–6; 9:6). In fact, its gold overlay has come to mean nothing to Israel, since they have to give that away, and Hosea rightly brands the calf a 'wooden' *idol*. This translation (*cf.* NIV) suits the context better than the more usual 'plan' or 'advice' (Heb. *'ēṣâ*) and can be justified from the feminine form of the word 'tree' or 'wood' that appears in Jeremiah 6:6. No matter how much the calf-idol glistened, its commonness was exposed when it stood mute and helpless as the Assyrians systematically dismantled Israel. Israel's glory had become her shame (4:7).

Samaria in (v. 7) seems to be a hanging nominative: 'as for Samaria, her king (*i.e.* not the temporal ruler but the calf-deity, called the *Inhabitant of Samaria* in v. 5) is being destroyed' (the verbal form is a passive participle of Heb. *dmh*; *cf.* on 4:5–6). The destruction wrought by the calf-idol (4:5–6) is being paid back in full. The helplessness, the insignificance of the wooden calf (v. 6) is pictured in the simile of the twig or wood-chip (Heb. *qeṣep̄* is a masculine form of the feminine word attested in Joel 1:7) bobbing out of control *on the face of the waters*, perhaps a reference to the churning unpredictable movements of history whose billowing waves would drown Israel completely.

Not only the calf but its revered habitat, Bethel, mocked by the prophets as *Beth-aven* or *Aven* (*cf.* 4:15; Am. 5:5), will be *destroyed* (v. 8). This is Hosea's only use of one of the Old Testament's strongest words for destruction, *šmd*, which was a favourite of Amos', always with Yahweh as subject (2:9; 9:8). Bethel is the locale of the devastation, but the precise object is the *high places* (Heb. *bāmôt; cf.* Am. 4:13; 7:9), the hill-top shrines which were the centres of the corrupt cult. So central were they that Hosea branded them bluntly *the sin of Israel*, the places that epitomized how far Israel had missed the target of divine truth (Heb. *ḥṭ'; cf.* on 4:7; 8:11; 13:2, 12) in its sexual, idolatrous lust for Baal. *Sin* here also furnishes a link to the Gibeah passage in verses 9–10. Bethel and Gibeah, ancient towns with many memories, are to be remembered in the end for their sin. The judgment on the shrines is capped with a curse. *Thorn and thistle* are elsewhere found as a pair only in Genesis 3:18, where they are part of the curse on the ground called for by Adam's and Eve's disobedience. Israel's fall at Bethel, like Adam's in Eden, is to be met by the invasion of enemy growth which inhibits the use of the shrine and symbolizes the divine displeasure. *Their altars* are again singled out as the precise prey of the thorny aggressors (*cf.* 4:19; 8:11; 10:1–2; *cf.* also the incursion of nettles and thorns that possess the tent-shelters used at the shrines in 9:6).

The call to the *mountains* and *hills* (*cf.* 4:11–14) is a death-wish, prompted by the shame of Israel and Ephraim (v. 6), by the collapse of their way of life, and by their fear of slow death by starvation. The grim terror foreshadows the sixth seal of the apocalypse (Rev. 6:15–16), where the captains of the earth take refuge in caves and beg the mountains and rocks to bring sudden death, lest they have to face further the unbearable wrath of the Lamb (*cf.* Lk. 23:30).

9–10. The lesson from history and geography switches its attention from Bethel to *Gibeah* (*cf.* on 9:9) and focuses again on its *days, i.e.* the notorious events in its past that were preserved in the records of Judges chapters 19–21. Israel is addressed in the second person and indicted for a pattern of sin that has stretched through four centuries. The accusation, *you have sinned*, together with the name *Gibeah* itself which means 'hill', serves to connect verse 9 to verse 8, where Bethel is called *the sin of Israel* and the *hills* are summoned to fall on the Israelites.

176

Only the first four words of verse 9 are addressed to Israel. The amplification of the indictment and its corresponding threat are in the third person as though Hosea was speaking to another audience, perhaps his disciples, about Israel.[1] *There they have continued* (or 'remained', lit. 'stood') seems to express the persistence of Israel's rebellion against the covenant: 'Things are still the same' (JB). The event of the past to which Hosea referred is the carnage of the civil war that nearly wiped out Benjamin's tribe when it sheltered the lewd men who had ravaged the Levite's concubine. The fact that nothing had changed right up to Hosea's day was proved by Gibeah's role in the conflict between Judah and Ephraim in the Syro-Ephraimite war (see at 5:8 – 7:16) – a conflict in which Bethel (*cf.* 10:5–8), Gibeah and Benjamin are all addressed in warnings (along with Ramah; 5:8). Did their hostility trigger Judah's northward drive? The sinful military action is, at its heart, disloyalty to the covenant and to the God-ordained unity of the people. The threat (verse 9b) pinpoints the place as *Gibeah* and the means as *war*. What the people of Gibeah had sparked at least twice in their long history will happen to them again: 'War will surely overtake them'. This intensive reading is reached by emending the word *not* (Heb. *lō'*) to *lᵉ*, the asseverative particle which reinforces a verb and gives the sense of 'surely' or 'indeed' (*cf.* Andersen, p. 565; Wolff, p. 178).

The phrase, the *wayward people* (lit. 'the sons of wickedness'), which ends verse 9 in MT, may perhaps be connected to verse 10 (*cf.* NEB; RSV;) as the target of God's coming ('come' is supported in the LXX and can also be defended from the Heb. which is sometimes read 'when I please'; *cf.* NIV) but can also be handled as part of verse 9b either by reading the preposition *'al* as 'because of', (making the phrase give the reason for the military takeover) or as 'against' (in which case the phrase loosely explains *them*, the object of *overtake*). *Wickedness* seems to be an eccentric spelling of a well-known Hebrew-Aramaic word (*'alwâ* for *'awlâ*, *cf.* v. 13; 2 Sa. 3:34; 7:10). 'Sons of (*i.e.* 'those characterized by', a standard Heb. idiom) wickedness' is an apt phrase for the criminals of Gibeah, whom Judges calls

---

[1] M. Gilbert and S. Pisano, *Bib*, 61, 1980, pp. 343–356, have cited a number of prophetic passages, including Ho. 10:9–10; Am. 9:7–8; Mi. 3:1–4 where the indictment is couched in second person terms and past tense, while the sentence is pronounced in third person terms and future tense.

'sons of Belial' (*base fellows*, RSV; 19:22; 20:13). Using strong language about Israel's past and present is a hallmark of Hosea in this section of the book. Each geographical site carries its own damning label:

> Baal-peor: Israel became *detestable* (9:10);
> Gilgal: *their every evil* is there (9:15);
> Bethel: the *sin* of Israel (10:8);
> Gibeah: home of the sons of *wickedness* (10:9).

God takes the podium in verse 10 as the threat of punishment continues. Two of the four main verbs begin with 'I', though none of them is without textual questions. The first verb is probably to be read either, 'I came' or 'when I come' (if the former, the root is *bw'*, the familiar verb for 'enter'; if the latter, the root is *'th*, a Heb.-Aram. root for 'come' to which the preposition *b* has been attached to signify the temporal clause). The spelling of the next verb needs to be changed slightly to give the meaning 'then I shall *chasten* them' (*cf.* on 5:2; 7:12). The next clause makes clear that God will use external means – *nations* (*cf.* 9:1, 17) – as part of the chastening, the implication being that he is the One who brings about the *gathering*. The gathering of the nations implies the gathering of Israel, as Hosea direly had prophesied (8:10; 9:6). The final verb restates the idea of chastening and is probably a passive infinitive, 'When they are chastened' (once more the verb needs correcting from a form that looks like it means to *bind*, Heb. *'sr*, to one that means 'chasten' or 'discipline', Heb. *ysr*). The verse may be read as follows:

> When I come, then I shall chasten them.
> And peoples will be gathered against them,
>> when they are chastened for their two iniquities.

The *double iniquity* (for root *'āwôn*, *cf.* on 4:8) may have a general reference like Jeremiah's 'two evils' – forsaking Yahweh and turning to idols (2:13). More likely, the words sum up the accusation of verse 9 which seemed to point to Gibeah's past crime of harbouring criminals and provoking civil war, and her more recent one of fostering ill-will and bloodshed in the Syro-Ephraimite clash. Like the ending of the previous section (9:17), this passage gives the *nations* a prominent place.

There they were the context for Israel's homeless wandering; here they are the agents of God's chastisement. Israel's bird-like hopping from one potential ally to the other ends in the net of captivity, a net held not only by Assyria's Great King (*cf.* 10:6) but by God himself (*cf.* 7:12). Or, to return to the metaphor that began this passage in 10:1, the nations led by Assyria are the grape harvesters, hired by God to strip the luxuriant vine of everything in which it prided itself and put to its persistent pagan purposes.

iii. A trained heifer (10:11–15). The metaphors continue but with a shift from vegetable (9:10; 10:1) to animal, and with somewhat different emphases: (1) the picture of God's elective grace is followed not by recounting Israel's abuse of his grace (*cf.* 9:10 – Baal-peor; 10:1 – altars and pillars) but by listing the divine demands on the whole people – north and south – to serve God's purposes at whatever cost; (2) the specified crime does not centre in the cult but in the royal policy that trusted military might, not God's power, for protection (v. 13); and (3) the chief geographical reference to an historical event – Beth-arbel – alludes not to Israel's acts of sinfulness but to a vicious episode of military slaughter (v. 14) which will recur when Israel is judged. The close ties between verses 11–15 and the preceding paragraph (vv. 1–10) are noteworthy; the *and*, with which verse 11 begins, signals a connection as does the use of 'calf' (*heifer*, v. 11) to describe an Ephraim who was about to be deprived of his calf-idol (v. 5); *Bethel* (v. 15; *cf.* vv. 5, 8) comes back into view as a centre of prophetic attention which had temporarily looked at Gibeah (vv. 9–10); the shadow of *war* as the means of judgment hangs over both sections (v. 14; *cf.* v. 9); a sign of the thoroughness of that judgment is the loss of Israel's *king* (v. 15; *cf.* v. 3).

The *trained heifer* is the most extended of the metaphors in Hosea. The figure of a work-animal involved in the various tasks of agriculture drives home the elective purposes of God. Israel was chosen to serve him. That service is described in agrarian terms: sowing, ploughing, harrowing, reaping, (vv. 11–13). The repeated pattern of these verbs, in varying combinations, depicts God's discipline of the people (v. 11b), his expectations of them (v. 12), and their failure to meet those expectations (v. 13). The speaker throughout the passage may well be Yahweh, though we can be sure only at verse

11. Except for verse 11, the people are addressed as *you*, whether in the singular as a collective entity (vv. 13b–14) or the plural with the individual members in mind (vv. 12–13a, 15). The general movement of the passage looks like this:

> Metaphor of past blessings (v. 11a);
> Threat of necessary discipline (v. 11b);
> Admonitions to responsibilities of their calling (v. 12a);
> Motivation to obedience (v. 12b);
> Indictment for disobedience (v. 13);
> Announcement of judgment with historical illustration (v. 14);
> Summary announcement-indictment (v. 15).

Ephraim (v. 11) must stand for the entire Northern Kingdom, since its reference is not to the present truncated territory around Samaria but to the past privileges of the northern tribes. It stands, then, for Israel, not in contrast to it as it does in other Hosean passages (*cf.* on 5:3, 5). *Trained* appears in contrast to *stubborn* in 4:15 and means tractable, responsive, useful (*cf.* its opposite in Je. 31:18, where Ephraim bemoans its lot as an 'untrained calf' that had to be chastened). The pet calf was given chores, especially the opportunity to *thresh*, either by treading the grain and loosening the chaff by the impact of the hooves or by drawing over the grain a sledge of slate fitted with shards of iron (*cf.* Is. 28:28; Am. 1:3). In either case, the animal enjoyed the opportunity to eat while working (Dt. 25:4; 1 Cor 9:9). Such work was far from onerous; the heifer's strong, well-proportioned (Heb. *ṭûb*, lit. 'good' or 'beautiful'; *cf.* on 3:5) *neck I* (the pronoun is emphatic, a reminder of divine grace), *spared* (*cf.* on Am. 7:8 where the same Heb. word, *'br*, is used: lit. 'passed by') the chafing rub of a rough yoke. This combination of *trained* animal and easy pull may have contributed to the imagery used by Jesus in Matthew 11:28–30.

All that was in the past now. The pattern has changed. God promises to 'harness' (*i.e.* to make ready for riding or pulling) Ephraim, probably fitting her with a yoke, as the two other verbs *plough* (with an oak handle and where possible an iron ploughshare) and *harrow* (an instrument of unknown composition, perhaps a sledge or log with iron teeth to break down the ground further after ploughing, or to make sure the seed is well-covered, *cf.* Is. 28:24) imply. The three proper names, *Ephraim* (Northern Kingdom), *Judah* (Southern Kingdom), and *Jacob* (the entire nation), are to be related to all three verbs. A specific agricultural task is given to each only for purposes of poetic parallelism. The gist of the whole threat is that from now on, since the nation has failed to appreciate God's benefactions and to put them to their appointed purposes, its lot – whether the northern part, the southern, or the combined peoples – will become much more harsh. Ploughing and harrowing were difficult tasks, thanks to the shallow, rocky, wind-swept soil of Palestine and the primitive character of the tools. Furthermore, nothing is said about harvesting or eating.

The interpretation of the agricultural language unfolds in verses 12–13. The admonition (v. 12), with its motivation clause promising the blessing of salvation as the result of obedience, seems to represent the *divine expectation* and could actually be a quotation of proverb-like instruction (*cf.* Pr. 11:18 and its antithesis, Pr. 22:8). The indictment (v. 13a) describes the *human reality*: the entire agricultural process from ploughing to eating has gone sour, presumably because the sowing was done with the wrong seed. To grasp the relationship between the admonition and the indictment we need to supply introductory rubrics like 'you know well the divine requirement' before verse 12 and 'compare that standard with your present conduct' before verse 13a. The differences in syntax and vocabulary between the divine imperatives (v. 12) and their faulty execution (v. 13a) should be noted: the nouns *righteousness* (*cf.* on 2:19) and *steadfast love* (*cf.* on 2:19) are modified by prepositions – 'according to' and 'in accordance with' in Hebrew (*cf.* NEB; NASB) and are not direct objects of the verbs to *sow* and *reap* (on this pair, *cf.* 8:7) but describe the manner in which true sowing and reaping take place. In contrast, *iniquity* (Heb. *reša'* is a standard word for violent, rebellious, wickedness; it is used only here in Hosea; *cf.* Pr. 4:17; 10:2; 12:3; Je. 14:20; Mi. 6:10–11), *injustice* (Heb. *'alwâ* also conveys a sense of violence in the doing of wrong; *cf.* the alternate spelling in 10:9; *cf.* also 2 Sa. 3:34; 7:10; Jb 6:29; 11:14; 15:16; 22:23; 24:20; Ps. 37:1; Mi. 3:10), and *fruit of lies* (Heb. *kāḥaš* connotes misunderstanding of God's will and ways that leads to a misinterpretation of it to the people; *cf.* 7:3; 11:12; Na. 3:1) are direct objects of their

181

respective verbs. Furthermore, verse 13 says nothing about sowing, the irreplaceable act if there is to be a harvest.

The upshot of these differences is an interpretation that can be paraphrased like this: 'You know now what God taught you – invest your lives (*sow*) in keeping with your relationship to God and all its implications (*righteousness*) and the result (*reap*) will be a corresponding measure of his *steadfast* (covenant) *love*. None of this is easy, and for it to happen you will have to change your patterns and be open to God's new ways (*break up your fallow ground*; Heb. *nîr*, untilled soil; *cf.* Je. 4:3); (Mt. 6:33 could be a free rendering of Ho. 10:12). But instead of all this, you have grooved (*ploughed*) into your way of life the seeds of *iniquity* (perhaps a reference to the ancient practice of sowing the land then ploughing the seed under) and accordingly have garnered a crop (*reaped*) of *injustice* and fed yourselves (*eaten*) and all your kindred on a diet of misunderstanding and misinterpretation of who God is and what he wants (*fruit of lies*)'.

Lest all of this look legalistic, the motivation of verse 12b needs noting. All times are ripe to *seek* (*cf.* 3:5; 5:6) Yahweh, since he alone – not Baal nor any other Canaanite deity – can bless Israel's endeavours and turn them into experiences of salvation (*cf.* Joel 2:23–24 for *rain salvation* or *righteousness*). The concept of salvation is near kin to *šālôm*, 'peace', 'complete well-being', and means that Yahweh will provide for the total needs of his people. The God-assigned tasks of sowing, reaping and harrowing were within their capability. The one thing they could not do for themselves and could not live without was the *rain* in the right season. Hosea would have understood Paul's conclusion: 'but God gave the growth' (1 Cor. 3:6), a New Testament example of an extended agricultural metaphor applied to the life and mission of God's people.[1]

The wicked harvest (of v. 13a) seems to be explained more

[1] Wolff's interpretation (pp. 180, 186, reads 'knowledge' for *time* in v. 12b (Heb. *da'at* [*cf.* 4:1, 6; 6:6] for *wᵉʻēt*) and renders the line, 'break up the fallow ground of *knowledge* and seek Yahweh', taking a cue from the LXX (*gnōseōs*) and seeking a parallel noun of covenant loyalty to match *righteousness* and *covenant love*. The LXX misunderstood 'till' and 'fallow ground' (confusing Heb. *nîr* with *nûr*, 'light') and may therefore have grasped at a way of rendering *wᵉʻēt*. More importantly, Jeremiah's (4:3) echo of Ho. 10:12 does not have an accompanying noun like *knowledge*; *cf.* Jeremias, p. 132, n. 7.

literally in verse 13b. The violent breach of the peoples' welfare and the lying deception that accompanied it (v. 13a) were the false trust, the misguided sense of security (*cf.* Am. 6:1 for Heb. *bṭḥ*), which Israel's leaders placed in their own 'power' (no need to emend to *chariots* with LXX; RSV; NEB; JB; if we read Heb. *drk* not as 'way' but as 'dominion', 'authority', 'power' as is the case in Ugaritic; *cf.* Andersen, p. 569) and in the *multitude* (another instance of the Heb. root *rb* as part of the motif of multiplication; *cf.* on 4:7; 8:11; 10:1) of their 'crack soldiers' (Heb. *gibbôr* powerful man, *warrior*; *cf.* Joel 2:7; 3:10; Am. 2:14, 16). Jeremiah (9:23–24 [Heb. vv. 22–23]) caught the danger of the self-reliance, symbolized in soldiers and fortifications, and denounced it in words that ring with overtones of Hosea's book: 'let not the mighty man (*gibbôr*) glory in his might . . . but let him who glories glory in this, that he understands and knows me that I am Yahweh, who practise steadfast love (*ḥesed*; *cf.* Ho. 10:12), justice (*mišpāṭ*; *cf.* Ho. 10:4) and righteousness (*ṣᵉdāqâ*; *cf.* Ho. 10:12) in the earth.' Preparation for warfare was the seed they ploughed into their sod (v. 13); the *tumult of war*, like the sound of the rush of mighty water (*cf.* Is. 17:12–13), was the crop they would reap (v. 14). All their hope of defence against their enemies – especially the *fortresses* (or fortified cities, *cf.* 8:14; Am. 1:3 – 2:5; 6:8) – would be vanquished (for *šdd, destroy, cf.* 7:13; 10:2).

The stern picture of destruction is made even more vivid by an historical illustration of a battle so savage that it left the bodies of *mothers* lying *in pieces* (*cf.* Ps. 137:9; Ho. 13:16) beside those of *their children* (v. 14c–d). The site is identified as *Beth-arbel*, connected since antiquity with Arbela (modern Irbid), located in Jordan, thirty-two kilometres northwest of Amman. *Shalman* does not seem to be Shalmaneser, whose name the Old Testament spells out in full (*cf.* 2 Ki. 17:3; 18:9). On the list of those who paid tribute to Tiglath-pileser III is a Moabite king, Salamanu, who may be a better candidate. Amos' record of horror stories that occurred in Gilead (*cf.* 1:3, 13) documents the tragic history of that region.

The events of the Syro-Ephraimite war (*cf.* on 5:8 – 7:16) in 733 BC showed how believable Hosea's prediction was. The blind arrogance that led Pekah to think that a western coalition, perhaps with Egypt's help, could withstand Assyrian assault was exposed as sheer folly. And the final attacks by

Shalmaneser V and Sargon II, toppling Hoshea, razing Samaria, were God's grave Amen to Hosea's words. No wonder military solutions had to be banned from the landscape of future salvation: 'I will break ... *war* (and its weapons) from the land' (2:18); 'upon the *horse* (the beast of military conflict, whether in chariotry or cavalry) we will not ride' (14:3).

Thus (Heb. *kākâ*; v. 15) makes clear the comparison ('just so', 'exactly like this') between the fate of Bethel and Beth-arbel. There is no need to emend 'Bethel' to *house of Israel*; (*cf.* RSV; JB). The attention by way of reprise returns to the cultic-centre (vv. 5–8) and coins a pun – Beth-arbel/Bethel – along the way. *Thus* also triggers the summary statement of judgment with which the sections in 8:1 – 10:15 close (8:14; 9:9, 17; 10:10). The verb should have God as implied subject and should be read as a prophetic perfect, used to describe the future but in such a way as to remove all contingency: 'He shall do to you.' Whether *Bethel* (RSV mg.) is the site of the judgment (NASB; *cf.* Andersen, p. 561) or the addressee of the threat (NEB; NIV), we cannot tell from the Hebrew text. What is clear, since it is reinforced by a repetition of the word, is how outrageous was the *wickedness* (lit. 'the evil of your evil') which God was punishing. Israel's calling was unfulfilled not by default but by deliberate and violent *wickedness* (Heb. *rā'â*; *cf.* 7:1, 2, 3; 9:15). This word, the most general, all-embracing Hebrew term for sin serves to wrap chapters 7–10 into a package which catalogues Israel's record of rebellion. In fact, Hosea's language reads like a thesaurus of words for sinful acts in this section of agricultural images: *evil*, 9:15; 10:15; *guilt*, 10:2; *sin*, 10:8–9; *waywardness*, 10:9; *iniquity*, 10:10; *wickedness*, 10:13; *injustice*, 10:13; *lies*, 10:13.

'At dawn' (no need to emend to *in the storm*; *cf.* RSV; JB) indicates a moment at the very start of battle, when the troops, waiting for first light, took to the field. It predicts a short encounter. With the *king utterly cut off* (Heb. *nidmâ*; *cf.* 4:5–6; 10:7), the troops will not be able to hold out. *King* may be the calf-idol (*cf.* on v. 7) but is more likely the monarch whose loss was anticipated in verse 3. The intensity of the description of his death (the infinitive absolute underscores the force of the verb) matches the intensity of the description of Israel's evil. The correspondence of punishment to crime is proof of the thoroughness and fairness of divine justice.

iv. The beloved child (11:1–11). The chain of images whereby God reflects on his expectations and Israel's failure reaches its climax: (1) the figure of speech turns personal – not Yahweh the farmer, tending Israel as his grapes (9:10), vine (10:1), or heifer (10:11), but Yahweh the parent, grieving over Israel, the rebellious child; (2) the picture of divine grace is expanded (vv. 1, 3–4); (3) the divine complaint expressed in self-directed questions lays bare the intensity of covenant love in terms unsurpassed in the Old Testament (v. 8); (4) the up-shot of this whole review of history is that there is hope beyond judgment (a note not sounded in the preceding metaphors) – hope based on the unique nature of God, the Holy One (v. 9); and (5) the form of that hope is conveyed in a leonine simile that depicts a reversal of the Exile, with Yahweh's roar summoning Israel back to its own land like a pride of skittish cubs (vv. 10–11). This speech draws to a close the second major division of the book which began at 4:1. Its final words of hope (vv. 10–11) recall the promise of 3:5: 'Afterward the children of Israel shall return and seek Yahweh their God.' They also anticipate Israel's penitent return predicted in 14:3: 'Assyria shall not save us, we will not ride upon horses. . . . In thee the orphan finds mercy.' The book of Hosea is about judgment and hope, about hope beyond judgment, and the great speeches in chapters 4–11 explicate that message in all its terror and poignancy.

God is the chief speaker of verses 1–11 as he has been through most of chapters 4–11. Yet only in verses 8–9 does he address the people directly. The account of his gracious treatment of them in their past history (vv. 1, 3–4), the accusations of sin (vv. 2, 7), the announcements of judgment (vv. 5–7), and the promise of future salvation (vv. 10–11) – these treat Israel in the third person. Again we have a scene that looks like a legal trial of some sort (*cf.* 4:18): Yahweh is both prosecutor and judge; Israel is the defendant; and an unnamed audience, perhaps Hosea, seems to serve as witness and jury. God presents his case to him, *except* he directs the verdict, with considerable pathos, to the judged people, whom he has loved and whom he will one day restore (vv. 8–9).

Since the heart of Yahweh's accusation is that his *child* has turned from him (vv. 2, 7) despite the boundless care and love poured out on that *child* (vv. 1, 3–4), the legal background that helped to shape this scene may be found in Deuteronomy

21:18–21. The law provided for the parents of a 'stubborn and rebellious son' (for 'stubborn', Heb. *sôrēr*, *cf.* Ho. 4:16; 9:15; for 'rebellious', Heb. *mrh*, *cf.* Ho. 13:16 [Heb. v. 15]) to bring him for judgment before 'the elders of his city'. If their case against the lad is sustained, the punishment is death by stoning. A society which had no provision for reform schools or probation officers and depended for its civility on respect for parental authority was forced to drastic means to deal with its incorrigibles. As in the case of Israel's adultery, the penalty of stoning which should have been invoked by law (Dt. 22:22–24) was suspended, and reconciliation with discipline was the verdict instead (*cf.* Ho. 3:1–5). Covenant love overrode covenant law, and mercy beyond judgment was promised. In each offer of hope, the language of Hosea turns intensely personal and familial: God is a disciplining but forgiving Husband in 2:14–23 and 3:1–5; he is a healing and reconciling Lover in 14:1–8; he is an authoritative yet compassionately forbearing Parent in 11:1–11. Whatever metaphors may describe the Lord's care for Israel, when it comes to future restoration – both its form and its motive – only the personal language of the family is intimate enough to carry Hosea's message of God's love for his people.

There can be little doubt that Hosea's own suffering over the lot of Gomer and their children contributed to the unparalleled insight he gives us into the heart of Yahweh. Yet the entire text of Hosea says nothing about the prophet's inner life. The focus is entirely on the acts and deeds of the prophet, not on his emotional responses. The reason for this seems clear: Hosea's book is not about Hosea; it is about God. The prophet's life was the record through which came the word of God (*cf.* 1:1–2) to the people. That word was not primarily about human response to betrayal and suffering but about perverse human behaviour and about the divine response, in suffering, outrage and compassion, to such disloyalty.

1–4. The tone of nostalgia which accented the entire speech beginning at 9:10 – 'Like grapes in the wilderness I found Israel' and proceeding through chapter 10 – 'Israel was a luxuriant vine' (10:1) and 'Ephraim was a trained heifer' (10:11) – reached its climax here, with the recounting of the Exodus and the personal nature of the relationship established by it (*cf.* 2:14–15). *Child* (Heb. *na'ar*, 'lad', 'youth') suggests an immaturity akin to helplessness, the inability to bear the responsibilities of adulthood (*cf.* Isaac's vulnerability in Gn. 22:12; Samuel's need of nurture in 1 Sa. 1:24; David's lack of military skill or experience in 1 Sa. 17:33; Jeremiah's unfitness to serve as prophet in Je. 1:6). *My son*, in contrast, describes both the intimate relationship with God and the sense of purpose which that relationship was intended to bestow on Israel. The verse rings with grace not only in the nouns which describe Israel but in the verbs – *loved* (*cf.* on 3:1–2) and *called*, which here may mean to 'summon' but more likely echoes Hosea's familiar use of the verb for giving someone a name (*cf.* 1:4, 6, 9; 2:16): *'out of Egypt* (the emphasis is probably on the act of rescue rather than the timing, 'from [the days of] Egypt') *I called him* (object pronoun supplied from *loved him*) by the name *my son'* (*cf.* Ex. 4:22–23 for use of *son* before the Exodus and Je. 31:20 for its continuity after Hosea). All of this testifies to the special covenant relationship – like an adoption – which was sealed at the Exodus and Sinai (*cf.* 12:9; 13:4).

Despite the tendency to emend the beginning word of verse 2 to *I called*, in keeping with LXX (*cf.* RSV; NEB; JB; NIV; Wolff, p. 190; Mays; Nötscher, p. 31), the MT can be readily handled if we see in verse 2 a second reference to an incident like the seduction to Baal at Peor (*cf.* 9:10b). The back-to-back records of the Exodus and the wilderness apostasy (Nu. ch. 25) are in keeping with the pentateuchal tradition as well as with the literary technique of Hosea in 9:10 – 11:11, where the metaphor (or simile) of past blessing is countered with a picture of defection from Yahweh (9:10; 10:1; 10:11–13; 11:1–2). The verse should be paraphrased like this: 'They ('the daughters of Moab', Nu. 25:1–2; or the Canaanites in general) *called to them* (by name; construction is parallel to v. 1), *i.e.* to the Israelites (described here in plural, despite the singular of verse 1; *cf.* v. 3); as a consequence, they strayed away (Heb. *hlk*; literally, *went* or 'walked', *cf.* 2:5, 13; 7:11) *from me*.[1] God's point is that the pagan call proved stronger than his own, leading to a complete capitulation to the wiles of *the Baals* (*cf.* 2:13 for the *burning of incense*, and 4:13–14; 8:13 for the *sacrificing*). The imperfect tenses of the two verbs in verse 2b

---

[1]The reading 'from me' involves a new word division in which *mipp^enêhem* 'from them', a rendering hard to fit into this context, becomes *mipp^enay hem*, 'they (an emphatic subject) from my presence [strayed]'. For readings close to this, see NASB; Andersen, p. 574.

may point to the beginnings of a practice that had persisted in varying degrees of intensity to Hosea's time: 'To the Baals they began to offer sacrifices and to the hewn images (Heb. *pāsîl*; here only in Hosea; *cf.* Is. 42:8; Je. 8:19; Mi. 5:12) to burn incense.'

The *I* with which verse 3 begins is emphatic. It contrasts with the 'theys' of verse 2. The structure seems intentional: the account of apostasy is sandwiched between descriptions of care. The picture of Israel's immaturity (v. 1) is amplified by what is best taken as an extended picture of God's tender parenting (vv. 3–4). *Ephraim* here is probably synonymous with Israel (v. 1) and names the whole Northern Kingdom, not just the rump state that clung to semi-independence from Assyria after the invasion of Tiglath-pileser in 733 BC. Hosea is surely recalling past redemptive history not the present political agonies. The unusual verb form built on the word for 'foot' (Heb. *tirgaltî* from *reḡel*) is generally translated, 'I taught to walk' (RSV; NEB; JB; NASB; NIV; Wolff, p. 191; Mays, p. 150; Nötscher, p. 31) but could also mean 'I walked in front of', so as to guide and protect (*cf.* Andersen, p. 579); such a meaning could account for the Hebrew preposition *lᵉ* that connects the verb to *Ephraim*.

The second clause of verse 3 seems closely connected to the first; no 'and' is found in Hebrew. The versions almost uniformly have Yahweh taking Ephraim up in his arms (RSV; NEB; JB; NASB; Wolff, p. 191; Mays, p. 150). The more normal words for this would be to 'lift up' (Heb. *nś'*) or to 'gather up' (Heb. *qbṣ*) both of which are used in Isaiah 40:11. 'Take' (the form is unusual, perhaps an infinitive absolute, *qḥ*), a shortened form of *lqḥ*, 'take', 'seize', 'grasp', probably explains the way in which God guided Ephraim – 'holding them by his (Ephraim's) arms' to steady or protect them while they were walking. Again, singular and plural pronouns alternate awkwardly to our ears, but are not out of phase with what happens in Hosea. The last clause of verse 3 indicates how intransigent Israel had become. They consistently misconstrued God's intent to treat them in tender ways that would mend their hurts and thus display his love (for *heal*, Heb. *rp'*, *cf.* 5:13; 6:1; 7:1; for the connection between *love* and *healing*, see 14:4). *Know* here means to admit the truth that should have been obvious, to acknowledge the Lord's pure motives and irreplaceable grace (*cf.* on 2:8; 5:4) in the Exodus deliverance and wilderness providence.

The question raised by verse 4 is whether the metaphor changes from parent-child to trainer-animal (*cf.* 4:16; 10:11). The keys to the answer are the meanings of *cords* (Heb. *ḥablê*; *cf.* Am. 7:17; Is. 5:18), *bands* (Heb. *ʿᵃbōtōt*; *cf.* Ex. 28:14; Is. 5:18) and the word frequently translated *yoke* (Heb. *ʿōl*; *cf.* Dt. 21:3; Je. 27:8). If we begin with the last word, we find available a cluster of words for 'nursing infant', or 'toddler' that, due to a similarity of root (Heb. *ʿl*), may readily account for the intrusion of *yoke* (Heb. *ʿûl*, Is. 49:15; 65:20; Heb. *ʿᵃwîl*, Jb. 19:18; 21:11; Heb. *ʿōlēl*, 1 Sa. 15:3; Ho. 13:16 [Heb. 14:1]; Heb. *ʿōlāl*, Ps. 137:9; Je. 6:11; Joel 2:16). If we choose one, *e.g.* *ʿûl*, whose spelling is closest to *ʿōl*, we may derive a sense like this for the third and fourth clauses: 'And I became for them as persons who lift a toddler against their cheeks. And I reached out to him and gave [him food] to eat.' If this understanding of the passage is correct (*cf.* RSV; NEB; JB: Wolff, p. 191; Mays, p. 150; Nötscher, p. 31), the two beginning clauses of verse 4 must describe the lovingly (*bands of love*; *cf.* on 11:1) humane ('cords of a man', lit.) treatment with which God taught and guided his people (v. 3). Even where redirection or restraint were called for, it was done gently and with their welfare in mind. In verses 1, 3–4 God has made the strongest possible case for his right to evoke full and terminal judgment on his rebellious child.[1]

Matthew uses Hosea 11:1 in his narrative of Jesus' infancy (2:15), because he finds much in that text that reinforces his understanding of the messianic office: (1) it is revealed in a context of conflict in which *Egypt* plays a key role; (2) it contains a divine *call* to purposeful service as did God's call to Israel; (3) it features a unique relation of *sonship* between God and his anointed one; (4) it intimates the *grace* by which the Father nurtured both Israel and the infant Jesus; (5) it

---

[1]Mention should be made here of Andersen's (p. 574) innovative reconstruction and interpretation of this difficult section. The outcome of his work is a revised picture of divine grace from the more usual one drawn above. It features images of redemption from bondage: 'I took from his arms the bonds of men' (v. 3a); 'I treated them like those who remove the yoke'; 'I heeded (his plea) and made (him) prevail' (v. 4b). The reordering and assigning different meanings to key words (*e.g.* 'made [him] prevail' for 'gave [him food] to eat') will spark considerable debate before his interpretation can replace the traditional understanding developed above.

recapitulates the *Exodus* and in so doing makes the Christ-child the *new, true Israel*; and (6) since Moses was involved in the first call from Egypt (*cf.* on Ho. 12:13), Jesus is spotlighted as the *greater Moses*.[1] The relationship of Old Testament prophecy to New Testament fulfilment is like that of seed to flower. What is potential in the seed becomes actual in the flower; themes latent in the Old Testament are bountifully disclosed in the New Testament. A relay race provides another image. The Old Testament writers, like Hosea, take their themes of divine grace and promise and thrust them forward like batons to the runners who succeed them; the New Testament writers, like Matthew, reach back and take those themes that suit their purposes, grasp them firmly, and run forward with them in ways that enlighten and strengthen the church.

5–7. Yahweh's case against the wayward son (vv. 1–4) has issued in a guilty verdict. Now the sentence is to be pronounced: invasion (v. 6), exile (v. 5), and burdensome captivity (v. 7).

The *lō'* ('not') with which MT begins verse 5 should be read as 'surely', an asseverative note of reinforcement and emphasis, showing how merited the punishment is. *Egypt* should be understood as a symbol of the Exile in *Assyria*, although undoubtedly some fugitives made their way to Egypt to avoid a more ruthless fate at the hands of the Assyrians against whom they had rebelled in 734 and 727 BC. *Egypt* and *Assyria* are fixed-pairs to Hosea; the mention of one almost inevitably calls for the other as part of the poetic parallelism (*cf.* 7:11; Assyria, 5:13 at beginning of passage, matched by Egypt, 7:16, at the close; 9:3; Assyria, 8:9, balanced by Egypt, 9:6; 11:11; 12:1). *Their king*, now to be *Assyria*, captures the earlier pathos of the collapse of their political leaders – 'we have no king' (10:3; *cf.* 10:15) – and of their calf-idol to whom they paid royal homage – 'Samaria's king shall perish' (10:7). And all of this because of Israel's rebellion against her true king. Andersen's (p. 584) alternative should be noted: 'his own king' (lit. 'his king himself') is made the subject of the verb

---

[1]On the relationship of Mt. 2:15 to Ho. 11:1, see F. W. Beare, *The Gospel according to Matthew* (San Francisco: 1981), p. 82; R. H. Grundy, *The Use of the OT in St Matthew's Gospel. Supplements to Novum Testamentum* 18 (Leiden: 1967), pp. 94–5, 175–6; R. T. France, *The Gospel according to Matthew*, TNTC (Leicester: IVP, 1985), p. 85–86.

return, with *Egypt* and *Assyria* as the possible destinations. Word order seems to favour the traditional reading. *Refused* (Heb. *m'n*), only here in Hosea, became a favourite word in Jeremiah to describe the reluctance of Judah to seek God's face and do his will (*cf.* Je. 3:3; 5:3; 8:5; 9:9; 11:10; 13:10; 15:18; 25:28; 31:15; 38:21; 50:33). For *return*, see on 3:5.

Having announced the more general theme of exile, Hosea moves to describe the specific havoc wrought on the *cities* of Israel (v. 6). They seem to be singled out for military destruction (*sword*) for two reasons: their fortifications had become abominable symbols of self-reliance (8:14; 10:14) and their palaces were centres of religious and political stratagems (Heb. *mō' ᵃṣ̌ôt*; *cf.* Mi. 6:16; Je. 7:24) or scheming plans. *Sword* seems to be the subject of all three verbs: (1) *ḥālâ* may derive from *ḥwl* to 'writhe' or 'whirl' (so NASB; NIV; Wolff, p. 192; Mays, p. 150) or from *ḥlh* 'to be sickly, weak'; Andersen (p. 585) reads the latter in an intensive form that translates 'will cause damage' or 'will damage'; (2) *klh* in the intensive form here means to 'bring to an end', 'finish off' (*cf.* Je. 9:15; 10:25; 14:12; Am. 7:2); and (3) *'kl*, literally 'to eat' (*cf.* the positive use of the root in 11:4) and then to 'consume' or *devour* in passages that smack of judgment (*cf.* 2:12; 5:7; 7:7, 9; 8:14; 13:8). The puzzling word is the noun that serves as object of the second verb, often translated 'its *bars*' (Heb. *baddāyw*) or the like (RSV; NASB; NIV). Recent interpreters have suggested that persons not things are meant here: (1) 'oracle-priest' (Mays, p. 150; NEB; *cf.* Is. 4:25; Je. 50:36 [RSV 'diviners']); (2) 'braggarts' (Wolff, p. 192); *cf.* Is. 16:6; and (3) 'strong men', 'heroes' (Andersen, p. 585). As frequently with obscure or ambiguous words, the choice hinges on the context. Andersen (p. 585) emphasizes the military notes in this verse and in Jeremiah 50:36, where *baddîm* occurs in parallel to *gibbôrîm*, 'warriors' (*cf.* Ho. 10:13). Yet the last word of Jeremiah 50:35 is 'wise men', a term also found with *baddîm* in Isaiah 44:25, where the context is *not* military action but oracular divination and advice. The use of the word in military passages can be readily accounted for: oracle-priests or diviner-prophets were an essential part of the teams that did Israel's battle-planning, playing a key role in deciding whether, when and how to engage the enemy in conflict (*cf.* 2 Sa. 16:23; 1 Ki. 22:6). Such an interpretation as 'oracle-priest' (*cf.* W. Holladay, *CHALOT*, p. 33) would suit well all three usages (Is. 44:25; Je. 50:36; Ho. 11:6) and would also help to explain the final target of the sword's devastation in verse 6, 'stratagems' or 'schemings' (RSV emends to *fortresses*), *i.e.* the fatal political and military plans which, having omitted God, were doomed.

Israel's wrong choices, to which diviners may have made their contribution (*cf.* on 4:11–12), were part of a persistent pattern of apostasy.[1] Hebrew *mᵉšûḇâ* (*turning away*) seems to mean the opposite of the divinely required *šûḇ*, 'turning' or 'return' to God (*cf.* v. 5). It connotes returning to old pagan ways and turning a back to Yahweh and his truth (*cf.* Je. 2:19; 3:6, 22; 5:6; 8:5; 14:7; Ezk. 37:33). God's label *my people* shows the perversity of their choice. It also both recalls the name of Hosea's third child (1:9) and prepares for the divine complaint in verse 8, which raises the ultimate questions about the restoration of the relationship between God and Israel.

The extreme depths of their apostasy seem to be described in verse 7b–c: 'unto their supposed high god, *i.e.* Baal, they have called and he can not at all lift them up.' For 'high-god' (*cf.* NEB; Andersen, p. 587) see on 7:16, where Hebrew *'al* also seems to stand for Baal. This reading removes any mention of a *yoke* (RSV) and makes verse 7b–c part of a summary-indictment not an announcement of judgment. It also dispenses with the need for emendation so prevalently used in treating *'al* here (*cf.* JB: Wolff, p. 192; Mays, p. 160; Nötscher, p. 32). 'Called' ties this passage to verses 1–2 which play on the contrast between Yahweh's call and the seductive calls of the Baals.[2]

8–9. For the first time, in chapter 11, God addresses Ephraim/Israel (the two must be synonymous here; *cf.* on vv.

---

[1] *Bent* (RSV; NEB; NASB) describes this pattern. Heb. *tl'* is 'to hang', as the Philistines suspended to public view the bodies of Saul and Jonathan (2 Sa. 21:12). The passive voice in Ho. 11:7 suggests 'being firmly attached to' 'hung up on'; therefore, *bent* or determined (NIV).

[2] The 'he' that serves as subject of the final clause is probably emphatic and underscores the importance of their alleged high-god. This interpretation is based on the emendation adopted by Wolff, pp. 192–3, that separates the suffix *hû* from the verb 'they have called' and makes it a freestanding nominative pronoun, *hû*. 'Lift them up' (Heb. *rwm* in an intensive form) means to 'rescue' or 'raise to a safe place' as in Ps. 27:5. 'Not at all' reflects the emphatic negative combination in Hebrew of *yaḥaḏ* which here as in verse 8 and Ps. 33:15 seems to mean 'totally', 'entirely'—a sense derived from its more common meanings, 'community' and 'all together'—and *lō* 'not'.

1, 3) in the second person singular; the entire Northern Kingdom is treated as a single, personal entity. More than that, it is
allowed as the defendant in the trial of the rebellious child (see
above at 11:1–11) to hear the pathos with which God partly
laments (for *how*, Heb. *'êk*, as a word of lamentation, *cf.* 2 Sa.
1:19, 25, 27; Mi. 2:4) the judgment he has already ordained
and partly deliberates (for *how* as an ejaculation of a self-
cautioning question, *cf.* Ps. 137:4; Je. 9:6, whose thought and
language are close to those of Ho. 11:8) the implications of
Israel's irrecoverable destruction. That destruction is phrased
here in personal language. It is not the *cities* (v. 6) but the
entire *people* that is the object, and it is not a swishing *sword* but
a complete act of *surrender* that is the fate. *Hand over* (*cf.* Gn.
14:20, where El Elyon is praised for turning over the enemies
into Abram's hand) and *give up* (*cf.* 1 Ki. 14:16, where God
promises to give Israel up for the sins of Jeroboam) have a
long history in political-military transactions. They mean
giving an enemy full right to do whatever the enemy pleases:
slaughter, exile, enslave, sell into slavery.

Historical allusions again are introduced in the form of
place names to reinforce the argument. The emphasis is on
places that have been utterly, irrevocably destroyed for their
persistent apostasy. Not even their rubble remains, only their
memory. *Admah* and *Zeboiim* (*cf.* Dt. 29:23; Gn. 14:2, 8) are
listed with Sodom and Gomorrah (*cf.* Gn. 10:19; 19:24–29) as
cities of the plain, erased by divine judgment in the days of
Abraham. Moses' speech warns of a curse so dreadful that
foreigners would find 'the whole land brimstone and salt, and
a burnt-out waste, unsown and growing nothing, where no
grass can sprout,' and he compares that moonscape desolation
with the four vanished cities. The site of these cities, which yet
awaits discovery, possibly lies under water at the southern end
of the Dead Sea.[1]

My heart speaks of the anguish of God's choice (*cf. heart* at
4:11); as he faces the momentous decision, his thoughts and
feelings have been 'turning over' (*recoils*) within him (*cf.* the
distressed thoughts of ravaged Jerusalem, La. 1:20; the same
root *hpk* was used for the overthrow of the wicked cities; *cf.*
Gn. 19:25, 29; Dt. 29:23), but, even more important, he
reveals that 'my sense of *compassion* (*cf.* Is. 57:18; Zc. 1:13; the

[1]See J. P. Harland, *IDB*, IV, pp. 395–397.

root *nḥm* suggests a desire to comfort and console) has been growing exceedingly (see on *yaḥad* at v. 7) *warm*' (*cf.* for Heb. *kmr* the pictures of Joseph's warm feelings at the sight of Benjamin, Gn. 43:30; the prostitute's yearning for the welfare of her baby, 1 Ki. 3:26; and the starving people's feverish skin in La. 5:10).

The wracking ambivalence reaches its conclusion with the verdict of verse 9, the first word of which is *not*: the verdict is negative. Not that God has had any change of heart about Israel's sin. 'The heat of my *anger*' (the phrase became a favourite of Jeremiah's *e.g.* 4:26; 12:13; 25:37; 25:38; 51:45; Is. 13:9, 13) is the way in which he describes the pent-up wrath, which he chooses not to *execute*. We have met that anger before (8:5) and will meet it again (13:11; *cf.* Joel 2:13; Am. 4:10). But its ultimate destination is not Israel; God's loving acts of healing will turn it away from them (14:4). Once the necessary judgment has been accomplished at the hands of Assyria, God *will not again* (so the Heb. *šûb*, 'return' signifies here; *cf.* BDB, p. 998) *destroy* (Heb. *šḥt* in intensive stem; *cf.* 9:9 for Israel's moral and spiritual destruction at Gibeah and 13:9 for Yahweh's devastation of Israel; *cf.* also Am. 1:11 where Edom destroyed his own pity) *Ephraim, i.e.* Israel, the entire northern people.

God's explanation (*for*; Heb. *kî*) of his commitment to continue the covenant beyond the judgment is both passionate and profound: the unique *holy* quality of his deity. His disposition and behaviour distinguish themselves (Heb. *qāḏôš*, 'separate from' 'incomparable', 'unique') from what would be the normal human pattern, whether of vicious revenge (*cf.* Lamech's song of massive retaliation in Gn. 4:23–24) or even of *lex talionis*, always exacting a punishment proportionate to the crime. The ultimate difference between God and a man (Heb. *'ēl* and *'îš*) is utterly basic to a biblical understanding of reality, whether in reference to creation, providence, sovereignty, or salvation. In each of these realms God has done and can do what no human being dare claim nor attempt. The blurring of the distinction sparked needless fear of other nations – 'the Egyptians are men and not God' (Is. 31:3) – or worthless arrogance toward the living God – 'yet you (the prince of Tyre) are but a man, and no god, though you consider yourself as wise as a god' (Ezk. 28:2).

The Holy One in your midst is a remarkable summation of God's transcendence and immanence. As the Holy One he has all the power, glory and awesomeness that Isaiah sensed at his commissioning (Is. 6:3) and that Jerusalem's citizens were to celebrate at the return from exile (Is. 40:25). Yet that Incomparable One is present and at work among his rebellious people, disclosing to them his innermost feelings, pledging his compassion (v. 8) despite their disloyalty (v. 7). And he defines his otherness, his divine uniqueness, not in terms of power, wisdom, or sovereignty but in terms of love – constant, sure, steadfast.

This revelation of holiness shed its light down the long path of biblical understanding through the New Testament and into the heart of the church. Acts of divine grace were seen as demonstrations of divine holiness (Is. 41:17–20). The hallowed name of the heavenly Father showed itself not only in the coming of the kingdom but in the provision of bread, the promise of forgiveness, the protection in temptation and the rescue from the evil one (Mt. 6:9–13). The apostle Paul prayed for his fellow believers to abound in love in order that their hearts might be 'unblamable in holiness' (1 Th. 3:12–13). John captured the essence of God's being with 'God is love' (1 Jn. 4:16). Holy love, loving holiness – these are the phrases that give us the clearest insight that we possess into the divine nature. No-one except Jesus the Christ has taught us more about this than Hosea.

The final word of verse 9 makes it difficult for us to affirm how this crucial passage ends. The three most frequent readings are (1) to derive the word *bāʿîr* from the root *bʿr* 'to burn', 'consume' (*cf.* 7:4, 6; Mays, p. 151); (2) to read a kindred root *bʿr*, to 'remove', or 'destroy', especially in the intensive form (*cf.* Is. 6:13; Nötscher, p. 32; RSV; JB); or (3) to treat the *b* as a preposition 'with' and read *ʿîr* as a noun meaning 'agitation' or 'wrath' (*cf.* Je. 15:8; Wolff, p. 193; NASB; NIV). A fourth possibility is to stick with the MT and translate the final clause simply, 'and I will not (again) enter into the city' (*cf.* LXX; Vulg.; AV). Divine judgment on the city is a familiar theme in Hosea (8:14; 10:14), and it may well be that Hosea intended an envelope pattern in which the threat of judgment (v. 6) and the promise of hope beyond judgment were bracketed by the word *city*, thus suggesting that what was the prime target of the divinely-wielded sword need no longer fear the threat of such terrible intrusion.[1]

10–11. The promise of restoration is couched in terms that flow out of the trial scene in verses 1–9: (1) the Israelites (*they, them* and *their* refer to the scattered people) are called *sons* or 'children' (v. 10; *cf.* v. 1); (2) their fearful walking *after* or behind Yahweh contrasts directly with their walking away from him (v. 10; *cf.* v. 2); (3) their *trembling* pilgrimage (Heb. *ḥrd* describes the quaking of Sinai, Ex. 19:18) implies an acknowledgment of God's intent to heal them that was absent in the divine complaint (vv. 10–11; *cf.* v. 3); (4) the specific sites of exile, Egypt and Assyria, are recounted as a reminder of the necessity of judgment (v. 11; *cf.* v. 5); and (5) the resettlement (Heb. lit. 'I will make them to dwell') in their own homesites (lit. 'houses,' which must include the properties they worked; *cf.* Andersen's 'estates', p. 575) pictures the restoration of the devastation of their cities (v. 11; *cf.* v. 6).

New in verses 10–11 are the *lion* simile for Yahweh (*cf.* Am. 1:2; 3:4, 8; Amos' language may have been known to Hosea) and the *bird* and *dove* images for Israel. Their role in this passage is to strengthen the pictures of divine authority, so badly violated by Israel's rebellion, and of Israel's obedient response to it. A wilful child may cavil at a parent's command; a bird or dove can scarcely ignore a lion's roar. Timorousness is the dove-like trait featured here, not silliness as in 7:11. God's authority, even sovereignty, is the leonine character here, not ferocity as in 5:14; 13:7–8.

The oracle formula, *says Yahweh*, marks the close of the salvation promises in verses 10–11 (*cf.* 2:16, 21), of the trial scene of 11:1–11, of the fourth major set of speeches whose metaphors described Israel's unfulfilled calling (9:9 – 11:11), and of the whole chain of messages which began at 4:1, conveying the nature of divine judgment. The carefully chartered course from judgment to hope has now been traversed a second time, and Hosea will yet take us again over its path before he draws his declarations to their conclusion.

---

[1]In his understanding of verse 9, Andersen (pp. 589–91) has again bucked the tide of scholarly consensus. His conclusion that the uses of *lō'* in the verse are not negatives but asseveratives to be translated 'certainly' is, of course, linguistically acceptable. What are harder to accept are his arguments that Yahweh demonstrates his holiness here not by compassion but by consistency of judgment and that verses 10–11 are not the logical consequence of a promise to forgive but an abrupt change to an eschatological situation.

III. HOSEA'S MESSAGES: PART TWO (11:12 – 14:9)

Hosea might have ended his book at 11:11 with the powerful, almost humorous, picture of God, the Lion, calling home his quivering family of birds. To that return the book has been driving relentlessly, reaching it once at 1:11, then at 3:5 and again at 11:11. But the prophecy has yet more to unfold of the nature of Israel's sin, the intensity of God's passionate judgment, and the glory of the ultimate reconciliation. So here, for the final time, it traces Israel's march from punishment to restoration. The main divisions of this final section are these:

> Ephraim and Judah, now – knaves and fools
> (11:12 – 12:1);
> Jacob, then and now – arrogance and self-reliance
> (12:2–14);
> Ephraim, then and now – idolatry and ingratitude
> (13:1–16);
> Israel and Yahweh, their future – repentance and
> restoration (14:1–8);
> Concluding admonition – walking and stumbling (14:9).

In the first division (11:12 – 12:1), which serves both as transition from the messages of Part One (4:1 – 11:11) and as introduction to the messages of Part Two (11:12 – 14:9), Hosea's eye is on the present corruption and the devastation that lies at the door. The Northern Kingdom is undoubtedly in its last decade, as these words are proclaimed. In the next two divisions (12:2–14; 13:1–16), Hosea draws on the past characteristics of the two great patriarchs of the northern tribes, Jacob (12:2–4, 12) and Ephraim (13:1), to account for the present behaviour of his neighbours. In the fourth division (14:1–8), the focus is almost entirely on the distant future when the wrath of judgment will have been spent and the lessons of contrition and devotion learned. (See the Additional Note on 'Fulfilment of Prophecy', p. 69, for the tenses that underlie Hosea's oracles.) In the fifth division (14:9), the proverb-like epilogue applies the book to the whole people of God, the author's eye seemingly on every era, including our own.

Hosea's use of the past to explain the present was well

illustrated in the chain of images that document Israel's failure to carry out her calling (9:10 – 11:11). What is new in this final section is that the *historical references* are not basically to *places* (*e.g.* Gibeah, 9:9; 10:9; Peor, 9:10; Gilgal, 9:10; Bethel, 10:5; Beth-arbel 10:14) but to *persons*, the heroic ancestors whose names their offspring bore. This change of focus (though Bethel, 12:4, Gilead and Gilgal, 12:11, are mentioned) means a shift in emphasis from *events* to *characteristics* that gauge Israel's behaviour. The placement of chapters 12–13 after chapter 11, then, may be strategic. In chapter 11, God has played upon the importance of the parent-child relationship to describe how tragically Israel had ruptured the covenant. In chapters 12–13, the parent-child relationship is again in view, but this time to show how mindlessly Israel had aped some of the worst characteristics of their ancestors.

In *literary form*, the three divisions are judgment-speeches, usually with greater attention given to the indictment and its description of Israel's sin than to the threats of punishment, although the latter gain volume and intensity in 13:14–16. The fourth division combines an admonition to return (14:1–3) with a promise of salvation (14:4–7) in the form of a love-song and with a final divine complaint (14:8). The last verse of the book is a wisdom admonition, proverb-like in its structure and message (14:9).

a. Ephraim and Judah, now – knaves and fools (11:12 – 12:1 [Heb. 12:1–2])[1]

As is his wont (*cf.* 1:7, 11; 4:15; 5:5, 14; 6:4; 6:11 – 7:1; 8:14; 10:11; 12:2), Hosea extends his horizons to include Judah, the Southern Kingdom. The fundamental errors that the prophet is constrained to point out – idolatry, political folly, military self-reliance – were not the private property of either realm. As divinely-commissioned messenger and covenant interpreter, Hosea's words could not be confined to the artificial boundaries that divided his homeland from his southern kin. But Israel's stubborn rejection of God's way had drawn her more rapidly than Judah into the vortex of divine judgment.

---

[1]This heading is borrowed from H. L. Ginsburg, 'Hosea's Ephraim, More Fool than Knave' (*JBL*, 80, 1961, pp. 339–347) who argues rightly that folly as well as treachery is Israel's crime, described in ch. 12.

And Yahweh saw to it that the first two writing prophets gave Israel not Judah their prime time. Israel's history was on a collision course with disaster, and the watchmen (*cf.* 9:8) had to direct their warnings almost exclusively to it. But the mentions of Judah are reminders that sin needs no passport but either crosses borders without customs' inspection or springs up endemically in any available soil. Moreover, God's long-term plans called for a people reunited (1:11), and Hosea's jabs at Judah in the judgment speeches kept that reality before his northern audiences.

11:12 [Heb. 12:1]. *Ephraim* and *house of Israel* must be synonymous here (*cf.* 11:1, 3) – the whole northern people, whatever their present legal status with Assyria may have been (see note at 5:8 – 7:16). *Lies* are a favourite object of divine wrath in Hosea (*cf.* 7:3; 10:13 for *khš*; but also *kzb* in 7:13; 12:1; *bgd*, 'to deal falsely', in 5:7; 6:7). *Deceit* (Heb. *mirmâ*) both interprets the intention of the lying and prepares for the description of Ephraim's crooked business practices in 12:7. Both the prior context (*cf.* 11:2, 7) and the parallel clauses that describe Judah's religious corruption suggest that *idolatry* is the deceitful practice indicated here. So widespread was the contamination that the speaker – *me* in verse 12a – was literally *surrounded* (Heb. *sbb*, *cf.* 7:2, where the wicked deeds of the priests hem them in and witness against them) by it. Though the prophet may be speaking of himself, it is more likely that it is Yahweh, the Holy One in the midst of his people (11:9), who is thus almost inundated by their spiritual deceit, which calls no-gods God and vice versa.

If we understand verse 12b correctly, *Judah* is in precisely the same predicament. Her behaviour is parallel to Ephraim's, not sharply different from it (despite the renderings of AV; RSV; Wolff, p. 205; Mays, p. 159; Jacob, p. 85). The key to our interpretation is the meaning of *god* (Heb. *'ēl*) and the *holy ones* (Heb. *q'dôšîm*). God here probably means El, the high-god of the Canaanites not Yahweh. And the *holy ones* are not a plural of majesty for Yahweh (note that the singular is used in 11:9), nor the cult-prostitutes (so Jeremias, p. 148), nor the true prophets (so Wolff, p. 210), but the Canaanite pantheon that comprises El's court (NEB; so Ward, p. 207; Andersen, p. 603).[1] The verb is to be read as 'roaming' or 'wandering'

---

[1] So also R. Coote, *VT*, 21, 1972, p. 389.

(Heb. *rwd*; *cf.* Je. 2:31) and need not be emended to 'know' (Heb. *yd'*) despite the tempting translation of the LXX: 'Now I God know them' (*cf.* RSV). The verse should then read:

> Ephraim has surrounded me with lying
> and the House of Israel with deceit.
> Judah yet roams with El
> and keeps faith with the 'holy ones' [of El's court].

Judah's faithfulness to the pagan deities worshipped in idol-form points to the topsy-turvy nature of the whole people's religious life. Where faithfulness was a virtue, it was lacking (4:1); where it was a vice it was pervasively present.

1. The treachery of idolatry was matched by Ephraim's (whether the rump state or the Northern Kingdom is meant, we cannot be sure) stupidity in foreign policy. *Herds the winds* and *pursues* (Heb. *rdp*; *cf.* 2:7; 6:3; 8:3; Am. 1:11) *the east wind* are images of futile, foolish endeavour akin to the Preacher's stock-phrase, 'striving after wind', literally 'a longing for wind' (Heb. *re'ût rûaḥ*; Ec. 1:14; 2:1, 17, 26; 4:4, 6; 6:9). Earlier Hosea used 'sow the wind' (or 'sow in the wind') for a similar figure of futility (8:7). In 13:15 *east wind* will be an instrument of judgment, as though what they ('all the day') pursued in 12:1 will ultimately catch up with them.

'Lying' (here Heb. *kzb*) and 'destruction' (Heb. *šōd*; *cf.* on 7:13; Am. 3:10; 5:9) may be read as a combined phrase (*hendiadys*, two words used to convey one meaning) 'violent falsehood', *i.e.* lying that results in violence (the latter word is sometimes emended to *šaw* 'vanity', 'futility' on the basis of the LXX.[1] The extensiveness of this harmful deception is again conveyed by the use of the *motif of multiplication* (*cf.* 4:7; 8:11; 10:1, 13). Exhibit A of their deceitful stupidity was their vacillating foreign policy (*cf. silly and without sense* in 7:11) in which they carried on negotiations (*bargain*) – even framed treaties (so *bᵉrît* 'covenant' means here; *cf.* 2:18; 6:7; 8:1) – with *Assyria* and simultaneously brought olive *oil* (*cf.* on 2:5, 8) as bribe or tribute to *Egypt*. On the circumstances see Additional Note on 'Possible historical backgrounds,' 5:8 – 7:16, p. 118. Courting two enemies at the same time was not

---

[1] See H. L. Ginsburg, 'Hosea's Ephraim, More Fool than Knave', *JBL*, 80, 1961, p. 340.

only an act of disloyalty to God but an act of political madness which was destined to bring down the wrath of both nations on them.

b. Jacob, then and now – arrogance and self-reliance (12:2–14 [Heb. 12:3–15])

Again Hosea moves to set the practices of wickedness summarized in 11:12 – 12:1 in their historical perspective. He does so by citing instances in the life of Jacob as explanations of the behaviour of both Judah and Israel. The development of the segments in this puzzling chapter is such that many interpreters have suggested massive rearrangements, but without scholarly consensus.

The most important issue is whether Jacob is being used as a positive or a negative example.[1] Hosea's general practice, the context of chapter 12 which is surrounded by the negative illustrations from history found in 9:10 – 11:11 and 13:1, and the wording of the text itself seem to tip the scales in the direction of a negative interpretation, despite Andersen's (pp. 597–600) apt warning that the text is less critical of Jacob than is often supposed. If there is a positive point to be made it must centre in verse 4, where the lesson may be either (1) Jacob's striving with God and/or his angel, understood as an example of repentance and return which Hosea's contemporaries were to emulate, or (2) God's forbearance extended even to a rogue like Jacob.[2]

The chapter can be divided into three sections without neglecting its overall thematic unity: the controversy with Judah and Israel – vv. 2–6; the empty boast of Ephraim – vv. 7–9; the parables of the prophets – vv. 10–14. Signs of unity are noted in the occurrences of Jacob's name (vv. 1, 12), the references to Egypt (vv. 9, 13), the use of the root *'wn* in various meanings – maturity (v. 3), wealth (v. 8), wicked futility (or false gods, v. 11), the dominant place given to

---

[1]Ward, p. 213, summarizes a number of the interpretative approaches of recent decades, including a suggestion of one of his students that verses 4, 8 which are sometimes read as speaking favourably of Jacob may be 'popular boasts made in debate with the prophet'.

[2]For the first possibility, see N. Peters, *Osee und die Geschichte* (Paderborn: 1924), pp. 14–15; for the second, see G. A. F. Knight, *Hosea*, Torch Bible Commentaries (London: SCM Press, 1960), *ad loc.*

accusation (vv. 2–3, 7, 11, 14), and the fact that the entire nation, both north and south, seems to be in view (*cf.* Judah, v. 2, Ephraim, vv. 8, 14, and references to the Exodus of the united people, vv. 9, 13).

i. Controversy with Judah and Israel (12:2–6). *Indictment* suggests that the legal setting of 11:1–11 is given fresh announcement in verse 2 (*cf.* on 2:2; 4:1, 4 for *rîb*, 'controversy', 'legal-contest,' or 'quarrel'). The threat of punishment is hurled at the defendant before the evidence is offered against him (v. 2b–c), though the accusations of 11:12 – 12:1 may carry over somewhat. Then the more specific evidence is cited, not from Israel's own behaviour but from that of his ancestor and eponym, *Jacob* (vv. 3–4); the hymn-like (*cf.* Am. 4:13; 5:8–9; 9:6) introduction of Yahweh's name (v. 5) serves to reinforce the sacral nature of Jacob's experience and to remind Hosea's hearers of the One who has entered into litigation with them; the admonition or instruction (v. 6) is a clear summary of their duty to the God of the hymn (*cf.* the similar admonitions in connection with legal proceedings in 10:12 and especially Mi. 6:8).

Judah (v. 2) is the first defendant, though many scholars have felt constrained to substitute Israel's name for Judah's on the assumption that a later Judean editor ignored the parallelism, Israel/Jacob, and inserted the name of the Southern Kingdom in an effort to use Hosea's text to expose Judah's crimes (*cf.* Moffatt; JB; Ward, p. 207; Wolff, p. 206; Mays, p. 161; Jacob, p. 85). Judah's name (*cf.* 11:12) is a reminder that the whole people inherited both the wicked or foolish characteristics of their common ancestor and the covenant promises which will make them one again. *Jacob* (vv. 2, 12) and *Israel* (vv. 12–13) refer to the father of both the northern and southern tribes and to all the tribes rescued from Egypt in the Exodus. *Ephraim* in this chapter (vv. 8, 14) means the northern kingdom and is the stylistic counterpart to *Judah*.

The threat of verse 2 is announced in familiar language found almost *verbatim* in 4:9: for *punish*, literally 'visit', *cf.* on 1:4; 2:13; 4:9; 8:13; 9:9; for *ways*, *i.e.* 'wicked ways' in this context, *cf.* 4:9; for *deeds*, *i.e.* the most general and encompassing description of the evil acts of all sorts, *cf.* on 4:9; 5:4; 7:2; 9:15; for *requite*, literally 'cause to return', *cf.* on 4:9; 12:15; as in Amos 1:3, the implied object is divine anger. The chiastic word order of the Hebrew – 'he will punish Jacob according to his ways; according to his deeds he will requite him' – puts the stress not so much on the sins as on the punishment which has first and last place in the sentence.

The absence of transition between verse 2 and verse 3 indicates that Jacob is still the subject and that the theme continues to be judgment and the grounds for it. Verse 3 transports us to the Jacob stories in Genesis. Two settings in Jacob's life are suggested by the prepositional phrases *in the womb* (*cf.* 9:11, 16) and *in his manhood* or maturity ('*wn, cf.* Jacob's use of the term '*wn* in reference to his virility to beget Reuben, his first-born, Gn. 49:3). The first setting is Jacob's birth-story, remembered for his grasping at Esau's heel (Gn. 25:26); the second seems to refer to his wrestling with God's angel near the Jabbok at the place that came to be known as Peniel (lit. 'God's face'; *cf.* 32:30). Puns on the double name of Isaac's son are the core of verse 3. The verbs are the clue. *He took* (grabbed) *by the heel* translates Hebrew *'āqaḇ* whose form in the imperfect tense is *ya'ᵃqōḇ, i.e.* Jacob. The negative force of the word would be even more clear to Hosea's hearers, as they recalled the instance in Genesis 27:36, where Esau complained to Isaac: 'Is he not rightly named Jacob? For he has supplanted (Heb. *ya'ᵃqōḇ*) me these two times. He took away my birthright (*cf.* Gn. 25:29–34); and behold, now he has taken away my blessing.' *He strove* (Heb. *śārâ*; *cf.* Gn. 32:29) is the basis of the explanation of the name change from Jacob to Israel (Heb. *yiśrā'ēl*; note the *śr* in the name) recounted in Genesis 32:28. It seems likely that the *striving* which is preserved in Israel's name was viewed negatively by Hosea. Both the heel grabbing and the striving were signs of Jacob's impulsive presumptuousness. Even though the Peniel event resulted in blessing for the newly named Israel, it also carried its pain as the price of brashness: Jacob's thigh was thrust out of joint, and he limped his way toward his meeting with Esau (Gn. 32:25, 31).

Verse 4 bristles with questions for the interpreter. What subjects do we understand for the chain of verbs? The absence of a signal that the subject has changed, the 'and' (omitted in RSV) that links verse 4 to verse 3, and the repetition of a verb with *śr* as prime consonants – all these point to Jacob as subject and some expansion of verse 3b as the intent of verse 4. It was Jacob who (1) 'contended with' (or perhaps

203

'lorded it over')[1] God – reading Hebrew *'el* (toward) as *'ēl*, not the preposition but the deity – and *prevailed* with *the angel* (*cf.* Gn. 32:28, where the language is almost identical); (2) *wept* (or 'perplexed him');[2] *and sought his favour* (for this stem of *ḥnn*, 'to be gracious', see Gn. 42:21; Dt. 3:23; 1 Ki. 8:33, 47); and (3) 'finds him at Bethel' (for Heb. *mṣ'* in the sense of meeting for worship, *cf.* 5:6) and speaks with him there (reading *him* with LXX and Syriac texts rather than 'us' with MT), promising his covenantal loyalty to God in exchange for divine guidance and provision (Gn. 28:18–22). Thus, we may read verse 4:

> And he [Jacob] contended with God
>   and with an angel [of God] prevailed.
> He [Jacob] wept and sought his favour.
> He met God [for worship] at Bethel,
> And there he spoke with him.

Such a reading keeps Jacob as the constant subject and God (or his angel) as the object and avoids much of the emendation involved in other ways of handling the verse (*cf.* RSV's double insertion of God in the text or Wolff's omission of *angel* (p. 206).

Can we harmonize Hosea's summary with events recorded in Genesis? Only in part. The plea for blessing seems to be set in Peniel/Penuel (Gn. 32:26) but no act of weeping is described there. Hosea may have added the word as a *hendiadys* to intensify Jacob's request. The only place name mentioned is *Bethel* (*cf.* 10:15; Hosea's usual names for the ancient, sacred town were the sarcastic Beth-aven, 4:15; 5:8; 10:5, or Aven, 10:8), whereas the struggle with the mysterious stranger took place at Peniel. The dramatic encounter with the angels of God at Bethel (Gn. 28:12–22) is tersely described as 'finding him' and 'speaking with him'. Hosea also seems to reverse the order of events, citing the Peniel episode before the Bethel meeting, probably because of the literary unity gained by the play on the roots *śrh* and *śrr* at the end of verse 3 and the

---

[1] The Hebrew root may be *śrr*; *cf.* Jdg. 9:22; Is. 32:1; Ho. 8:4; if so, the punning not only involves Israel's name but also the 'princes' or 'military leaders', *śārîm*, whose complicity in Israel's evil Hosea has so often noted; *cf.* 3:4; 5:10; 7:3, 5, 16; 8:10; 9:15; 13:10.

[2] *Cf.* R. B. Coote, 'Hosea XII', *VT*, 21, 1971, p. 395, for the suggestion that the root here is not *bkh* but *bwk*, as in Ex. 14:3; Est. 3:15; Joel 1:18.

beginning of verse 4. The possibility must be left open that Hosea had access to traditions about Jacob in forms different from those preserved in Genesis.[1]

How did Hosea intend to relate Jacob's behaviour to Israel's situation in the closing years of the Northern Kingdom? Gingerly we venture a three-part answer. First, Jacob's *presumptuousness* about his rights and role as Isaac's son, Esau's rival sibling and God's covenantal heir, had their counterparts in Israel's easy expectation that their elect status could never be jeopardized, no matter how like that of the dwellers of Canaan their comportment became (vv. 7–9; *cf.* their insincere claims to divine grace in 6:1–3; 8:2). Second, the meeting of Jacob with God at *Bethel*, landmark that it was, did not guarantee the patriarch's obedience to God, as later episodes in his life attest (*e.g.* the idolatry that had corrupted his household in Gn. ch. 35). *Bethel* was not an ultimate solution to Jacob's covenantal infidelity and certainly was not to Israel's, once it became a centre of calf-worship. Third, and perhaps most important, Jacob did not keep the vow of constancy to God made at *Bethel*, and his progeny had more than followed in his train. Whatever bond was forged at *Bethel*, when Jacob spoke with God, was shattered to bits by Israel's foolish understanding that ritual acts (*cf.* 5:6) were sufficient to fulfill their covenantal obligations.

This three-part approach to Hosea's intent in verses 3–4 gains some support from the hymn-fragment and admonitions in verses 5–6. The hymn which features Yahweh's name in contrast to *ʾĕlôhîm* and *ʾēl* in verses 3–4 is a reminder of the dangers of confusing Israel's Lord and Saviour with the gods of the land, even with the high-god El. The use of the full title *Yahweh God of hosts* (*i.e.* armies of heaven and earth, [2 Sa. 5:10] found here only in Hosea) moves the focus away from any local sacred sites like *Bethel* and centres attention on the universal power and glory of the Lord. The fact that *name* in verse 5 is not the more common *šēm* (*cf.* Am. 4:13; 5:8; 9:6) but *zēker* which literally means the 'title to be remembered by' (*cf.* Ex. 3:15; Ho. 14:7) may be Hosea's way of underscoring how crucial it is not to forget the knowledge of Yahweh's unique identity.

The admonition of verse 6 may be an example of lawsuit

---

[1]See Andersen, pp. 597–615, for extended comments on the relationships.

instruction, a solemn reminder of covenantal duties like Micah 6:8. The God with whom Israel deals insists that the stipulations of any agreement with him include the covenant-love (Heb. *ḥesed*; 2:19; 4:1; 6:4, 6) and regard for human-rights (*mišpāṭ*); which are so central to his own behaviour (*cf.* on 2:19). Jacob's ambitions put him out of phase with God's character right at the start of his life (*cf.* v. 3). His offspring, whether as individuals or collectively – the emphatic *you* is singular – had to be redirected from their ancestral pattern to *return* (again Hosea's favourite word for a penitent renewal of covenant responsibility; *cf.* on 3:5; 11:5). Here *return* is used absolutely without an expressed target (*cf.* 14:1–2 [Heb. vv. 2–3], where the phrase *to Yahweh* occurs; the prepositions are Heb. *'ad* and *'el*). The preposition *b* with *your God* probably means *by the help of* (Mays, p. 161; RSV; NEB) and is a reminder that even repentance is impossible without the divine grace that enables it. The emendation of *your God* to 'your tents' (*cf.* Ward, p. 207) is readily understandable in Hebrew (*bē'lōhêḳā* becomes *bᵉ'ōhālêḳā*) but unnecessary here and anticipates too quickly the announcement of a new wilderness relationship sounded in verse 9. The fruit of the return is not only the loving and just conduct so lacking in Jacob and his heirs (*cf.* Ephraim in vv. 7–8) but also a patient, expectant dependence (Heb. *qwh*, 'wait for', 'hope in'; *cf.* Pss. 25:5; 27:14; 37:34, where 'wait' and 'keep' [Heb. *šmr*], are found in parallel as in Ho. 12:6; *cf.* also the noun *tiqwâ*, *hope* in Ho. 2:15 [Heb. 2:17]). Jacob had snatched at his destiny time and again; so had Israel and Judah with land-grabs (5:8–10), rash treaties (10:4; 12:1), and pleas to Baal (7:14–16). Their renewed style was to *wait* in full hope for the divine Redeemer to meet their needs.

ii. Empty boast of Ephraim (12:7–9). The previous two verses have shifted our attention from Jacob's dubious conduct to the needs of Hosea's contemporaries. The target narrows in verses 7–9 from the entire people who call Jacob father (*cf.* 11:12; 12:2) to the Northern Kingdom, *Ephraim*, a name recalling its most famous and dominant tribe (*cf.* on 4:17; 5:3, 9, 11, 13). The transition from entire people to the core of the northern cluster is artful. Ephraim's characteristics are described (v. 7) before Ephraim's identity is revealed (v. 8). Moreover, the prophet's strategy is to link *Ephraim* with the corruption of the Canaanites – *trader* or 'merchant' (*kᵉna'an* in

Heb; *cf.* Zp. 2:5) – while at the same time building on the biographical sketch of Jacob (vv. 3–4), whose ambitious greed, even towards his brother, set the pattern for *Ephraim. False* (*i.e.* 'deceitful'; Heb. *mirmâ; cf.* 11:12) *scales* speak of crooked business practices against which Amos inveighed (8:5–6) and the sages warned (Pr. 11:1; 20:23). Ephraim was even-handed in his crooked greed – he *oppressed* (Heb. *'šq;* 5:11; *cf.* Dt. 24:14; Je. 7:6; Am. 4:1) even his 'friend' or 'ally': *loves* should not be an auxiliary verb here (*cf.* RSV; NEB; JB; NASB; NIV) but should be translated 'loved one' and made the object of the infinitive, *to oppress.* The clause then echoes Jacob's treacherous treatment of Esau (v. 3).

The cheating trader is not only identified in verse 8 but is made to testify against himself (*cf.* 2:5, 12; 10:3) with a boast as foolish as it is evil. He claims to have made himself rich (Heb. *'šr*). The use of the verb 'found' (Heb. *mṣ'*) for the acquisition of *wealth* (for the progressive pun on the meanings of *'wn,* see v. 4 and v. 11) is surely designed to contrast with Jacob's meeting (Heb. *mṣ'*) at Bethel (v. 4). Whatever failings the patriarch had, he certainly encountered something more important than the wealth in which his children trusted. The boast, which is a self-indictment, continues to the end of verse 8 (as in NIV and contrary to RSV; NEB; JB) and seals its arrogance with what is either a claim to innocence or to impunity: '(In) all my gains (Heb. *yāgîa'* describes the produce of wearying toil; *cf.* Dt. 28:33; Hg. 1:11) they will not find (again *mṣ'*) in me any crookedness (Heb. *'āwôn; cf.* 4:8; 5:5; 7:1; 8:13; 9:7, 9; 13:12; 14:1–2) that is a sin' (Heb. *ḥēṭ'*; Is. 31:7; Hosea frequently uses the root but not the word in this precise form; *cf.* 4:7; 8:11; 10:8, 9; 13:2).[1] Reading the text this way (so Andersen, pp. 593–594; Wolff, p. 207; Jacob, p. 85; Jeremias, p. 148) both intensifies the boast and delays the announcement of judgment so that we can hear it from Hosea's own mouth in verse 9.

God's self-introduction (v. 9 *cf.* 13:4) is the logical response to Ephraim's boast. It reminds us, as did the hymn-fragment in verse 5, of who is truly in charge. The people's destiny lies not in their Jacobite genes nor in their commercial cunning. They were from the beginning – *the land of Egypt* (*cf.* on 2:15) – and will be until God says differently, the people of *his*

[1]The translation is Ward's, p. 208; the parenthetical annotations are mine.

election. And what he elects for them in judgment is an abandonment of their prosperity and a return to the austerity of their wilderness *tents*. The crucial events of the Exodus and its subsequent wanderings have to be replayed, so that Ephraim may learn how dependent he is on Yahweh and how grateful he must be for such dependence. The *days of the appointed feast* may be an allusion to the temporary huts used for camps near the shrines (*cf.* on 9:6). But, since God's aim is to wipe out every vestige of Baal worship (2:16–17), more likely they continue the wilderness theme and refer to the festal use of the Tabernacle as described in Numbers (so Andersen, p. 618).

iii. Parables of the prophets (12:10–14). God, having introduced himself in verse 9, proceeds to describe his relationship to the prophets and the nature of their ministry (vv. 10, 13). The usefulness and faithfulness of their work contrast sharply with the selfish greed and foolish ambition of Jacob and his look-alike, Ephraim. The context, alight with references to the Exodus (vv. 9, 13), illuminates the role of the prophets in the founding and preservation of the nation. Nowhere does Hosea argue more forcefully for his own right to be heard. In intent these verses are identical to Amos 2:11–12; 3:3–8; 7:10–17: they describe the prophet's role as God-given and, therefore, unassailable. In the long run, prophets count for more than patriarchs, kings or princes. *To* (Heb. *'al* 'upon', 'against', 'over', 'unto' is unusual here and seems to contrast with *bᵉyad* in the final clauses; *'al* then, would mean *to* and *bᵉyad*, 'by' or 'through') them God has spoken his judging, guiding, saving word, and *multiplied* – note the contrast between their multiplication (12:1) and God's – *visions* (Heb. *ḥāzôn*; for the relationship between prophetic *vision* and speech, see Am. 1:1; 'vision' is the title of the books of Isaiah, Obadiah, and Nahum). *Through* (Heb. *bᵉyad*, lit. 'by the hand' of; perhaps a contrast with Ephraim's *hand* which held the cheating scales, v. 7) them God uttered *parables* (Heb. *dmh* does not here mean to 'silence' or 'destroy' as in 4:6; 10:7, 15 but 'to resemble' or in the intensive stem as here to 'devise comparisons' or 'similitudes', or 'set forth examples' [NAB]). The term is found in a wide range of literary forms with a spectrum of meanings, reminding us that content and form are both divinely given in the Scriptures.

The seeming disjointedness between verse 10 and verses 11–13 may become more understandable if we follow the suggestion that the mention of prophetic comparisons or similitudes at verse 10 leads to some examples of them from the prophet's own lips.[1] (Note that Yahweh is mentioned in the *third* person throughout vv. 11–14.) *Gilead* and *Gilgal* (see on 4:15; 6:8; 9:15) are introduced here abruptly for several reasons: (1) to show how widespread Israel's idolatry had become; (2) to resume and reinforce the theme of deceit and lying – both in religion and politics – with which chapter 12 was introduced (11:12); and (3) to demonstrate the sarcastic punning which was part of the prophetic style as God had ordered it – the punning that itself was part of the proclamation of judgment on the wicked folly of the people.

Before we can look at the puns in detail, we need to tackle the translation of verse 11. The *Gilead* clause is usually rendered either as a condition (RSV) – *If there is iniquity* (Heb. *'wn*; *cf.* on vv. 3, 8) – or a question (NEB; NASB; NIV) – 'Is Gilead wicked?' It is probably clearer to read the particles that suggest question or condition as intensive or emphatic (so JB; NAB; Andersen, pp. 594, 619). *Gilgal* and *Gilead* should be read in closer parallel than do most versions. The last two clauses should be read in parallel to each other with the place names as the double subject of both and both translated in past tense:

> They were certainly in Gilead with a worthless idol (*'āwen*)
> surely in Gilgal with an empty image (*šāw'*).
> (To) bulls they sacrificed.
> Indeed their altars were like cairns beside the fields' furrows.

In this reading the final clause is not a prediction; that would jar the tenses by inserting a future note in a verse that contains none. The point is to mock not to predict: the altars are as worthless as stones piled up by a farmer at the edges of his field (for 'furrows of the fields', see 10:4) when he clears his land (*cf.* Is. 5:2). Whether *bulls* should have the preposition *to* is an unanswerable question. Since Gilgal ends with the letter that is also the preposition *to* (Heb. *lᵉ*) the text may have accidently dropped it or else assumed that its force would

[1]See R. B. Coote, 'Hosea XII', *VT*, 21, 1971, pp. 397–402, for the identification and analysis of these 'similitudes'.

carry over. At stake is whether Hosea is speaking of calf-worship *per se* – *to* the bulls – or of sacrifice in which bulls were slaughtered (*cf.* 8:11–13; 10:1; 11:2).

The puns, which may be illustrations of the parables or similitudes (v. 10), begin with the description of Gilead's idolatry as *'wn*, a catchword in chapter 12 which has three separate meanings: *manhood*, mature virility (v. 3); *wealth* (v. 8); 'idolatry' (v. 11). Coote's conclusion seems correct. 'The deprecation of *'ôn* in any sense is the intent of the saying as of the chapter as a whole'.[1] Presumption and folly lie at the heart of all three behaviours – Jacob's struggle, Ephraim's avarice, Gilead's paganism. The word-play also focuses on the connection between the names Gilead, Gilgal and cairns or stones (Heb. *gallîm*), since all three terms feature the consonants *gl*. The worthlessness of the places is a chief thrust of this 'similitude': Gilead and Gilgal sound like and therefore are as empty of life and purpose as the piles of stone they use for altars.

The final 'similitude' employed by Hosea to demonstrate his prophetic role is in verses 12–13, where Jacob's service for a wife is made an illustration of Yahweh's rescue of his bride. The link between these verses has been so puzzling that the RSV has wrapped parentheses around it to suggest that it interrupted the flow of the text, while numerous commentators have moved it to the other Jacob section in verses 3–4. We see the placement of verses 12–13 as intentional: both verses tell the story of the way in which a bride (or in Jacob's case, brides) was obtained from a foreign land – Jacob/Israel's (note the double name in the parallelism, which serves further to interpret the verb-puns of v. 3) from *Aram* (Gn. 28:5; 29:15–30); Yahweh's from *Egypt* (*cf.* the bridal language in 2:14–15).[2] One sign of the parallel between the two episodes is the use of the verb 'watch' or 'keep' (Heb. *šmr*; RSV *herded*) which described Jacob's care of Laban's sheep (v. 12) and God's guarding of his people (v. 13).

The prophet's point here is more than comparison; it is also contrast. Jacob did what he had to do on his own. God rescued and preserved his bride by the use of prophets. The climax of the argument then is not that Ephraim has followed in the footsteps of Jacob, though that is surely part of the story, but

---

[1] R. B. Coote, *op. cit.*, p. 398.   [2] R. B. Coote, *op. cit.*, p. 401.

that Yahweh was again ready to work through a *prophet*. He had used Moses, as the prophet of the Exodus, and Samuel, as the prophet of the settlement in Canaan by whom Israel *was preserved*. Now another *prophet* held centre-stage, Hosea, whom the Israelites had previously deemed mad (9:7). The book began with the story of the prophet's mission in and through his marriage and family. It cannot conclude without a further word on the crucial role that God's called servants, however powerless and irrelevant they seemed, had played and would play in his redemptive work. Hosea's lineage as a prophet ultimately outweighed Ephraim's descent from Jacob. Each stood in continuity with ancestors, and Hosea knew which 'tribe' could truly draw on God's help.

The concluding verse (v. 14) tells us why Hosea went to such pains to explain and defend his role as God's agent. Ephraim had opposed the divine word to the point of *bitterness* (Heb. *tamrûrîm*; *cf.* Je. 6:26; 31:15), *provoking* (Heb. *k's*; *cf.* 1 Ki. 14:9; Je. 7:18, 19) Hosea and Yahweh beyond what they could suffer by flagrant disregard of their instruction. To be called as a prophet and put through excruciating pain is bad enough; to have words thrown back in your face is utterly insufferable. To have redeemed a bunch of slaves and settled them in a land they could have neither won nor bought was a demanding task; to find them incorrigibly ungrateful was provocation indeed. The language of this verse is intense. *Murders* (lit. 'bloodshed'), are counted among Ephraim's crimes (*cf.* 1:4; 4:2, 6:8), and God offers not relief but full accountability; the whole weight of such wrong is to be settled squarely on Ephraim's shoulders (Heb. *ntš* means to 'leave with' or 'entrust to'; *cf.* 1 Sa. 17:20). Ephraim's conduct has been a source of shame and reproach (Heb. *ḥerpâ*; *cf.* Je. 15:15; Joel 2:17, 19) to himself and his Sovereign. Since Ephraim's fate has been self-chosen, God will not avenge the abuse Ephraim has borne. Instead its full measure will be heaped (lit. 'made to return'; *cf.* 4:9; 12:2) upon him. Fittingly the last Hebrew word in the chapter is *his lord* (Heb. *ʾadōnāyw*; only here in Hosea; but frequently in Amos; *e.g.* 1:8; 3:7, 8, 11; 7:1, 4; 9:1). The acknowledgement of God as Master was not Jacob's nor Ephraim's strong suit. But in the end they would learn that covenant-privilege lasted only so long as did covenant-submission. Prophets like Hosea understood this. And, even more, when they bowed to the painful costs of saying yes to their commissions, they demonstrated what others would learn only through judgment – that Yahweh is the living Lord.

c. Ephraim, then and now – idolatry and ingratitude: (13:1–16 [Heb. 13:1 – 14:1])

Once more Hosea looks at Israel's impoverished present against the background of the lavish past (*cf.* 9:10; 10:1, 9; 11:1; 12:13). As in chapter 12, the focus is not on geographical sites (although note 12:11) but on the behaviour and reputation of a patriarch – this time *Ephraim*, which in verse 1 must stand for the original descendants of the strong son of Joseph, who counted among their ranks powerful leaders of the nation like Joshua (Jos. 24:30) and Jeroboam I (1 Ki. 11:26; 12:20). This chapter complements chapter 12 by stressing the announcements of judgment (vv. 5, 7–8, 9–10, 14, 15–16) as forcefully as chapter 12 emphasized the accusations of sin (11:12 – 12:1; 12:2–4, 7–8, 11, 14a). Yet the accusations that trigger the announcements in chapter 13 should not be overlooked because they recapitulate a number of dominant themes in Hosea and thereby set the stage for both the final word of judgment in verses 15–16 and the last call to return in 14:1–8. The themes summed up in chapter 13 are these: *idolatry by calf-worship* (v. 2; *cf.* 8:5–6; 10:5, 7; for idolatry in general, *cf.* 2:8; 3:1, 4; 4:12, 17; 8:4; 9:6, 10; 10:2, 6; 11:2); *ingratitude for the Exodus* (vv. 4–6; *cf.* 8:14; 9:10; 11:1–2; 12:9, 13); *foolish trust in political leaders* (vv. 10–11; *cf.* 7:7; 8:4; 9:15; 10:3, 15); *complacency in the face of judgment* (v. 13; *cf.* 4:4, 16; 5:6–7; 6:1–3, 4–5; 7:2, 9–10; 8:2; 9:7; 12:8–9). They not only recapture Hosea's major emphases, but also prepare for the precise words of penitence spelled out in the call to return with which the book closes: *idolatry* must be renounced (14:3c, 8), *gratitude* expressed (14:2c), *trust* in political alliance and military might rejected (14:3ab), *complacency* replaced by dependence on God (14:3d).

Chapter 13 is a series of short judgment speeches, each of which is reinforced by literary devices that intensify the indictments or sharpen the threats. If Hosea deliberately restates a number of his major themes, so he seems to display again an array of his literary techniques.

Ephraim's tragic fall (vv. 1–3).
   The accusation is heightened by the note of *tragic reversal*
in Ephraim's power and prestige (v. 1); the announcement (v. 3) carries a note of *irony* in its similarity to God's
description of the inconstancy of the people in 6:4.

God's ferocious judgment (vv. 4–8).
   The accusation (v. 6) is strengthened by the *self-
introduction* of Yahweh and the stinging reminder of his
grace (vv. 4–5); the announcement is made bold by the
similes of wild beasts to whom God likens himself (vv.
7–8).

Ephraim's total vulnerability (vv. 9–11).
   The judgment threat is fortified by *rhetorical questions* that
highlight the impotence of Israel's military-political structures (v. 10).

Ephraim's foolish stubbornness (vv. 12–14).
   The accusation is couched in a *double metaphor* that conveys a picture of intentional yet stupid refusal to repent
(vv. 12–13); the announcement is empowered by the
pathos of *divine complaint* followed by the fatal *rhetorical
questions* which summon the forces of 'Death' and 'Sheol'
to execute their gruesome task.

Samaria's fatal rebellion (vv. 15–16).
   The announcement of judgment is sounded in the
combination of *metaphorical and literal* accounts – the 'east
wind' (v. 15) is interpreted by the 'sword' (v. 16).

i. Ephraim's tragic fall (13:1–3). The judgment speech
(accusation, vv. 1–2; announcement, v. 3) uttered by the
prophet *about*, not *to*, the people, virtually repeats the tragic
story of 9:10, except that, in the earlier passage, the emphasis
was on Israel's potential fruitfulness in doing God's will. Here,
however, the point is Ephraim's prestige and leadership
among the tribes – expressed in terms of the awesome impact
on others, the *trembling* (Heb. *rᵉṭēṭ*; found here only; Vulg.
reads 'horror', a meaning confirmed in the Qumran scrolls;
1QH 4.33) caused by Ephraim's presence and the elevated

role allotted to him (Heb. *nś'* is to be pointed either *niśśā'*, Niphal participle 'lifted up'; or *nāśî'*, 'key leader'; *cf.* Gn. 23:6; frequently in Numbers, *e.g.* ch. 2 and Ezekiel, *e.g.* chs. 45–48). If *Ephraim* in this instance describes the tribe in its prime, *Israel* may mean the entire people, not just the northern tribes. If so, the chapter has a further tie to chapter 12 where Judah is specifically mentioned (12:2) and the whole people is in view, at least part of the time, in the references to Jacob and the Exodus. As chapter 13 progresses and the attention shifts from past to present, *Israel* means the Northern Kingdom (v. 9) and *Ephraim*, the beleaguered enclave around Samaria (vv. 12, 16), the last region to capitulate to Assyrian rule.

As in 9:10, *Baal* (*cf.* 2:13, 16–17; 11:2) was the cause of defection, and the results were disastrous: Ephraim 'became detestable' (9:10), *died* (v. 1), *i.e.* ceased to play any productive part in God's programme and consequently was headed for the judgment of full covenant annulment described in the names of Hosea's three children (*cf.* ch. 1). If a specific historic occasion is needed for Ephraim's fall from grace and glory, it would be the seizing of the throne of the northern tribes by Jeroboam I, some two centuries earlier, and his prompt establishment of shrines to rival Jerusalem in which Baal came to be worshipped in the guise of the golden calves (1 Ki. 12:16, 26–30).

All this is a reminder of the stages in Israel's devotion to Baal: (1) Baal-peor (9:10; Nu. 25:3) suggests some kind of beginning spark in Moses' day; (2) Jeroboam I lit the fire afresh when he divided the kingdom after Solomon's death; (3) Ahab and Jezebel fuelled the flames until Elisha and Jehu doused them with a vengeance (2 Ki. chs. 9–10); (4) Jeroboam II and his successors seemed to have fanned the smouldering embers to life once more as the pages of Hosea describe the situation; and (5) though the Assyrian invasions and deportation forever changed the life of the northern tribes, Baal worship survived in Judah until its surrender to Nebuchadrezzar (586 BC) as the speeches of Jeremiah attest (7:9; 9:13; 11:13, 17; 32:29, 35). Hosea's wrath against the calves (*cf.* 8:5–6; 10:5, 7; 13:2) is to be explained in part by the fact that they always threatened to misrepresent God and lead the people into paganism even when the name of Baal was not specifically invoked. We note from 2 Kings 10:28–31 that Jehu was faulted because he retained Jeroboam's calf-images at Dan and Bethel even after he had 'wiped out Baal from Israel'.

What Jeroboam I had begun and Jeroboam II sponsored, the people of Samaria continued with unbridled enthusiasm (v. 2) in Hosea's time. The prophet describes their passion bluntly. It is sin (Heb. *ḥṭ'*, *cf.* 12:8), described as: (1) making a cast or *molten image* (Heb. *massēkâ*; here only in Hosea; *cf.* Ex. 32:4, 8 and the story of Aaron's golden calf) of *their silver* – a symbol of high value, perhaps worth more than gold in Hosea's day (*cf.* 2:8); *their* speaks of high arrogance, since any wealth belonged to God (Ps. 24:1) or was his gift (Ho. 2:8) – and set up to serve as *idols* (Heb. *'āṣāḇ*; *cf.* 4:17; 8:4; 14:9; the root means 'to shape or form') *i.e.* symbols of, or substitutes for God, which they could never be because they were entirely the work of mere *craftsmen* (*cf.* 8:6), no matter how skilled (Heb. *tᵉḇûnām* is probably a shortened form of *tᵉḇûnātām*; so BDB, p. 108; not a derivative of *tabnît*, 'pattern', 'form', or 'model', as Wolff, p. 219, reads it); (2) speaking to the images, *i.e.* in prayer and petition (reading with Andersen, p. 624; most commentators and versions make this clause the introduction to a quotation that follows, but doing so entails an emendation of the 'those sacrificing' from participle to imperative and, often, a juggling of the word order); the last two lines of v. 2 may be read:

> to them [the idols], they – those who sacrifice a human
> being – are speaking.
> They kiss [the] calves;

(3) engaging in human sacrifice – a picture both horrible and ludicrous is drawn of persons talking to idols and at the same time being 'sacrificers of a human being' (for other possible references to human sacrifice, usually child-sacrifice, in Hosea, see 5:2; 9:13); and (4) kissing calves; *calves* may describe the form into which the images were moulded, while *kissing* is an act of devotion, adoration or appeasement, (*cf.* Ps. 2:12). Viewed together, the sin is a total perversion of values. A craftsman's work is elevated to divine status; human beings sacrifice their offspring to a metal object from whose lifeless form they also beg help; persons embrace with adulation the images of the very animals that they use for ploughing, threshing and hauling.

The inevitable (*therefore*; *cf.* on 2:6, 8) judgment for such worthless worship is to become worthless, in fact, to vanish (v. 3). A four-fold simile of fading into nothingness is Hosea's powerful way of intensifying the picture by multiple repetition. *Morning cloud* and *dew* that evaporates early described Israel's fickleness in 6:4. See Psalm 1:4 for the *chaff* that is sent spinning away from the *threshing floor* (*cf.* 9:1–2) in a storm-wind (so Heb. *s'r*, 'storm' or 'rage' depicts). *Smoke* is a second subject of the verb *s'r*; a strong wind would suck the smoke from the lamps that illuminate a room through any orifice, whether a latticed opening (*window*) in the wall or a chimney on the roof (Heb. *°rubbâ*, *cf.* Is. 60:8; Gn. 7:11; 8:2, may mean either). The point is that idolatry carries its own punishment: you worship nothing; you get nothing; you end as nothing.

ii. God's ferocious judgment (13:4–8). God will now speak and continue through verse 14; then the prophet's words will close the judgment speech in verses 15–16. The divine self-introduction (*cf.* 12:9) is expanded to remind Israel of the prologue to the ten commandments and of the first commandment itself (Ex. 20:2–3). *No God but me* (*cf.* Joel 2:27) speaks to the idolatry described in verse 2 and recalls to Israel the exclusiveness of the covenant relationship (on *know* as the symbol of that relationship, see 2:20; 4:1, 6; 6:6; for Israel's claim to know God, and his denial of that claim, see 5:5; 6:3; 8:2); 'No *saviour* besides me' condemns Israel's foolish dependence on foreign alliances and impotent kings (*cf.* Samuel's conviction that setting up a king entailed rejecting God as Saviour, 1 Sa. 10:19; also Ephraim's failure to be Jephthah's saviour or helper in his battle with the Ammonites, Jdg. 12:3) and prepares the way for verses 10–11. In *knew you in the wilderness* (v. 5), *you* is singular and must refer collectively to all the people who descended from the Exodus tribes and by a kind of corporate personality experienced those events that their forbears went through five centuries earlier (*cf.* Levi's paying of tithes while yet in Abraham's loins, Heb. 7:9–10). *Knew* describes God's gracious care that derived from his special relationship to his people. For *know* in this sense, *cf.* Psalm 1:6; Amos 3:2. The emphasis on God's provision is reinforced by the phrase *the land of drought* (Heb. *tal'ubôt*, only here in the Old Testament, may be related to an Akkadian word for 'fevers'), whose meaning seems to extend the notion of desolation inherent in the *wilderness* experience (*cf.* 2:3, where a similar phrase means 'parched' or 'arid' land).

The accusation, charged with intensity by the reminder of Exodus-grace, comes to its climax (v. 6) in a manner identical to 2:13: *therefore they forgot me* (*cf.* 4:6; 8:14, for Hosea's use of this verb as a symbol of ultimate and absolute rejection – the term directly opposite to the verb *know* which expressed divine love and care in verse 5). Self-reliance – including reliance on their self-adopted and self-sustained religion (*cf.* 2:13) – lay at the heart of the crime. *Full* stomachs were its primary cause. God traces the steps in their downfall: (1) 'when I fed them' (Heb. *kᵉmô rᵉᶜîtîm; cf.* NIV; JB; Andersen, p. 633) a word division that makes better sense than MT's 'according to their pasture' (*cf.* NASB; Ward, p. 218; Wolff, p. 220); (2) 'they grew satisfied' (Heb. *śbᶜ* was used as part of a judgment announcement in 4:10; when satisfaction leads to sin, frustration may become the proper punishment); (3) 'they stayed satisfied' (the lack of conjunction between the two uses of *śbᶜ* emphasizes both the repetition and the connection of the second form with what follows); (4) '*and* then *their heart*' (*cf.* on 2:14; 4:11; 7:2, 11, 14; 10:2; 11:8) became haughty (lit. *lifted up,* 'high'; *cf.* 11:7 for an intensive-causative form of the word; Heb. *rwm*); and (5) *therefore they forgot me*.

The announcement of judgment (vv. 7–8) is alive with pictures of vicious animals, whose ferocity Yahweh threatens to emulate. *Lion* (Heb. *šáḥal,* one of the less frequent words for lion; *cf.* 5:14, for a similar passage) sets the scene of savagery. The *leopard* (*cf.* Je. 5:16; Hab. 1:8) is watchful along the path of its enemy (LXX; Vulg. incorrectly read Heb. '*šwr* as Assyria rather than 'I shall keep watch', *lurk; cf.* the same verb used more positively of Yahweh's vigilant care in 14:8). The bereaved *bear* (*cf.* on Am. 5:19) heightens the action from stalking to attack, as inferred from the verb (Heb. *pgš,* 'meet', 'fall upon'), and from the adjective 'bereaved' (Heb. *šakkûl; cf.* Je. 18:21), which describes a female bear in a frenzy either to recover her cubs or destroy their attackers (*cf.* 2 Sa. 17:8; Pr. 17:12) – a destruction further described as 'ripping open (Heb. *qrᶜ; cf.* Gn. 37:29; Joel 2:13) the enclosure of their heart' (*i.e. breast,* the chest cavity). 'Heart' here recalls verse 6, where the 'haughty heart' led to the final forgetfulness; the punishment corresponds to the crime. *Lion* (Heb. *lābî '; cf.* on Joel 1:6), sharpens the picture of savagery, as do the verb *eat* (*cf.* on

2:12; 11:6), the adverb *there* (*i.e.* right on the spot, not bothering to haul the carcass away), the further description of the lion as 'beast of the field' (*cf.* 2:12), and the final verb, 'split them open' (Heb. *bq'* in the intensive stem; *cf.* Gn. 22:3; 1 Sa. 6:14).

The contrast between the threats of judgment in the first two speeches (vv. 1–3, 4–8) is informing. Where the *folly of idolatry* was involved – the crediting of divine status to an artisan's handiwork – the punishment was expressed in terms of natural phenomena like disappearing clouds, vanishing dew and wind-whipped chaff or smoke. The crime virtually carried its own penalties and no divine intervention was described. Where the crime was the *spurning* of the grace proffered in the Exodus and the personal rejection of God, the corresponding punishment was ferocious destruction, wrought in scene after scene by Yahweh, who assaults Israel like a pack of wild animals. This is a reminder that Israel's theologians believed in two kinds of punishment: (1) an automatic or dynamistic pattern in which breaking the patterns set by the order in God's creation had predictably bad results, like defying the law of gravity by jumping off a roof; and (2) a legal, personal, or forensic retribution in which God kept careful records and personally executed the punishment. The dynamistic pattern is more characteristic of wisdom literature, though found at times in the prophets (*cf.* the woe oracles of Hab. ch. 2), while the forensic form is more frequent in the prophets.

iii. Ephraim's total vulnerability (13:9–11).

God continues to threaten judgment. And he addresses Israel directly – *I will destroy* (Heb. *šḥt*, intensive stem; *cf.* 9:9; 11:9) *you, Israel*, or following a recent reconstruction, 'Should I destroy you, Israel, who, please, will be your helper.'[1] The chief crime, the prime folly, had been arrogant self-reliance (*cf.* on vv. 4–8), whether expressed in confidence in man-made idols (vv. 1–2), in crops garnered with Baal's alleged help (v. 6), or in the imperium of Samaria's monarchs (vv. 10–11). That foolish crime is to be exposed and avenged by the withdrawal of the

---

[1] M. Dahoud, *Bib*, 60 (1979), pp. 573–4. This reading hinges on interpreting *kî* as interrogative *who*? not causal or emphatic, and *bî* not as prepositional phrase, 'against me' (NASB; NICOT) but as a precative particle, 'please'.

HOSEA 13:9–11

help that made possible everything good in Israel's life (*cf.* Pss. 33:20; 70:6; 115:9–10; 121:1–2; 124:8). By this threat God himself was removing from Israel's experience the marker stone set up by Samuel and named Ebenezer, stone of *help*, to commemorate the constant availability of divine aid in Israel's struggle to secure its national identity in the face of Philistine harassment (1 Sa. 7:12). One of the terrifying aspects of God's judgment on his people is that when he, the Redeemer, becomes the oppressor there is no help at all on which to fall back.

The rhetorical questions of verse 10 sharpen the point. The destruction is going to be wrought by military means (*cf.* v. 16, *the sword*). The logical defence against such a threat would be the king – 'who would *save you*', *i.e.* 'bring you victory' (Heb. *yš'* might involve a pun on the name of Hoshea, Israel's last king to whom no permanent victory was given) – and his cadre of military commanders, called here 'rulers' (lit. 'judges'; *cf.* on 7:7) and *princes* (*cf.* on 3:4; 5:10; 7:3, 5, 16; 8:10; 9:15). But they are *nowhere* to be found. Such is the expected answer to the questions. 'In all your cities' (no need to emend the text as do RSV; JB) adds bite to the sarcasm. Great investment in their fortifications would prove fruitless when God marched his Assyrian troops against them (*cf.* 8:14; 10:14–15). The quotation of Israel's plea for a monarchy summarizes conversations between Samuel and the people in the last days of Israel's judges (1 Sa. 8:4–9), in which the people seemed to override the senior prophet's misgivings (1 Sa. 8:10–20). God had acceded to their begging for a king (1 Sa. 8:22). The monarchy as a whole was established in ambiguous circumstances which help to account for Yahweh's anger: the people had brushed aside all its potential pitfalls, especially the competition it offered to God's own kingship (1 Sa. 8:7). If our interpretation of *Gilgal* as a symbol of the brash beginnings of the monarchy is correct (*cf.* on 9:15), then verses 10–11 are further comment on it. The imperfect tense of the verbs, 'I was giving' and 'I was taking', suggests that the statement describes an historical pattern not just the enthronement or removal of a single controversial king, like Saul or Jeroboam I. Indeed, verse 11 is a succinct summary of the role of divine sovereignty in exploiting, for purposes of instruction and judgment, the political chaos of the Northern Kingdom, especially during its last three decades (*cf.* on 6:11b – 7:7).

Hosea notes the human initiative with all the rebellion inherent in it (8:4) and the divine providence which made use of the rebellion and controlled its shape and form (13:11).

iv. Ephraim's foolish stubbornness (13:12–14). The first metaphor (v. 12), with its verbs of 'tying up' or 'wrapping' (Heb. *ṣrr*; *cf.* on 4:19) and 'hiding' (Heb. *ṣpn*; *cf.* Ex. 2:2; Jos. 2:4) so as to guard or treasure, suggests how firmly and intentionally *Ephraim, i.e.* Israel, cherished his sinful behaviour (on *iniquity*, Heb. *'āwôn, cf.* 4:8; 5:5; 7:1; 8:13; 9:7, 9; 12:9; 14:1, 2; on *sin*, Heb. *ḥaṭṭā't, cf.* on 12:8). He bundled it up and stored it away like a precious scroll or a family heirloom. Other readings see the metaphor as symbolic of a document of judgment that records Israel's sins (so NIV; Jacob, p. 93). Our interpretation is based on the conclusion that Ephraim must be the implied subject of the passive verbs in verse 12, as he is the clear subject of the birth-metaphor in verse 13. God is speaking – the form is probably a *divine complaint* (so Jeremias, p. 165) in which is contrasted the foolish stubbornness of Ephraim (vv. 12–13) with the gracious, redemptive intentions of Yahweh (v. 14) – in a vein similar to 4:16; 6:4–6; 7:13c, 15; 8:5b; 9:10; 10:1; 10:11; 11:1–9, although his focus is more on Israel's present than past.

The timing of this seems clear in the second metaphor (v. 13), where the imperfect verbs should probably be translated as future, 'labour pains *will come* for him' and he '*will not present* himself'. It is possible, however, that what God describes is not just the final instance of intransigence, in the face of imminent disaster at Assyrian hands, but a characteristic pattern that could be rendered, 'The labour pains keep coming ... but he never presents himself ....' The *pangs* (Heb. *ḥᵃbālîm; cf.* Is. 13:8; Je. 13:23) connote here not so much anguish as *timing*, (*cf.* the prominence of *time*, Heb. *'ēt*, in the sentence), since the focus is not on the mother but on the *son* needing to be born. In the normal process of birth those pains in their rhythm of contraction would cause the child to surge inch by inch through the cervix and vagina to daylight. Not so with Ephraim. The time of his birth – his rejection of his haughty independence and the declaration of his total commitment to Yahweh – was being strongly and regularly signalled both by historic events and prophetic proclamation. But he was not moving – a stubbornness that endangered the life of both mother and child (*cf.* Gn. 35:16–19; *cf.* Is. 66:7–11, where the joy and relief of a rapid, painless, birth are featured). *Present himself* (Heb. *'md*, lit. 'stand') probably means 'stand ready' but could also be read as 'should not delay', since the time of birth has come (*cf.* NASB). The closest parallel to this birth analogy is Hezekiah's complaint (2 Ki. 19:3; Is. 37:3) that Judah's time of birth has come and they do not have strength to push through the cervix (Heb. *mašbēr*; probably the same word used in Ho. 13:13 and to be translated 'mouth of the womb', lit. 'the place of breaking-through') to be born. In verse 13 the problem is not lack of strength but absence of wisdom – a trait of Israel well documented in Hosea (*cf.* 'without sense', lit. 'heart' in 7:11; 'take away the understanding', lit. 'heart' in 4:11; 'a people without understanding' 4:14, Heb. *yābîn*; its cognates are frequently used in parallel to 'wise' in Proverbs and other wisdom literature). It is the inability to make the right decision – the decision to trust God and return to him – that stands at the core of Israel's folly. The need for wisdom, stressed here, will be the dominant note on which Hosea's book is ended and its message extended to the whole believing community: *Whoever is wise* . . . (14:9).

The divine complaint gathers pathos in the first clauses of verse 14, the exact force of which has divided interpreters. Most (RSV; NEB; JB; Ward, p. 219; Wolff, p. 221; Jeremias, p. 160; Jacob, p. 91) read them as rhetorical questions that insist on negative answers. Wolff suggests that the questions counter pleas or protests that *Yahweh* intervene in the blocked birth process (v. 13). Absence of any overt sign of a question places such interpretations in question. Some (NASB; NIV) read as promises: 'I will ransom' (for the Heb. *pdh*, *cf.* 7:13); 'I will redeem' (*g'l*, lit. to act in rescue or ransom as a kinsman toward a relative in difficulty; used only here in Hosea; *cf.* Gn. 48:16; Ex. 6:6; 15:13; Is. 43:1; Je. 31:11). The imperfect tenses allow that, but such bold assurance of rescue jars the context. Andersen (p. 625) read the tenses as past, in what he must deem to have been an account of deliverance already wrought (p. 628) but with no explanation of its setting or its role in the chapter.

If we take our cue from an earlier statement about God's desire to redeem (7:13), we may see in verse 14a an expression of his compassionate intent which has been frustrated by

Ephraim's foolish stubbornness: 'From the hand (*i.e. power*; *cf.* Am. 9:2; 2 Ki. 13:5; Pr. 18:21) of *Sheol* (*i.e.* the grave, the realm of the dead; here virtually treated as a personal entity over which God claims absolute power; *cf.* Am. 9:2; Ps. 16:10; 139:8) I wanted to *ransom them*; from *Death* (not only the experience of death is described by Heb. *mwt* but probably the Canaanite god of death and drought, *Mot*, as well) I longed to *redeem them.*' This combination of sovereignty over the powers of death and of frustration at Ephraim's failure to avail himself of this power – which failure turned his mother's womb into his grave – lies at the heart of the divine complaint (*cf.* 11:1–9) and issues in the sharp commands implied in the rhetorical questions with which verse 14 closes. In reverse order from verse 14a, *Death* and *Sheol* are addressed by Yahweh and ordered to do their dastardly deeds to the people in judgment by *plagues* (*cf.* Am. 4:10; a standard term for disaster, the word may here mean 'thorns'; *cf.* Ps. 91:3, 6) and by *stings* (Heb. *qeṭeb* occurs in Dt. 32:24; Ps. 91:6; Is. 28:2, parallel to *deber, plague*; the occurrences are too scarce and too uncertain to allow a confident translation), perhaps the stings of hordes of insects like mosquitoes. Andersen's suggestion (p. 640) that some demonic connotation may be present in this combination of terms should be borne in mind.

The introductory question word 'Where?' (Heb. *ʾehî, cf.* v. 10), is found only in Hosea and seems to be an alternative (dialectical?) form of the standard word for 'where?', *ʾayyēh*, and should not be connected with the verb *hyh*, 'to be' (*cf.* Ward, pp. 220ff.). The force of the *where* here is something like, 'Bring them on; let your smiting, stinging scourges do their work. I am at my tether's end. Having rejected my intent to redeem him, Ephraim can now bear the full brunt of your assault, O Death and Sheol' (note the pairing of these forces in Rev. 6:8). The final clause of verse 14 clinches the matter: 'Compassion (Heb. *nōḥam*, only here in the Old Testament, must be from *nḥm* 'to feel sorry'; *cf.* the kindred *niḥûmîm* in 11:8; LXX and Vulg. both use words for *comfort* to translate) will be hid from my eyes.' Judgment is announced as the climax of the complaint, and forces irresistible to any but God will be summoned to inflict it. The New Testament use of these questions capitalizes on their ambiguity and hears in them words not of threat but of triumph (1 Cor. 15:55–57) – a reminder of the difference that Christ has made. In Christ's resurrection, the ransom and redemption that God intended for Israel (Ho. 13:14a) have been fulfilled. The backs of Sheol and death have been broken. When summoned now they come not as marauders to terrorize but as vanquished enemies to be mocked.

v. Samaria's fatal rebellion (13:15–16). This last judgment speech of the book voices no accusation, only the threat of judgment. The target of the divine wrath is narrow, since the judgment by enemy invasion and political subjugation has apparently descended already on the bulk of the Northern Kingdom. *Ephraim*, the central hill country now invested and insulated by Assyrian troops, is the subject of the attack described metaphorically in verse 15. *Samaria*, its capital and only major city as yet unscathed by foreign assault, is the object of the savage siege detailed in verse 16. The movement from metaphorical to literal is one key to understanding the speech. Another is the *pun* on the name *Ephraim* contained in the word *flourish* (Heb. *pr'*, whose consonants play on the *pr* which stands at the heart of Ephraim's name, may be a deliberate or a dialectical misspelling of *prh*, the more normal verb form; *cf.* the familiar formula in the command to populate: 'be fruitful', Gn. 1:22, 28). The picture of fruitfulness is a preparation for the judgment by the east wind as well as for the final pun on Ephraim's name at 14:8.

A third key is the reprising of earlier words and themes to sum up the message: (1) Ephraim, who pursued the *east wind* in treaty-making with Assyria (12:1) will now be scorched by that same *east wind* (v. 15); (2) the *wilderness*, the site of Israel's original (9:10) and future (2:14) encounters with God, will become a source of the judgment (v. 15); (3) the idols (2:8) and cultic ornaments (2:13) – their *treasury* (*cf.* Joel 1:17) of *precious vessels* (*cf.* 9:6) – which Israel fashioned from God's gifts and used to adore Baal will be *plundered* (Heb. *šsh*; *cf.* 1 Sa. 14:48; 23:1; 2 Ki. 17:20; Is. 42:22); (4) Ephraim's boast of purity in spite of ill-gotten wealth (*cf.* 12:8) is put down by the exposé of Samaria's *guilt* (Heb. *'šm*; *cf.* 5:15; 10:2; and especially 13:1, where Israel's guilt through Baal leads to death), the full consequences of which are announced in verses 15–16; (5) the utter destruction of the populace, with the dashing of the babies (*cf.* 10:14) and the disembowelment of the pregnant women (*cf.* Am. 1:13; *cf.* Ho. 13:8 for Yahweh as the implied subject of the same verb *bq'* to 'split open') becomes a literal fulfilment of the 'Not-my-people' judgment (1:9) in which not only is the covenant annulled, but the people itself is wiped out, with no chance of survival – children gone and pregnancies aborted; (6) *sword* in verse 16 (*cf.* 1:7; 7:16; 11:6; not until the sword has done its appointed task will it be abolished, 2:18) indicates how *east wind* in verse 15 should be heard: judgment by literal drought is not the point here (though it certainly can be in the Old Testament *cf.* Joel chs. 1–2; Am. 4:6–8); the Assyrian invasion under Shalmaneser V is the *east wind*, with the result that *east wind* and *sword* mean the same thing – military invasion of earth-scorching, life-denying proportions; (7) Samaria's rebellion (Heb. *mrh* only here in Hosea; *cf.* the wilderness traditions of Nu. 20:10, 24; 27:14) sums up a whole series of indictments against the capital – both political (the 'wicked deeds' in 7:1) and religious (the 'calf' in 8:5–6; 10:5, 7); and (8) the historic role of Ephraim as the prominent and admired tribe of the Northern Kingdom (*cf.* 13:1) seems to underlie the description of his flourishing 'among the brothers' (v. 15a) and suggests that the familiar emendation of 'brothers' to *reed plant* (*cf.* RSV; NEB; JB; NASB; Wolff, p. 222) does little to improve our understanding of the passage.

The intricate relationship between the metaphorical *east wind* (described as *Yahweh's wind* to feature both its origin and its terrifying effectiveness) and the literal *sword* raises the question about a possible connection between the disastrous effects attributed to each instrument of destruction: the *east wind* (v. 15) destroys Ephraim's *fountain* and *spring*, while plundering the *treasury* of every *precious thing* (lit. 'vessel'); the ravaging *sword* (v. 16) attacks inhabitants in general (*they shall fall*) and then singles out *little ones* and *pregnant women*. It is just possible that the objects of verse 15 are metaphors for the persons of verse 16, just as the *east wind* seems to be poetic imagery for the military invasion summarized in *sword*. *Spring* (Heb. *ma'yān*) is used three times to describe a wife as a source of life and refreshment to her husband (Pr. 5:16; Song 4:12, 15); *pregnant women* (and perhaps *little children*) may well be called the *spring* from which fresh life for the nation should flow. *Precious things* is literally 'vessels of desire', *i.e.* delightful vessels. While the phrase probably means images, art objects, jewelry and serving vessels (*cf.* Je. 25:34; Na. 2:9), we should not overlook Hosea's own use of a related phrase 'delight of their womb' to describe new-born babies (9:16; *beloved children*, RSV). It is worth noting, further, that the word 'vessel' (Heb. *kᵉlî*; Gr. *skeuos*) in Rabbinic writings is used on occasion as a metaphor for a woman, particularly in contexts where sexual activity is in view. Paul's admonition to marital chastity may reflect this Rabbinic imagery in 1 Thessalonians 4:4.[1]

If Hosea has some such close links in mind between verse 15 and verse 16, we have (1) strong evidence for the unity of this judgment speech; (2) a further example of Hosea's pattern of using imagery and then interpreting it (*e.g.* the Gomer/Israel pattern of chapters 1-3; the oven figures of 7:3–7; the foreign alliance metaphors of 7:8–9, 11–12); and (3) a clear illustration of the 'similitudes' (or *parables*) in which God enabled his prophets to speak (12:10).

d. Israel and Yahweh, their future – repentance and restoration (14:1–8 [Heb. 14:2–9])

The threats of judgment in the third section of the book (11:12 – 13:16) have brought Israel to its nadir: the Northern Kingdom is pictured as consisting first of Ephraim, the remnant state (13:15), and finally of Samaria alone (13:16), whose destruction is pronounced to be total and irreparable, with no possibility to rebuild the kingdom. No time is left to avert the judgment; no way is open to skirt the will of God, announced throughout the book from the naming of Jezreel (1:4) to the picture of Samaria's demise (13:15–16). Consequently, the prophet speaks again of Israel's distant future, after the judgment has had its way (1:10; 2:14; 3:5; 11:8–9). His aim has been to transcend the judgment. His hope is that the divine constancy that has insisted on punishing a people who have abandoned their calling will reveal God's holy love in forgiveness when the tattered remnant of his people seek it. His approach to the future, then, begins with a *call to return* (14:1–3), spelling out in detail the steps Israel must take to leave the days of judgment behind and move towards reconciliation. That call is complemented by a record of God's *response* in the form of a love song (14:4–8).

[1]*Cf.* C. Maurer, *TDNT*, VII, pp. 361–362, 365–367.

i. Israel's call to return (14:1–3). Each term of the call (v. 1) is chosen to recall and distill major aspects of Hosea's message. *Return* (Heb. *šwb*) has been the characteristic way of stating God's unfulfilled desire for Israel throughout the book (2:7, 9; 3:5; 5:4; 7:10, 16; 11:5; 12:6). It occurs four times in this concluding chapter (vv. 1, 2, 4, 7) which pictures what will happen at Israel's return – both as to requirements and results – and which stands as a deliberate contrast to the half-hearted return which Israel proposed in the earlier song (6:1–3). *Yahweh* is named specifically as the *destination of the return*, since confusion as to his nature and exclusive sovereignty over Israel has been the bone of contention between prophet and people (*cf.* 2:16–17, where the very names of the Baals have to be eradicated in order that Yahweh's true lordship be honoured). His exclusive right to their loyalty is reaffirmed in the words *your God* (*cf.* 4:6; 9:1; 12:6). The cluster *Yahweh your God* is found in the two self-introductions preserved in Hosea (12:9; 13:4). *Israel* – here most likely the entire people, though with a focus on the northern tribes, as Ephraim's name suggests (v. 8) – is called to respond to the One who has so forcefully presented himself as Lord and Saviour in the two previous chapters.

The need for return is compressed into two main terms. *Stumbled* embraces the multiplicity of consequences that have accrued to the defiant people, whose whole national life has been a tissue of instability – whether the fabric is political, economic, or religious (4:5; 5:5; 14:9). Given the paths they chose, Israel simply could not walk steadily and uprightly. What they tripped over was their *iniquity*, a word (Heb. *'āwôn*; *cf.* on 4:8 and 13:12, where Ephraim clung to it as though it were a priceless treasure) which catches the rebellion, deceitfulness, perversity and crookedness of Israel's life. With a whole repertoire of terms at his disposal, Hosea chose this as the most encompassing and effective way of describing the endemic and manifold evil he decried (*cf.* also v. 2).

The terms of the return are listed with almost telegraphic brevity in verses 2–3: the issues are too clear to need expansiveness; the stakes are too high to risk obscuring the main points by embellishment. The mood remains imperative: urgency makes politeness irrelevant; all other options have long ago been exhausted. The doctor knows what must be done and wastes no strokes in performing his surgery. *Take*

with you words. The grammar switches from the singular of
verse 1 to the plural, not only to include all segments and
persons of Israel but also to set up a contrast to the singular
that is used to address God. The first three imperatives in
verse 2 are plural, directed to Israel; the next two are singular,
addressed to God. *Words* describes the pleas and the vows
contained in verses 2b–3 (*cf.* Jacob's words with God at Bethel,
12:4). Israel's crime was not just breach of law; it was an
offence against the divine person, the Husband of chapters
1–3, the Parent of chapter 11. As such it could not be dealt
with by the offering of sacrifice and the payment of fine (*cf.*
6:6; Mi. 6:1–8). The personal relationship could be restored
only by words that make a personal commitment, words so
important that the prophet could not leave them to chance but
listed them precisely in a litany of contrition.

Take away all iniquity (v. 2); the Hebrew construction is
unusual (*all* precedes the verb which is followed by the noun,
as though the *extent* of Israel's iniquity is featured) and may
well be connected to the final clause of verse 3 – *since by You the
orphan is pitied* – and thus form a frame for the other lines of
the prayer-vow (so Andersen, p. 642). The forgiveness pled
for here is precisely what was denied in 1:6 and can be offered
now only because judgment is complete. Forgiveness deprived
of justice would be a travesty of divine righteousness. As
1 John 1:9 puts it, 'he is faithful and *just* and will forgive our
sins'. The cross is the ground of forgiveness because it is also
the seat of judgment. *Accept what is good* pleads with God to
take the words of contrition and pledge at their face value.
They are words well-meant and to be trusted. For *good* (Heb.
ṭôb) as a virtual synonym of *word*, see Nehemiah 6:19; Psalm
39:2, 5.[1] A second, though less likely, possibility is to understand *good* as an epithet for deity, 'Accept (us), O Good One'
(Andersen, p. 645).[2]

In support of these basic requests Israel is called to make
pledges to God about their conduct. The first of these pledges
is a blanket commitment to keep all the pledges: *And we will
render* (Heb. *šlm* in the intensive stem means to 'compensate' or
'pay', a frequent term in the laws of Exodus; *cf.* 21:34, 36; and

[1] R. Gordis, 'The Text and Meaning of Hosea 14:3', *VT*, 5, 1955, pp. 89–90.
[2] Andersen, *loc. cit.*, cites W. Kuhnigk, *Nordwestsemitsche studien zum Hoseabuch*,
Biblica et Orientalia, 27 (Rome: Pontifical Biblical Institute, 1974), pp. 154–
156, as the source of this suggestion.

especially ch. 22) *the fruit* (Heb. *prym* should be read as *fruit*, *pᵉrî* RSV; *cf.* 13:15 and 14:8, not *bulls* [*pārîm*], the *m* being an enclitic *m*, added for emphasis or a case marker and common in Canaanite dialects) *of our lips* describes the promise to fulfill their promises, including the paying of the obligations to pray, worship and keep vows.

The three pledges of verse 3 wrap up the major needs for reform. Each contains a *not* and represents the turn in Israel's behaviour. *Assyria will not save us* is both a statement of fact and of commitment. The silly dove has finally come to his senses and ceased his flitting (7:11); the unturned loaf of bread is finally done to a turn (7:8); the chronic sufferer has decided to change doctors (5:13); the wild ass is seeking to eat from the Trainer's hand (8:9); the true identity of the Great King has been discovered, and his palace is not on the Tigris (5:13; 10:6). *Upon horses* (the noun in Hebrew is singular and probably collective; for the military significance of the horse, see on 1:7; Joel 2:4) *we will not ride* is the graphic way of denouncing all trust in military might for survival or expansion (*cf.* 8:14; 10:14). Since the kings and the military commanders are often linked in Hosea as sources of national weakness or wickedness (7:7, 16; 8:4, 10; 10:3; 13:9–11), this vow may carry with it an unspoken commitment to a different role for the monarchy – a role briefly spotlighted in 1:11 and 3:5. *We will not say again 'Our God'* (LXX uses plural, our gods, as a true reflection of Israel's religious fickleness) – the importance of the use of the name of deity is stressed here as in 2:16–17 and probably 4:2, 'swear' – *to the work of our hand* epitomizes the folly of idolatry as Hosea saw it: human beings worship what they outrank; they use the creativity granted them by their Creator, in whose image they are made, to fashion images to pray to – a blatant case of a creator bowing before a creature and hence turning all of reality topsy-turvy (*cf.* on 2:8; 4:12; 8:5–6; 13;1–2). The tragedy is that the idol lacks the capacity of inter-personal exchange: We may say 'Our God' to what we make; it can never say 'my people' to us (*cf.* 2:23).

The closing confession of trust (v. 3d) apparently completes the prayer, connecting with the first line, 'Take away all iniquity', and grounding the right to pray in the best possible reason (Heb. *ᵃšer* of the clause's beginning probably stands for *yaʿan ᵃšer*, 'because'; *cf.* 1 Ki. 3:19; 8:33): the plentiful

mercy of God towards those who acknowledge their helplessness (*orphan* implies lack of clan ties and, therefore, lack of
identity, power and care in Israel's society; *cf.* Ex. 22:21; Ps.
68:5; Is. 1:17, 23). This clause heads us full circle towards the
opening of the book. It says, in effect, that Not-pitied is
counting on divine pity (the Heb. verb *rḥm* is used here in the
same stem as in the daughter's name, 1:6; 2;23) and that
Not-my-people, orphaned by the severing of the covenant, is
trusting for restoration to the family (1:9–10; 2:23).

ii. Yahweh's loving response (14:4–8). The form and content make clear that God is speaking. In verses 4–7 he seems
to be talking *about* Israel, as though telling the prophet how he
intends to answer their prayer. In verse 8 he seems to address
Ephraim directly, although we cannot be quite sure of the force
of verse 8a. The passage begins in verse 4 with the promises of
love bestowed and anger withdrawn. It turns figurative and
highly poetic in verses 5–7, where God sings of Israel's future
prosperity in the freshly formed covenant of love. In verse
8a–b, the language is literal again, while in verse 8c, God's
self-description is a simile. If we are right in hearing verses
4–7 as a love song and verse 8 as a divine complaint, then we
are once again privy to the divine pathos – the profoundly felt
and poignantly voiced affections of God as he experiences the
tensions between what ought to be and what is in his dealings
with Israel.

Hosea likens divine judgment to inflicting wounds or
imposing illness (5:12–14; 13:7–8). Consequently, he may
compare restoration to *healing* – healing which Assyria could
not effect (5:13), which Israel sought but not sincerely (6:1),
which God passionately wanted to bestow (7:1), to which Israel
remained resistant (11:3). Here the healing is openly
promised (v. 4) – and not just the healing of the wounds of
judgment but the healing of the cause of judgment, the *faith-
lessness* or 'apostasy' which led them further and further away
from their covenant in the waywardness of rebellion. Their
bent to such conduct is part of what Yahweh lamented in 11:7.
What they cannot cure, he will heal. The restoration is deeply
personal – not only an illness cured but a relationship
renewed: *I will love them.* God's love was expressed in the
Exodus in 11:1 and maintained even in days of apostasy with
the Baals (3:1), while Israel's love was being squandered on

false gods (2:5, 7, 10, 12–13) or treacherous allies (8:9). *Freely* (Heb. *nᵉdābâ*; *cf.* Ps. 54:6; 110:3) connotes initiative, joy and alacrity in the love-relationship. God, despite all of Israel's rebellion, will move into the reconciliation without grudge. The last line of verse 4 gives the reason: God's *anger* (*cf.* on 11:9) has done its righteous work in judgment and can now be directed away (on Heb. *šwb* with anger as its implied object, see Am. 1:3) from Israel, viewed collectively here in singular (lit. 'from *him*').

The bursts of song both reverse the judgment of Israel and in verses 5–7 drink deeply of the same springs of love poetry that watered the Song of Solomon: (1) *Dew* (v. 5), elsewhere in Hosea a sign of Israel's fickleness (6:4) that will lead to his complete evaporation (13:3), here describes the refreshment of God's love; its use in Song 5:2 is literal; (2) *blossom* (vv. 5, 7), used sarcastically in 10:4 to picture Israel's bountiful crop of injustices, here describes Israel's bountiful prosperity which results from his restored favour with Yahweh; in Song 6:11; 7:13, the verb occurs in the context of an erotic, verdant setting for love; (3) *lily* (v. 5; also 'crocus' or 'lotus'), only here in Hosea, depicts the bride's beauty (Song 2:1–2), the bride's and the husband's lips (2:16; 5:13; 6:3), the bride's light and delicate breasts (4:5); (4) *strike root* (v. 5), not found in the Song of Solomon reverses the judgment of barrenness – 'their root is dried up' (9:16); (5) *Lebanon* (vv. 5, 6, 7), the final word in each verse, symbolizes the acme of verdure and fertility in dramatic contrast to the bleak, almost treeless, terrain of Palestine in Hosea's day, and may well modify the earlier nouns in the two verses where it seems unaccompanied – lilies of Lebanon (v. 5), olive of Lebanon (v. 6; *cf.* Andersen, p. 642); Lebanon's prominence in Solomon's Song is evident: a trysting place (Song 4:8) known for its streams (4:15), wood (3:9), mountain (7:5; lit. 'tower'), cedars (5:15), and fragrance (4:11; *cf.* Ho. 14:6); (6) the *olive* (v. 6), cherished for its oil (*cf.* on 2:5, 8) and its bountiful foliage (here called *shoots* or *suckers*) is not mentioned in the Song of Solomon, but seems to be used as love imagery in Jeremiah 11:16, where God is quoted, in what may be a snatch of love poetry, describing Israel: 'A green olive tree, fair with goodly fruit', *cf.* Ps. 52:8; (7) *fragrance* (v. 6), here probably the scent of the Lebanon olive, is a dominant word in oriental love poetry (Song 1:3, the charm of the man; 1:12; 4:10–11; 7:8, the scent of the woman stimulated in love; 2:3, springtime, the season of love; 7:13, mandrakes); (8) *return* (v. 7; *cf.* the theological significance discussed at 14:1–2) may also echo the language of love; *cf.* Song 6:13 [Heb. 7:1]; it possible to read *return* as an auxiliary verb meaning 'to do something, *i.e. dwell*, again'; (*cf.* Wolff, p. 232; Andersen, p. 642); (9) *those who dwell in his shadow* (v. 7; or 'shade'; the participle in construct with the prepositional phrase serves as the subject of the sentence; *cf.* Ps. 24:1; Andersen, p. 642) describes an intimately protective relationship *cf.* Song 2:3; the *his* of verse 7 seems to be God not Israel, another instance of the sudden switches in grammar – God is I in verses 4–5 and (probably) 8; (10) *grain* (v. 7; RSV has needlessly emended to 'garden') should probably be modified with a preposition 'like' in parallel to like *the vine*, leaving Israel as the subject of *flourish* (lit. 'bring to life') and keeping the focus on Israel as the recipient of God's prospering love rather than on any individual crops (though the many earlier references to *grain* are certainly in view; *cf.* 2:8, 9, 22; 7:14; 9:1, where a chief purpose of the Baal-cult was to assure the annual grain supply);[1] (11) the *vine* (*cf.* 2:12, where Israel was to lose her vines in judgment for her spiritual harlotry; *cf.* also 10:1 where Israel herself was compared to a luxuriant vine) served in the Song of Solomon as a sign of spring (Song 2:13), as part of a site for erotic encounter (6:11; 7:12; both use *vine* with the verb *blossom*, as does Ho. 14:7); (12) *wine* (*cf.* 7:5; 9:4), which here is a figure of Israel's restored reputation (on 'remembrance' or 'name', Heb. *zēker*, *cf.* 12:5; no need to read 'fragrance' here as do Ward, p. 226, and RSV), the vintage name they will gain, like Lebanon's fine wine, plays a standard part in the language of love describing its value and exhilaration; *cf.* Song 1:2, 4; 2:4; 4:10; 5:1; 7:9; 8:2.

In an extraordinary way, the poet-prophet has interwoven in these verses *recollections* of Israel's past relationship to God as olive tree and grapevine, *renunciations* of the fertility powers of Baal, whom Israel wrongly credited with gifts of grain, wine and oil (ch. 2), and *recitations* of love-lyrics, whereby he dramatized the promise to *love them freely* (v. 4) which is the centrepiece of chapter 14. By implication, this love music recalls not

---

[1] R. B. Coote's ingenious reconstruction of the text, on the basis of the LXX, though remaining hypothetical, does point out how strongly these verses aim at polemic toward the Baals. See Hosea 14:8: 'They who are filled with grain shall live', *JBL*, 93, 1974, pp. 161–173.

only to our minds but also to our emotions all that the divine Husband promised more specifically in 2:19–23. The relational thrust of the book, which took such fierce forms, when God used bestial language to describe his judgment in 5:14–15 and 13:7–8, is again filled with warmth and tenderness when God likens himself to the dew (v. 5). The language is agricultural; but its intent is not like those of Joel's promise of full threshing floors and vats (2:24) after the years of locust invasion, nor like that of Amos' oracle of teeming vineyards and lavish gardens (9:13–14). The language is agricultural; but its meaning is not material provision so much as enriching love. It is not God the Husbandman who sings this final love-song but Yahweh the Husband. The 'I am' (*I will be*; Heb. *'ehyeh*, v. 5) that introduces the love lyrics, with their horticultural images, seems to be a reversal of the disinheritance (or divorce) formula, 'I am not (Heb. *lō' 'ehyeh*) your God,' which capped the first announcements of judgment (1:9). Like the promises that remove the Nots from the children's names (2:23), it speaks of a restored relationship as Husband and Parent, a relationship guaranteed by history's ultimate personal declaration, 'I am' (see Ex. 3:6; Jn. 6:35; 8:12, 58; 10:7, 11; 11:25; 14:6; 15:1).

It is possible that Israel/Ephraim utters the first words of verse 8; so the Targum reads it: 'And some from the house of Israel said.' If so, the first sentence would be Israel's affirmation of their fidelity to God and the abandonment of their idols, an appropriate response to God's song of love. It is more likely, however, that God is speaking to Ephraim in a question that carries a hint of divine complaint (*cf.* 11:8). If this is the case, the time-frame has shifted from the picture of bliss in the distant future to the present realities of Hosea's day (*cf.* the note at 1:10 – 2:1), when Ephraim yet found himself in league with idols (*cf.* 13:1–2). Once more God, from a heart wracked in agony, drives home the major messages of the book: my love and care – expressed here as *answering* (*cf.* the uses of Heb. *'nh* in 2:15, 22; 5:5; 7:10) their pleas and *looking after* their needs (*cf. šwr* in 13:7) – are your only hope; to reject them is suicide; no other gods are worth the material from which you make them.[1] Only in 14:8 is God compared to a tree in the

---

[1] The conjecture of Wellhausen, appropriated by Jacob, p. 95, that the verbs 'answer' and 'look after' should be read as the Canaanite divine names Anat

Old Testament. His desire to wipe the land clean of the fertility cult has led him to strong, almost risky, language. He borrowed the enemy's sword to make his final thrust.

In a chapter that excels in summary statement, the pithiest of all may be the last line of verse 8: 'from me your fruit is obtained.' Who is the true source of Israel's livelihood? That has been a major question of the book. The wrong answer led to the religious harlotry, political instability, and international chicanery that are Hosea's major themes. God's last words are the correct answer. The pun on Ephraim's name implied in the word *fruit* (*p^erî cf.* on 8:9; 13:15) only serves to strengthen that answer. *Yahweh*'s covenant call carried with it the responsibility to produce the fruit of full obedience to him (*cf.* on 9:10; 10:1). That productivity became impossible when Ephraim forgot the source of all true fruit.

e. Concluding admonition: walking and stumbling (14:9 [Heb. 14:10])

The literary form is like the admonitions of Proverbs (*cf.* 4:20–23), where imperative or jussives (third person commands, usually singular) that map out the way of wisdom are followed by the reasons that support the commands, usually introduced by *for* (Heb. *kî*). The vocabulary as well as the style reflects the influence of wisdom literature: *Wise* (Heb. *ḥākām; cf.* 13:13), *understand* (Heb. *bîn; cf.* 4:14), *discerning* (also from *bîn*), *know* (a key catchword in Hosea; *cf.* on 2:8), *ways* (*cf.* 4:9; 10:13) as descriptions of conduct; *right* (used in Proverbs more than twenty times; *e.g.* 2:7; 3:32; 8:9), *upright* (Heb. *ṣaddîqîm*; lit. 'innocent of crime'; *cf.* Am. 2:6; 5:12; used more than fifty times in Proverbs, often as a synonym of *wise*, with a meaning close to 'loyal to Yahweh and his will'), *walk* (as a verb of behaviour, *cf.* 5:11; and about twenty times in Proverbs), *transgressors* (lit. 'rebels'; Heb. *pš^e*; *cf.* 7:13; 8:1; the noun 'transgression' is found about a dozen times in Proverbs). The first four words cluster as part of the introduction to Proverbs (1:1–6) and are sprinkled liberally through the book, while the fifth (*way*) occurs about seventy-five times.

---

and Asherah again catches the anti-Baal intent of the passage but stretches credibility by asking us to believe that Yahweh, whose plan was to obliterate the names of pagan deities (2:16–17) and who had clearly introduced himself as Yahweh (12:8; 13:4), would now call himself Israel's true Anat and Asherah.

The contrasts between the nouns *the upright* and *the transgressors* and the verbs *walk* and *stumble* (Ho. 4:5; 5:5; 14:1; Pr. 4:12, 19; 24:16–17) form an antithesis in the last two lines. The poetic structure, found dozens of times in Proverbs (especially chs. 10–15) and frequently in 'wisdom' Psalms (*e.g.* Pss. 1; 37), underscores a doctrine of *the two ways*, which makes clear the absolute consequences of loyalty or disloyalty to God. Jesus' use of 'wide gate' and 'narrow gate' (Mt. 7:13–14), 'good fruit' and 'evil fruit' (Mt. 7:15–18), and 'house upon the rock' and 'house upon the sand' (Mt. 7:24–27) are a few of the New Testament expression of *the two ways*.

It is evident in Jeremiah's frequent use of Hosea's words, images and ideas that the advice of this verse was heeded by the believing community, who sensed, probably as early as the fall of Samaria (722 BC), that Hosea had spoken and lived the truth.[1] This closing admonition, whether added by the prophet or one of his followers, viewed the whole book as Scripture and urged the hearers of whatever place and season to heed the warnings of judgment and the promises of hope.[2] The correct response to Hosea's words then, now, and in every era between, has been the difference between walking safely and stumbling tragically.

---

[1]For evidence of the influence of Ho. 13:4 – 14:9 on the so-called 'apocalypse' of Isaiah, especially 26:13 – 27:11, see John Day, *JTS*, 31, 1980, pp. 309–319. Some eight verbal and thematic parallels are listed.

[2]C. L. Seow (*CBQ*, 44, 1982, pp. 212–224) has argued for a 'foolish people motif' in Hosea, which makes plausible the conclusion that 'the presence of a sapiential exhortation at the end of Hosea may not seem as out of place as it had been supposed' (p. 223).